No Fats, No Fems

No Fats, No Fems

A Guide to Queer Empathy and Unpacking Prejudice

Max Hovey

HARPERONE
An Imprint of HarperCollins*Publishers*

 For information, address HarperCollins Publishers, 195 Broadway, New York, NY 10007. In Europe, HarperCollins Publishers, Macken House, 39/40 Mayor Street Upper, Dublin 1, D01 C9W8, Ireland.

HarperCollins books may be purchased for educational, business, or sales promotional use. For information, please email the Special Markets Department at SPsales@harpercollins.com.

hc.com

FIRST EDITION

Designed by Jason Kayser

Library of Congress Cataloging-in-Publication Data has been applied for.

ISBN 978-0-06-342346-6

Printed in the United Kingdom

26 27 28 29 CPI 10 9 8 7 6 5 4 3 2

No Fats, No Fems

Contents

Introduction

No Fats, No Fems

We have rightfully dedicated so much of our time to protesting against the way society treats us. But in the process, we've neglected how we treat each other.

The title of this book likely evoked some form of emotional reaction within you. Maybe it was a little triggering because you've encountered the use of this phrase online or you've felt excluded from some spaces because of this mindset. Maybe you felt some offence because this is a phrase (or a variant of it) that you have used online yourself. Now you're wondering why it's on the cover of a book about queer empathy. Maybe you felt some confusion because you've not encountered this before, and the title itself without context reads like I'm about to indoctrinate you with the ideas by prominent so-called alpha males. You could have even felt a bit of solace and relief that a topic such as this might finally be addressed in a constructive way rather than the 'that's just how it is' mindset we've become all too familiar with. Or maybe you're not queer at all, and you want to learn more about us and how we work. If that's you, hey! Welcome, you're in for a ride.

'NO FATS, NO FEMS', for those who don't know, is an all-too-common phrase that frequents the profiles of many gay men on dating and hookup apps. It is a blatant, instant rejection of anyone who is remotely fat or feminine. Some don't see the harm in this. But in reality, gay men grow up feeling emasculated just for being attracted to other men and at the same time are constantly pressured to compare themselves (and their bodies) with the same men they are attracted to. To then see a string of profiles automatically rejecting men for this reason or that, it's going to take a toll on their self-esteem. As a result, our community becomes ever divided and fragmented.

No matter your initial emotional reaction, it's valid. Having spent two years living in a big city and building connections with incredible and diverse queer people, I have learned that whilst we may share the umbrella experience of being 'queer', our individual experiences often differ dramatically. Our home lives, our school years, our families, our professional lives, our social circles, our heritage, our relationships, our sex lives, our desires, our expressions, and so many other differences that make us who we are.

And yet, queer people have a lot more to process and work through than our non-queer counterparts. You may even be reading this thinking, 'I don't have anything to work through, I'm fine!' But it is impossible to grow up queer in a straight world without any baggage at all. So even if you think you got out unscathed, that might just mean you need to dig a little deeper. Sometimes the impact is so embedded into our psyche that we're not even aware, and it can manifest subconsciously in ways that are not only detrimental to ourselves but to those around us. An important thing to note when first understanding empathy through queerness is that we, as humans, have as many similarities as we do differences, and both are equally important.

Same Experiences: Surrounding ourselves with those who have been through similar experiences can help us feel seen and heard or better understand ourselves and why we think, act, and react the way we do. It can also help us feel less alone: an incredible support system of people can help even the scales when we're struggling. We can develop a true sense of community and unity in finding others who can truly relate and sympathise with our lived experiences in a way that others cannot.

Different Experiences: Being exposed to other ways of thinking and life experiences can help us develop a stronger sense of empathy. Growing up feeling like we're misunderstood or don't fit in can feel pretty isolating. Surrounding ourselves with people different from us can help us develop into an empathetic and caring individual who strives to actively include others and help them feel heard. We can also learn to listen to differing perspectives in a way that makes it easier for us to learn and grow, rather than believing that our view alone is the correct one.

We rarely feel completely supported by those who don't fully understand us. But by surrounding ourselves *only* with people who share our experiences, we set the foundation for being less tolerant to those who are different.

No one is born homophobic, or transphobic, or racist, or with any other prejudice – these views are taught. Whether it's directly or indirectly. Whether it's because we have never seen people who are different, or because when we have, we've been told by those we're meant to look up to that it is wrong. Experiencing homophobia in schools is a direct result of poor representation and low tolerance levels for those who are different, often through parenting and wider societal views. Think back to being in school: whilst kids are often carefree, they are also often quick to question those who are different – if that difference hasn't been adequately represented. If kids are shown early on that there are many kinds of people, relationships, interests, and forms of expression, they're more likely to grow up with understanding for those who are different, rather than disdain. Queer people specifically know the isolating feeling of not 'fitting in', so you'd think we'd have empathy and compassion for others experiencing the same, right?

Not always.

I've found that once we come out, it feels easier to, at last, find a community. This is instantly validating, as though we've escaped the isolation that has plagued us for most of our lives. People finally understand us; they truly know what it feels like to be us. But for some, the journey stops there.

Queer rights did not progress through the efforts of one individual; we stood together as an entire community, and what binds us together is that whilst we all have our own different lived experiences, we as a collective will always be different from everyone else. Those who oppose our very existence view us all the same. Whether we're gender non-conforming with different-coloured hair and piercings or we present in a more conventional way – if they see us holding hands with someone they feel we shouldn't be, they will always think that we're doing something wrong, that we need fixing, that we're setting a bad example for kids, that we should keep it behind closed doors. No matter how you dress, present, or walk through life, our identity will be the deciding factor for how people treat us. To those who do not understand us, we *are* the same.

What I learned from living in a big city with a much larger queer scene is that our minds are very easily influenced by our environment. After spending the first twenty-two years of my life in a quiet, conservative coastal town, my mind was very narrow. I was almost never exposed to different kinds of people or ways of thinking. Yet, during my time in London, I met people who I feel will be in my life forever. I met people who opened my eyes to the beautiful spectrum of queerness and the importance of acceptance and allyship. *Twenty-one* of these trailblazing individuals will be speaking in this book and opening up about topics that are important to them. The multitude of identities and queer experiences that need platforming cannot be done by me alone, so I feel honoured to have such incredible people share their experiences with me and you so candidly. I hope to elevate these conversations and help us all better understand our differences and how we can truly have more empathy for our queer family.

'When you don't share stories, you're just this isolated person in one village, whereas when you can communicate, you're an army. When you've got your community, you're a whole tribe.'

Le Fil (he/they),
artist and drag performer

'I'm Gay, Not Queer!'

The LGBTQIA+ community has spent decades fighting against an oppressive system set out to eradicate us. The word *queer* gained its initial notoriety as a homophobic slur, dating back as far as the early twentieth century. Generations have felt the potent sting of being labelled as queer and the horrendous treatment associated with the word.

Over time, many of us have begun reclaiming the use of *queer* and now label ourselves with it as a sign of pride and defiance, a way to solidify us under a broader identity. I vividly remember that when I first accepted being gay, I still distanced myself from the community. I used to take 'you don't seem gay' or 'you have a "manly" voice' as a compliment. I was gay, but I just didn't want to look or sound like it. I still saw heterosexuality as superior. Now, I take pride in my sexuality and the beautiful fluidity that comes with it. I embrace the absolute joy that queer friendships bring me and happily 'queen out' with my friends without spending a second of my time worrying if people think I'm 'too gay'. Queerness is more than an identity; it's an entire culture. I feel so embedded in our community that I am more than just a gay man: I am queer.

In many societies, you are free to embrace your queerness. You can embody everything beautiful about being different whilst empowering others to feel the same. But some tend to forget that whilst on the surface many of our rights are equal, there is still an ever-persistent tremour of prejudice that is able to crack the ground beneath our feet at any moment. We're told to feel safe and accepted in a society where global multibillion-pound companies change their logo to rainbow colours for a month once a year – whilst simultaneously hate crime rates against the community are increasing. We're told that 'love is love' – whilst we watch the rights of queer people rolled back around the world. The reason for some being unaware of these threats is that they're much less likely to be the target or they simply feel they don't impact them. For queer people, our very uniqueness is what makes us special and what solidifies our bond as a community. But there are some LGBTQIA+ people who see our uniqueness and non-conformity as a threat to their own existence.

To this day, I get hundreds of comments from gay men criticising me simply for having my nails painted, feeling it is 'too fem' or 'too gay' – neither of which actually exists. This is just one way people express their resentment for anyone deviating from the norm, even if they are gay themselves. They will reject the entire concept of community in an attempt to say, 'I'm not part of that lot. I'm a normal straight guy except I just sleep with men!' or 'I'm gay, not queer!' And these commenters aren't just correcting someone on how they identify; they're using it as a way of distancing themselves from the wider community and subsequently berate anyone who is part of it. Being gay is a sexual orientation; being queer is an entire cultural identity – and it's queer culture they want to steer clear of. Doing so may provide a temporary reprieve from the onslaught of hatred by people they're aiming to stand with. But in the long term, they're just as much a target as us.

I want you to approach this book with an open mind and understand that these topics are going to be discussed with empathy at the forefront. This is a book on queer empathy, after all. The title does not mean I'm about to spend hundreds of pages adding to the negativity. I'm hoping it will be controversial enough to call a lot of queer people into this conversation, especially gay men. Why did I specifically mention gay men? Because as one myself, we are seen to some as (and often are) the top of the queer food chain, and with that comes a lot of privilege. Now before you run away at the mention of privilege, it might not mean what you think.

The Privilege Is Mine

Having privilege doesn't mean that life has been easy, it just means that certain elements of our identities haven't made life more difficult. Feel free to read that as many times as you need.

Acknowledging your privilege is just about reading the room. Say at your job you work Monday to Friday. Then one day you're asked to come in on Saturday as a one-off, and you decide to complain about this to your friend, who at their job works Monday to Saturday every single week. Sure, having to work that Saturday may be inconvenient for you, but your friend who already works six days a week probably won't have much sympathy for you. Whilst this is a very simple example, you get the gist.

When you're a queer person just trying to navigate the world, and a very difficult world at that, often the last thing we have the capacity to do is think of others. When we have so much to work through, often we need to put ourselves and our healing first. I myself have had multiple rounds of therapy and likely even more in my future. I am still trying to work through stuff, but having my own struggles does not make me incapable of seeing things from other perspectives.

I've heard the phrase 'oppression Olympics' multiple times, the feeling that one person is claiming to be a 'better victim' over another. When some people are informed of their privilege or told they have it 'easier', they feel it minimises and invalidates their own struggles. They view it as a personal attack on their morals or an attempt to disregard whatever struggles they may have endured. They hear 'privilege' and assume it means they have a very comfortable, carefree life. Recognising our own privilege means that we are aware of our position and can also acknowledge the difficulties others face. We can have empathy for those who may be at a greater disadvantage and not make it worse for them or, better yet, actively participate in supporting and uplifting them.

I once heard a gay man get pretty frustrated when feminine gay men called out his privilege. They claimed it was easier for him to address certain things about being queer because of the way he acted and looked. He was a tall, very well-built, masculine, and conventionally attractive cis white gay man. This would have been an opportunity to acknowledge his privilege, but instead the callouts were seen as an invalidation of his own struggles.

Who do you think is more likely to feel comfortable walking into a very traditional British pub full of football fans? A masculine cis gay guy who might even enjoy football himself, or someone more effeminate who may be physically non-conforming – have a more slender build, an effeminate voice – and may have no interest in football at all? Naturally, the masculine guy will be more likely to fit in. Sure, he may experience some discomfort. He may worry a little about being judged. But he's masculine presenting; he can conceal his queerness in a way that causes less discomfort in those who resent non-conformity.

> **'There's a certain type of gay man where they don't really understand their privilege. They've not had the journey I've had. I can't physically hide I'm gay. When I walk into a barber shop, I can put a deep voice on, but I look like a faggot, and I'll always be a faggot.'**
>
> Danny Beard (he/they),
> drag queen and performer

I remember speaking with a friend about his experience with verbal homophobic abuse on public transport when presenting more feminine. 'It happens every time I go out', he told me.

Yet I recall only two occasions in the past five years when this has happened to me. One was when I was walking down the street holding hands with my then boyfriend, and the second was when I was walking down the street wearing a crop top. As someone who often presents more masculine, I'm privileged to receive a fraction of the verbal abuse that effeminate gay men are subjected to. The point is that existing as certain identities in a world designed for men, specifically straight white men, can be a lot harder. We're all in the same boat. But some people on this boat don't have to put in as much work to stay afloat. This is where intersectionality comes in.

Intersectionality describes the way in which a person's differing characteristics in their identity can lead to a greater level of disadvantage in society. Some people might experience prejudice based on their sexuality, but their race, gender expression, and body image might also contribute to making their lived experience far more difficult. A muscular gay white man has privilege in that he won't be subjected to systemic racism or fatphobia, but a straight white man will always have greater privilege over a gay white man, as his sexuality is not a stressor. The Wheel of Power and Privilege is a concept that perfectly illustrates how our individualised characteristics can contribute to the level of disadvantage we may be subjected to in society. The characteristics closer to the centre are closer to privilege, and those further out experience greater disadvantage.

It Starts with Us

Some might think that by specifically mentioning cis white gay men, I am stoking even more division within LGBTQIA+ spaces. I completely see why some people have this perspective, and often these people are cis white gay men themselves. The

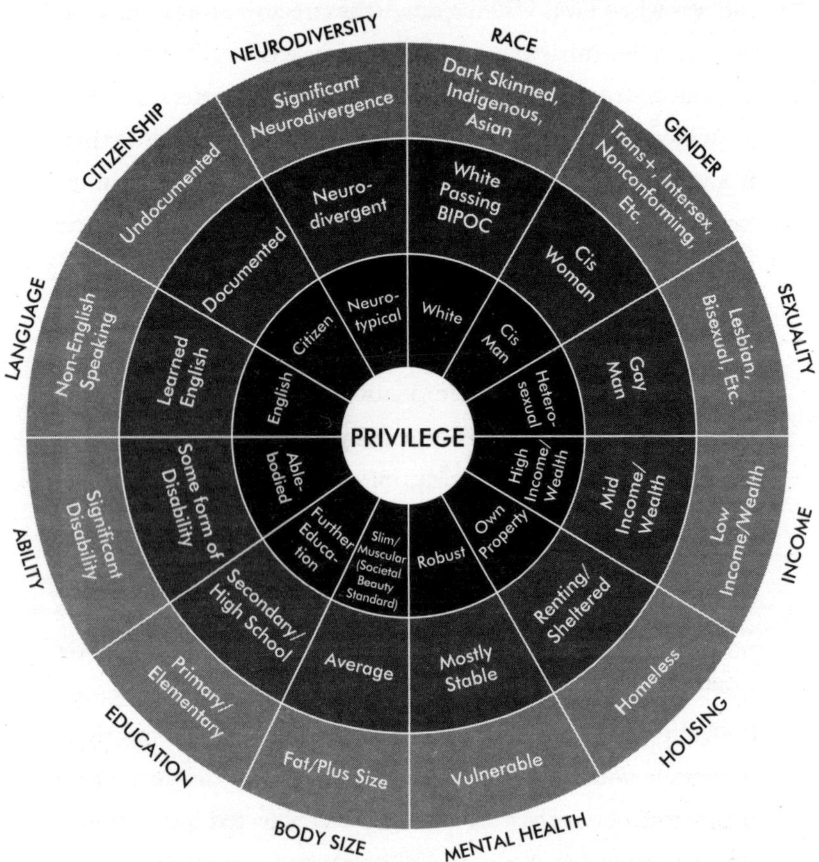

reason they feel it's stoking more division is that, as cis white gay men, the division within the community often doesn't negatively affect us. It's usually cis white gay men who are causing the division in the first place, and that's something they often don't wish to admit. If you are this identity whilst also being muscular and masculine, the divisions within the community almost won't at all negatively impact you, therefore you won't be aware of them. If you're this identity and do not have any feminine queer friends, you're probably completely unaware of what it's like to navigate queerness as a feminine person.

Unfortunately some gay men will, instead of using their privilege to uplift the same people who fought for our rights, distance themselves in an attempt to be closer to the norm. 'I'm not like other gays', they'll say. Just because you don't watch *RuPaul's Drag Race* or frequent Soho bars on the regular, doesn't mean you're not chowing down on a man's ass at the end of the night. Homosexual acts were only legalised in the UK in 1967, and even then the age of consent was only equalised with heterosexual acts in 2000. Decriminalisation of homosexual acts was the very first step. Section 28 was a piece of legislation that outlawed even mentioning the existence of LGBTQIA+ people in UK schools, and it was fully repealed only in 2003. Same-sex marriage was fully legalised in the United Kingdom in 2014 and the United States in 2015, and to this day there are still those fighting for this to be overturned. That is how recent some of our rights have been won. And unfortunately, some privileged gay men are happy to revel in these hard-fought rights whilst dismissing or publicly denouncing the same people who fought for them.

> **'Loving and uplifting gay men has been central to most of our experiences. But we've now reached a point where gay men have been lifted up, and we kind of need you to throw a rope back down for us to get up there with you.'**
>
> Dani St James (she/her),
> chief executive of the trans+ charity Not a Phase

I saw the negative impact of femphobia in our spaces only when I started experimenting with makeup and feminine clothing. I lost twenty thousand Instagram followers in a few months and was continually messaged hateful things by other gay men. I became aware of the racism people face within our spaces only when I moved to London and became friends with queer people of colour. Division already exists, the lines have been drawn, and we've been put into our boxes. Naturally, those who are most negatively impacted by these divisions are going to be the most aware of them. Being made aware of these boxes and how we fit into them is the first step, and the next is what we do with them.

You may also be wondering why, as a cis white gay man, I am even talking about privilege. Despite me not having washboard abs, my privilege is still very intact. There is a responsibility of those in a position of privilege to platform and pass the proverbial and literal mic to those with less privilege. The reason I personally am having this conversation is because who I am today is entirely different from who I was when I first came out.

I used to think the only men I'd ever find physically and even emotionally attractive would need to have the body of a swimmer and the mindset of a 'jock'. My top priority when dating was how someone looked, not how they made me feel, and as a result I've probably missed out on connections with some incredible people over the years. To this day, I'm ashamed to admit it, but it's also one of the reasons I am committed to bringing about change. I am not speaking from a pedestal; I am speaking from experience.

Now if there were a lineup of the people I have dated (or slept with), there would be absolutely zero consistency. I changed what I found attractive. It truly is possible. I discovered that I am in fact attracted to a range of different guys, to different gender expressions, body types, and races. I realised that I didn't need to aspire to have the physique we have thrust in our faces by the media in order to be happy and to feel desirable. I realised that embracing the things I was taught to suppress in fact brought me great joy, instead of the shame I was told I'd feel. The queer people I'd been told were 'too much' have become people I would now consider family.

My past mindset towards different identities, bodies, and expressions wasn't my fault. It was instilled in me over the course of my closeted life by the poor representation of diverse queer people. Whilst my prejudices weren't my fault, my failure to address them was. We all have internalised prejudices, and we all have it within us to unpack and unlearn them. In a society deeply rooted in bigotry and social hierarchy, it's going to take generations to rip it out root and stem. But I know first-hand that these damaging mindsets can and should be unlearned.

These prejudices can be referred to as our 'unconscious bias'. This is where we make judgements and/or decisions based on our predetermined views stemming from our experiences or what we've been taught. A very simple example: we may assume that someone smaller or more effeminate is a bottom and that their partner, who is much taller or more masculine, is a top. Whilst this can be true, it may not be. We are making an assumption based on what we've been taught – masculinity is dominant, and femininity is submissive. Masculinity is strong, femininity is weak. Masculinity is to be praised, femininity is to be ridiculed. We owe it to the community to sit with our unconscious biases and unpack why they exist.

My own unconscious bias reared its ugly head a few years ago over this exact topic. I dated a guy who, up until this point, had been the top in our relationship. One day, he told me he no longer had any interest in topping and wanted to start bottoming. I believed that this was something we could work on as a couple. Whilst topping wasn't my preference, I believed in compromise and exploring our sexuality as a team. However, when I explained that I was more than happy to try, he responded by saying he didn't like the idea of bottoming for *me* personally, stating that 'it cringed him out'. This came shortly after being told that my shift to expressing myself in a more feminine way had made me less attractive to him.

At the time, I was experimenting comfortably with femininity and didn't feel much pressure to uphold masculinity, as I was the bottom in the relationship. Once the conversation about wanting to change positions had occurred, I subconsciously started changing who I was. I dyed my hair back to my natural brown from bright, vibrant purple. My nails went from being long and having a regular multicoloured manicure to being cut back to the shortest length and stripped bare. I began dressing in less feminine, less colourful clothing and even started really pushing myself at the gym to get bigger and more muscular. Most gay men feel pressure to present more masculine at some point, including me. But this time, I subconsciously felt this immense pressure to become more masculine purely to be seen as a desirable top.

Having a preference over your bedroom role is perfectly okay, and I personally still very much prefer to bottom. However, I recognised my unconscious bias and realised that we shouldn't have to express ourselves in a specific way to be valid in the bedroom role we enjoy. We shouldn't need to shift to a more masculine presentation to be perceived as a desirable top, and vice versa.

I'm not perfect. I'm far from it. I have my flaws, as we all do, and sometimes my unconscious bias will still creep in. Sometimes a thought will pop in my head when I see someone different from me. But now, instead of reacting to it, I notice it, halt it, and let it go. I've learned that even if I do have a judgemental thought based on how I've been taught to feel about certain people, I don't have to verbalise it.

Unconscious bias takes time to unlearn. Even just by picking up this book you've taken an important first step in having more empathy and understanding for our queer family. This has nothing to do with being 'woke' or a 'snowflake'. These are real issues that have real consequences. We need to work together to help make our generation, older generations, and generations to come feel welcomed into the community with open arms.

The aim isn't just to help us garner a greater sense of empathy and understanding for those who are different, but also patience and grace for those who want learn. Putting the work in to actively dismantle our own views on the world is not something that warrants a pat on the back. We should not unlearn problematic mindsets with the aim of receiving praise, but some people don't allow others the time for unlearning to happen at all. The slightest mistake is met with anger, often without any chance of forgiveness (i.e., cancel culture). We may pride ourselves on our differences and on accepting each other's so-called imperfections, but we often allow next to no room for error.

There will always be those who act out of malice with zero desire to change – these people are willingly ignorant and never worth our time. But maybe someone is from a small rural town and hasn't shaken their instilled views, maybe they are new to the queer scene and are unintentionally ignorant. These people need to be given time to learn, grow, and evolve.

> **'It's important to remember that sometimes when people say things that come across as small-minded or bigoted, it's maybe just because they've never had to think about things in the way that you've always seen the world, and it might take them time to catch up.'**
>
> Shiv (they/them),
> journalist and broadcaster

It is my hope that this book with help you understand three main things: where our prejudices come from, the impact they have, and finally what we can do about them. Each of the earlier chapters will focus primarily on the first two understandings, giving each topic the depth it deserves and giving each incredible interviewee their time to speak. The majority of actionable steps will be laid out in our final chapter. You may be thinking "surely unpacking our prejudices needs more than just one chapter?", and you're right. It requires *you* putting in the work. But when it comes to unpacking prejudice and understanding those who are different, the advice often has a lot of similarities, only focused on a different identity. So, if when reading the following chapters you start to think "well, what now?", don't worry, it's coming.

I'll be honest, I'm going to detail many harsh truths in the upcoming pages. Some of the topics, behaviours, and attitudes discussed in this book may make you feel 'called out' or challenged. For some of you this book will be uncomfortable to read. I know if I picked this book up ten – hell, even five – years ago, I would've felt *very* uncomfortable. But I've learned that when something makes us uncomfortable, it's triggering an emotional response. That means it matters to us in some way. Whether it's positive or negative, it matters. When this happens, I want you to consider three things:

Why? Without judgement, I want you to think critically, objectively, and honestly about why what you're reading matters to you and why it makes you feel uncomfortable. You'd be surprised how much can be uncovered about our psyche with the simple question 'why?' If you ask enough, and keep asking, you'll realise your normal thought process is being challenged, which means there is work to be done and unlearning to do. This is okay, it will take time.

It May Not Be About You. Contrary to the above, some of what we'll talk about simply won't be about you, and so the discomfort may be unwarranted. When I discuss cis white gay men, it's not going to mean every cis white gay man. Just because a certain group is mentioned doesn't mean everyone is automatically guilty. You can acknowledge your own privilege without invalidating your own experiences. You can acknowledge the problematic behaviours of your peers without feeling you're being accused of them yourself. Just because *you* don't exhibit the problematic behaviours being discussed doesn't mean other people don't. So when certain behaviours and mindsets are being called out and you feel uncomfortable, consider if you actually take part in them. If you don't, then that's great, it's not about you personally. But that doesn't mean the issue doesn't exist and we shouldn't take the time to learn about it. Or better yet, actively work to dismantle it.

Experiences Differ. Fundamentally, we should care about other people. We should empathise with those whose experiences differ from our own. If you're going to take anything away from this book, I want it to be this: just because something doesn't impact you, does not mean that it doesn't impact others. Developing a strong sense of empathy means taking a step back and listening to the experiences of others and their impacts. If even after this you still don't care, then that is another conversation entirely that cannot be solved in this book (but maybe in therapy).

As a community, many of us work tirelessly for mainstream acceptance whilst simultaneously rejecting each other – this is something I want to work to change.

Judgement comes from a place of insecurity.

Acceptance grows from a place of self-love.

I hope this book helps us all be a little kinder to ourselves and, in turn, share this kindness with others. So, let's get started.

Chapter 1

I Don't Want to Be Gay

What Is Internalised Homophobia?

Queer people are often seen as just the butt of a joke rather than people with a rich history and culture to be celebrated. For men in particular, the idea of being gay is automatically an insult and seen as derogatory. Any glimpse of femininity is ridiculed to the point that having sexuality even questioned is considered being 'less of a man'. Heteronormativity is thrust in our faces from an incredibly young age. For those who don't know, heteronormativity is the idea that being heterosexual and binary in gender are the inherent 'norm' with everything else being seen as 'other'. Classmates, friends, family members, strangers, the media, and even governments expect us to act in a very particular way, whether through more subliminal messages or outright prejudice. When we grow up seeing difference in others as something to shame and fear rather than embrace and celebrate, it's going to take its toll.

This fear shows us not only how we should feel about others but also how we should feel about ourselves. We're told that relationships look a specific way and that to be desirable we need to conform to what it means to be a 'man' or a 'woman'. That certain clothes and colours are for people born with certain anatomies, and that some activities are only for certain genders, as well as an unquantifiable number of other norms and restrictions that will determine who we are allowed to be. We're told that we cannot deviate from any of these ideals at any point in our lives. To deviate from any of these norms and socially constructed rules is to be different, and being different is inherently wrong and therefore something to be shamed.

But what if who we've been told we must be our entire lives just doesn't quite feel natural? For example, when everyone's hormones start flying about and someone starts talking about the opposite sex in a more sexual way, and we have to pretend to join in even though we just don't share those feelings. Instead we may experience different feelings entirely. 'Why don't I feel the same way as everyone else?' we begin to think. 'What's wrong with me?' we ask ourselves. These questions often become more frequent and more self-deprecating. We haven't seen any other forms of relationships. We haven't been told that sometimes boys like boys, girls like girls, some like both, some like neither, some like everything, and some like nothing. So, who are we?

In time, those niggling thoughts at the back of our mind become harder and harder to ignore. By this point, our views on the world have well and truly formulated to become the very thing that plagues almost every queer person alive: internalised homophobia. This often seeps into other prejudices you might encounter within queer spaces. And so, this feels like a natural place to start. The struggle with internalised homophobia is a pretty universal experience for queer people and refers to how we can have internal prejudices that influence the way we see ourselves and the wider community. It doesn't necessarily mean someone doesn't accept being gay but refers instead to the internalised negative perceptions of being gay.

One of the easiest ways to understand the impact of internalised homophobia is the concept of cognitive dissonance, which is the discomfort and shame that can arise from having conflicting beliefs and/or actions existing simultaneously. Having homosexual feelings whilst still internally believing that homosexuality is wrong creates cognitive dissonance. Internalised homophobia is the internal prejudice; cognitive dissonance is the discomfort that arises as a result. Because our homosexual desires and actions conflict with our internalised view of homosexuality being wrong and something to be ashamed of, the two beliefs clash. Months turn into years, and, for some people, years turn into decades. Soon we truly do believe that being different, specifically being queer, is something to be ashamed of. Whatever path we choose next will determine how much we let internalised homophobia control us, or if we can learn to control *it*.

Where Does Internalised Homophobia Come From?

At a younger age it's more subconscious. We're told pink is for girls and blue is for boys. We're shown model families, which will often be a mum, a dad, three children, maybe a family pet, and a perfect picket-fence life. Some children may even be asked if they have a boyfriend or girlfriend before they're even capable of experiencing any form of sexual feelings. We're shown in older Disney films that princesses are damsels in distress to be rescued and that princes are to be strong, brave saviours and protectors. Even when looking at kids' clothes, we'll often see a cute fluffy animal, like a bunny or kitten, for girls and a predator, like a lion or dinosaur, for boys. On the surface it may not seem that deep, but from an early age we're told what we're meant to like and who we're meant to be.

As we get older, especially when we start to hit puberty, these expectations become more specific. Boys become men. Boys are supposed to become even more athletic and better at sports. They're supposed to become taller, their voices deeper, and their muscles bigger. Most importantly, boys' desire for girls changes from having a cute playground 'girlfriend' to a more physical and primal urge that they may not yet understand. Simultaneously, girls start to become women. Most begin to experience the menstrual cycle and develop breasts, ultimately beginning physical changes that prepare their bodies for carrying and raising children. Girls aren't expected to work with tools; instead they should learn about sewing or cooking or 'home economics'. Their education becomes geared towards being a homemaker, whilst the boys are taught how to be a provider. All of us become slaves to a body we no longer have control over, and the expectations of how we're meant to present ourselves to the world become even stronger. At that age, kids and teenagers are still figuring out who they are, what they like, and what they want to become. Figuring out who you are may be encouraged, but only as long as it stays within very strict, arbitrary rules set by society. Deviating from these rules often leads to shame and ridicule, whether we experience them ourselves or witness them used against others. These expectations are upheld in three ways, often in a perpetual cycle:

'Gay Is Wrong'

We may see strangers, peers, friends, and even family members all exhibiting negative views of queer people. Negative views could range from sly comments of disapproval to more overt fuelled hatred, both of which we can begin to internalise.

Having attended an all-boys school myself, hearing homophobic comments was almost inescapable, even if they weren't directed at anyone. In religious studies class, the same boys who had always been homophobic used the class as an opportunity to be even more so. Somehow gay adoption was brought up, and one loudly proclaimed, 'It was Adam and Eve, not Adam and Steve! It's wrong!' The guy who said this wasn't even religious, and neither am I, but my shame doubled, and I just sat silently. Not only did I not want to become a target myself, but I felt such deep-rooted shame in my sexual feelings towards men that I wanted to pretend they didn't even exist.

> **'My growing up was definitely being amongst people where you're afraid to even tempt the idea that you're gay, queer or attracted to men. It was definitely used as a taunt to your manhood.'**
>
> Uzo Emenike (he/she/they), musician

The complicated reality is that homophobia stems from religion, or at least religion is used as a guise for homophobic views. The idea that any form of queerness (or non-conformity) is a sin remains the root cause of prejudice, even from those who do not actively practise a religion. The negative views of queer people have been so heavily engrained in society over centuries of religious propaganda that there is this generational view that being queer is innately wrong, with no evidence based in reality to support it. Quite often people's homophobic views will be so intrinsic, without really knowing why, that they will go out of their way to *find* reasons to support homophobia. The funniest example of this was when someone attempted to justify their homophobia by saying that gay men were more likely to experience fecal incontinence because of anal sex. Imagine being so homophobic that you pretend to care about a man you don't know potentially shitting himself? Whilst we can laugh at the feeble attempts to justify homophobia, the prejudice still exists. So long as it exists on a societal level, the cycle will continue in the next generation.

Poor Representation

Char Ellesse, a queer Black woman, is an incredible advocate for uplifting the underrepresented voices in our community, or, as she says, 'passing the mic'. During our interview she quoted something a friend said to her: 'Representation is an antidote to shame' – and I have never heard truer words spoken.

Representation is twofold:

1. It helps the people being represented feel like they're seen, heard, and truly not alone.

2. It helps educate people that various other identities exist and helps them to understand, respect, and empathise with those stories.

The unfortunate reality is that without sufficient representation, those who are underrepresented do not feel seen, do not feel heard, and more often than not feel alone in who they are. And less representation means less understanding, less respect, and less empathy.

For Char in particular, growing up as a Black woman in a society with white-centric beauty standards, she never felt represented. Her love for fashion at a younger age led to her collecting a variety of different fashion magazines. Yet despite the broad collection, the common theme throughout was the focus on a very particular type of model: white and skinny. Pair these specific physical representations with a lack of queer representation, and what we're left with is a collective of underrepresented queer people who never truly feel like they belong. The queer people who begin to break those boundaries with non-conformity are then met with the secondary result of poor representation: ridicule from those who haven't been exposed to difference.

Retaliation to Non-Conformity

'You're all right because you're a normal gay guy, not an annoying feminine one.' I remember hearing someone say this to one of the gay kids in my school. Though I wasn't out at this point, I internalised this idea. 'If I ever come out, I have to be masculine in order to be accepted', I thought. The main indicator people saw for potential queerness was gender non-conformity. Not two days into starting at an all-boys secondary school, I had my voice mocked for being high and effeminate. Femininity made me a target. And this isn't exclusive to men: Shell Rowe, a cis woman and lesbian, admitted she too worried about being seen as 'too gay' for being masculine, as it would make her a target. If queer men are too feminine, they're clocked. If queer women are too masculine, they're clocked.

> 'I used to have really long hair, and then I got diagnosed with cancer when I was twenty. I was told that I was guaranteed to lose my hair. I was really terrified of that and it was one of the first things that I thought about. I have always been a bit of a tomboy; I would wear men's clothes, boys' football kits, and I had a very boisterous personality. But I'd really held on to my long hair because it felt like this shield of femininity. This way I could be palatable if I wanted to be. You know, you're gay, but you're not "too gay".'
>
> Shell Rowe (she/her),
> content creator

Hiding who we are to any degree only reinforces the shame we're made to feel about our true selves; it reminds us that there is something to be ashamed of. Attempting to blend in means we are also more likely to be exposed to homophobic viewpoints and discussions from our peers.

Queer people often have different levels of internalised homophobia depending on our upbringing, school life, and general surroundings in our earlier years. Some will suffer on a less grand scale, but the impact can still be severe.

> 'When I was younger, I would dance to the Bollywood songs from films that always had a powerful female lead, and I was always drawn to female actors. I'd learn the choreo and dance for my family, and they would encourage me to do that, until I started hitting the age of about twelve or thirteen, where I started to grow up to them. I was becoming a man, going through puberty, and I would still be shaking my hips and dancing to these songs in a way they used to encourage. But then a time came where they just went, "No more of this. You're a boy. You don't do this anymore." I stopped dancing. I stopped having fun. It was just a part of my identity that I didn't know was so core to me, just being silly, goofy, and feminine, which I just completely stopped doing. Because I was told that's "not what boys do".'
>
> Asad Zafar (they/them),
> queer charity worker

You're Not Exempt from Misogyny

Misogyny is defined as prejudice, dislike, or hatred against women, and anyone can be guilty of it. Anyone has the capacity to perpetuate the idea that women are in some way inferior, even women themselves (the red hat brigade, for example). But more specifically, there is a strong undercurrent of misogyny within queer spaces that tends to sweep the rest of our community away, leaving only gay men standing. It is therefore no surprise that at the top of the queer iceberg sits the most masculine and muscular men, while queer women, feminine men, and gender non-conformists are pushed below the waterline. This is a prejudice that plagues all corners of society, and the queer community is no exception.

> 'I think it's about not listening and not valuing female voices, and that kind of thing happens a lot.'
>
> Shell Rowe (she/her), content creator

For a lot of gay men, the negative feelings surrounding femininity aren't just internalised homophobia but also misogyny. The vein of misogyny in our spaces is often overlooked by gay men but incredibly apparent to the rest of the community. Some gay men have genuine disdain for anything feminine, including women. Their priority is to be in all-male spaces, and they do not believe lesbians or other genders/sexualities should share the same spaces as them.

> 'You throw a stone in Soho, you will hit three gay bars. We deserve to be able to have a space that we can see from the street and not have to walk past five times till we realise where it is. We deserve better. But it also is a magical space and was a

magical space before there was anywhere else, because it was like the only place you could go to and have a drink.'

Shiv (they/them),
journalist and broadcaster

Shiv is a trans non-binary queer person, and having spent a great deal of time in Soho (London) myself, their above description is very accurate. If I go out with a friend or on a date, there are a multitude of gay and queer venues to choose from. I want to state that there is a difference between gay and queer venues; gay venues are often centred around (white) gay men, whereas queer venues tend to embrace far more corners of the community. I can think of three venues off the top of my head that are incredibly male dominated. Even in the 'queer' spaces, the number of men still outweighs the women.

Shiv explained how being in gay bars often leaves them feeling like a minority within their own spaces, saying they'll rarely see another lesbian. Sometimes even if Shiv does encounter a woman in queer spaces, upon chatting the woman will realise that Shiv is queer and almost respond in shock that they're being hit on by a queer person in a queer venue and swiftly declare that they're straight, being there only as an 'ally' of gay men. The bar Shiv mentioned is quite literally hidden away: I discovered the existence of this bar only when a friend pointed it out to me. The bigger gay bars frequented by predominantly gay men have bold appearances, large logos, and prominent pride flags. Yet a bar dedicated to lesbians is hidden underground and needs to be actively looked for.

'Everyone has their own need for feeling safe, for feeling seen. If we've got so many queer spaces that are male dominated, we should have spaces that are female dominated.'

Shell Rowe (she/her),
content creator

There is also some controversy around cisgender heterosexual (cishet) women being allowed in queer spaces. Some believe they are welcome and deserve to share our safe space because of the allyship they offer us. They may be accompanying one of their queer friends. Maybe their queer friend didn't want to go to a 'straight' club and feel unsafe, or hasn't been to a queer bar before and hasn't built a queer circle of friends yet. And sometimes the person you are perceiving as cishet may actually not be. We cannot automatically assume how a person identifies. What some also forget is that a space feels only as safe as we make it. More importantly, who we make it safe for. Some of our so-called safe spaces, as discussed, are still very white gay male – centric. Many queer people, specifically women, in fact do not feel safe in those spaces.

There are other occasions when a group of cishet women will enter a queer venue *without* any queers and walk around like they own the place. They become the loudest and drunkest group there and treat queer people like props or animals in a zoo, feeling that because it is a 'safe space', it gives them the green light to act however they see fit. The bar becomes overcrowded and there is nowhere for queer people to sit.

Queer spaces should be a place for *all* queer people and allies. The key term there being *ally*. Having a gay friend does not automatically make someone an ally. Actively standing up for *all* queer people in the face of oppression makes you an ally.

> 'When you [non-queers] think "Let's go to a queer bar and watch a drag show", and the queers almost become animals in a zoo, the reaction of them [gay men] is to kind of push back. And that's when I think we start to see the misogyny really boil its ugly head.'
>
> Danny Beard (he/they),
> drag queen and performer

The thing to consider when feeling negatively towards non-queer people being in a venue, specifically women, is *why* you feel negative. Is it because of the way they are acting, or is it because they're women? As you may find, it's actually not about protecting queer spaces but internalised misogyny.

One concept we need to leave in the past is the levels of 'gay':

Gold-Star Gay: Never had sex with a woman.

Platinum-Star Gay: Same as above, but was born via a C-section, therefore never coming into contact with a vagina.

Diamond-Star Gay: Same as above two, but was conceived via IVF, meaning that even conception didn't involve being inside a vagina.

Whilst to some it is used as a joke, to others it is a system of ranking they take quite seriously. This concept implies that the less contact you have with a woman, the 'higher-ranking' gay you are. Some gay men even become so repulsed at the thought of intimacy with a woman that they in turn are repulsed by men who have slept with women. They may also refuse to sleep with a trans man, despite sexual attraction, because they wish to retain their 'gold-star' status by refusing to come into contact with a vagina. This specific concept is one that thankfully feels much less prominent in today's culture, but the impact of misogyny is still very much felt in queer spaces.

> **'I think that my chosen family all of a sudden being populated by queer women almost made me realise that I had ingested a lot of misogyny that exists in gay male culture . . . It seems sad for me to admit this, [but] I'd almost overlooked queer women, as it's like I was blind to the fact that queer women were even around me because my circle was so gay male heavy.'**
>
> Dani St James (she/her),
> chief executive of the trans+ charity Not a Phase

Misogyny, like most prejudices, has become more covert. It's easy for us to hear words such as *misogyny*, *transphobia*, and *racism* and assume that people are accusing us of an active and unshakeable hatred for a group of people, but this isn't always the case. Our unconscious bias can create views that tie back to prejudice without us even realising it.

'For a lot of gay men, they may have experienced a level of misogyny with their femininity, effeminate ways of speaking or acting, the way they carry themselves, or the way they want to dress, and so that might, in some ways, feed into the misogyny that a gay man might experience.'

Shiv (they/them),
journalist and broadcaster

Not long after coming out, I started speaking to a guy on a dating app. He mentioned that he was considering getting a nose ring. I can't recall if I vocalised this or merely thought it (I really hope it was the latter), but I remember thinking that I wouldn't find him attractive anymore, as I saw a nose ring as being too feminine. Andrew Gurza, a queer disability advocate, recalled a time long ago where they had hooked up with an incredibly sweet guy, yet Andrew felt some unease around the guy's voice, which they thought was too high and 'feminine'. On reflection, Andrew admitted his horror at this past mindset but understood its origins. Queer people, mainly men, are often so shamed for femininity, and see no positive or desirable representations of male femininity, that we project these thoughts onto others.

'We don't see enough representations of feminine as desirable. We don't see enough representations of queer men as desirable.'

Le Fil (he/they),
artist and drag performer

Nature or Nurture?

Representation can teach kids from a young age to be tolerant, understanding, and empathetic towards those whose experiences differ from their own. They can grow up in a world free of shame. They won't project shame onto others, as they won't have any themselves.

The harsh truth is, we will unlikely feel the true effects of authentic representation, as the shame runs too deep. For us, it may feel like the damage has already been done, and in a lot of ways it has. Trauma runs deep and truly never goes away; we just become better at coping with it and the pain of it gradually subsides. The wound can heal, but a scar will remain. For us, representation provides more of a comfort than anything else. But once we are fully grown and internalised homophobia has embedded itself within our psyche, seeing someone who looks, acts, and sounds like us on TV isn't quite going to cut it.

In the long term, representation will echo down for generations and will hopefully eradicate internalised homophobia altogether. This is our hope, but something that many of us won't see in our lifetime. Instead, it is our job to lay down the foundation. It is our job to create the antidote that is representation, to help reduce the shame of internalised homophobia for future generations.

And it really does work. Le Fil is a British-born Chinese artist and drag performer who grew up in York, with little diversity around him. He told me how he joined the choir at school and met three other boys who weren't like the typical boys he'd been told he had to aspire to. One was very flamboyant and embraced camp, one was a bit geekier, and one was just a lover of music and very theatrical. They helped Le Fil embrace more of his authentic self at a young age. Seeing different representations of what we can be helps validate our authentic selves and helps beat back the shame instilled within us. It is the first step in learning that who we truly are is okay and that there are others just like us.

> **'That was the first time that I felt that masculinity had different interpretations other than what I saw in PE [gym], around school, and on TV, like it was something that I could experience. It was just really refreshing for me to hang out with people that weren't boys I'd seen or boys that I thought I had to be like.'**
>
> Le Fil (he/they),
> artist and drag performer

Believe it or not, representation also plays a part in what we find attractive. No, I'm not saying we're indoctrinated into being queer, but instead how we navigate our queerness. Our teen years are also our most sexually formative. It is here that we, for the very first time, begin to experience sexual feelings and to uncover more about who we really are. Our relationship with sex at a younger age is often a lot more puritanical and is seen as something to be ashamed of. Poor sex education delivery leads to young people feeling a great deal of anxiety around sex, and for queer people who are taught nothing, this shame is magnified.

The combination of internalised homophobia, sexual shame,

idealised masculinity, and the ridicule of femininity sets us on the path of friction with our perspectives on queerness. It is therefore no surprise that often some of the younger queer people who we see on dating apps or social media may display some of these narrow-minded viewpoints. They've had much less time to truly explore what it is they like, and their main points of reference are the representations of purely idealised standards.

But positive representation is not something that can be worked towards alone, it is a community and societal effort. In the meantime, there is work that can be done on a personal level to begin to unpack our unconscious bias and tackle internalised homophobia. We can apply what I spoke of at the end of the introduction by asking ourselves 'Why?' If you have negative feelings towards certain community members for being non-conforming, ask yourself 'Why?'

A lack self-awareness can mean we allow what we find attractive to shroud our judgement. Some of us become too well acquainted with our so-called preferences, and we allow them to dictate the way we treat others, much like the individuals who will say 'no fats, no fems' or its equivalent in their bios. We allow them to dictate who we are friends with, who we value, who we respect, and generally who we give our time to. Some won't even entertain a conversation with someone unless they deem them to be of value to them, primarily by being attractive, even in a nonsexual manner.

We often have the idea that we cannot help what we find attractive, which to an extent is true. We do not make a conscious choice to find some things attractive and some things not. Queer people have a better understanding of this than most, as much of our fight is trying to explain to others that our sexual orientation is not something we have any control over. However, the various words used to describe our likes and dislikes are used interchangeably and often incorrectly. Sexual attraction, sexual arousal, sexual orientation, and sexuality are all different:

Sexual Attraction: This focusses purely on our ability to feel desire for sexual interactions with a specific individual. Who we are sexually attracted to can help us understand our sexual orientation through our attraction to specific gender(s); however, we are highly unlikely to experience sexual attraction to *everyone* within a specific gender. For example, a woman may be a lesbian if she is attracted to women, but she may not be sexually attracted to *all* women. It is highly unlikely that anyone who experiences sexual attraction is going to be sexually attracted to everyone who crosses their path.

Sexual Arousal: This explains our mental and physical responses to sexual stimuli (bluntly, what makes us horny). Arousal can occur without sexual attraction being present, as it can be a result of physical stimulation. It can also occur without physical stimulation, as our arousal could be because of something that is visibly arousing, such as someone we find sexually attractive or being aroused by certain body parts. This can also contribute to discovering our sexual orientation but, again, not necessarily determine it.

Sexual Orientation: This is a broader term used to describe the gender(s) we are romantically and/or sexually attracted to, which contributes to our overall sexuality. Sexual attraction and arousal can *help* us understand our sexual orientation, but our sexual orientation is determined by more than those two factors. For example, asexuality is a sexual orientation that involves a lack of sexual attraction to any gender. However, a woman can be both a lesbian and asexual, as she may be romantically attracted to women whilst not experiencing any sexual attraction. Some straight men are aroused by receiving anal stimulation but are not aroused by a dick or sexually attracted to men. Some straight men have this itch scratched by solo play or being pegged by a cis woman (using a strap-on). This does not make them gay or bi. A man can be completely heterosexual while also aroused by the stimulation that comes from bottoming.

Sexuality: This is the *big* one, the main umbrella term that encapsulates all elements of sex for an individual. This includes our sexual behaviours, such as things we like to do or don't like to do, as well as kinks and fetishes. It also includes our attitudes and beliefs towards sex – being sex positive, for example, or experiencing shame around sex – and our sexual orientation and the gender(s) we are attracted to, as well as who we are more specifically sexually attracted to and what makes us sexually aroused. This is what's most used interchangeably to discuss our sexual orientation, which technically isn't incorrect, as our orientation is part of our greater sexuality.

The issue arises when people use the same logic that's used to explain sexual orientation being out of our control to justify sexual attraction being out of our control. Despite many research attempts to prove that we choose to be queer, there is no convincing evidence that our sexual orientation is in any way, shape, or form influenced by our social environment – so no, it isn't a choice.[1] However, sexual attraction is both biological and environmental, and for this I am speaking from experience. My sexual orientation was predetermined for me. Before I had a single sexual encounter, I was already experiencing sexual attraction to men. This sure as hell wasn't environmental, because every single fibre of society was telling me that those feelings were wrong. This is one of the many reasons why claims that queerness is a 'choice' and that we 'indoctrinate kids' fall completely flat. You don't need indoctrination for queer people to exist. Our sexual orientations grow and develop despite society's stark opposition to our existence.

Yet, who we find sexually attractive within a specific gender has a much clearer positive correlation with our social environment and representation we see. I want you to think of every time you have seen a man be portrayed in a sexually desirable way, and not even necessarily a gay man. What did he look like? What was his demeanour? How did he dress? How did his body look? How did his voice sound? I can almost guarantee that he would have been muscular, if not at least slender, and masculine both aesthetically and vocally. More often than not he was probably white too. Think back to any time you've seen a male model for underwear or on the poster of a club night, or a male actor in almost any porn. There is a very clear pattern in aesthetics, one that idealises masculinity in every form. This can be unintentionally internalised and heavily influence the types of people we are attracted to, and this certainly happened to me. As I detailed in the introduction, the types of men I am sexually attracted to has changed; I went from having an aversion to feminine men to now finding them actively attractive. The reason being I grew up not being shown feminine men in a desirable way, yet once I exposed myself to different kinds of people, how I view others, including my capacity for attraction, changed.

Prejudice Isn't Your Fault. Refusing to Work on It Is.

Much like privilege, some people feel affronted when internalised homophobia, misogyny, or other prejudices are brought to their attention. I remember being in one class as a teenager where my friend and I were discussing an upcoming project. I was still figuring out who I was at this point and ironically had a little crush on the friend I was working with. We spent the two-hour lesson brainstorming various ideas, and I remember, after I made one suggestion, I instantly dismissed it by saying, 'Nah, but that's gay.' My teacher was stood in front of me on the other side of the desk, organising some papers, and without even turning his head he said, 'We don't say that, do we, Max? What you mean to say is that you don't like it. But that doesn't make it gay.' I apologised instantly and sheepishly got back to brainstorming with my friend. This memory has stuck with me ever since. The irony is that while I knew I wasn't straight, I still used *gay* as an insult. I had become so accustomed to hearing it that I too thought it was okay; I'd never heard someone be called out for saying it before. It was also a way of distancing myself from the idea of being gay, as I honestly believed it would make people suspect me less or less likely to target me.

That behaviour is something many people unfortunately

don't ever unpack, or at least not for a long time. When I first wrote that sentence, I originally used the phrase 'grow out of' instead of 'unpack'. But it's not something we ever 'grow out of'; it takes time and hard work to change the way we view ourselves and queerness as a whole. We must actively dismantle our unconscious biases and rebuild our relationship with ourselves, and in turn develop a true love for who we are and for our community. Without this, some will instead distance themselves from perceived queerness to feel less of a target. It can be as simple as a 'no fems' bio to denouncing the entire community.

The most common example of this is that some believe that certain queer people, namely the less conforming, give us a 'bad name' to those who already dislike us. They believe that those who are even further from the norm make the entire community a target for ridicule by the masses. 'Why does being gay need to be your entire personality?' is one of the most common things we hear from non-queer and even some queer people. It's also a mentality I used to share. I didn't understand why being queer was something to be proud of, let alone something that was completely integral to some people's identities. My view was that who we are sexually attracted to and who we love shouldn't change who we are, and I know why I came to this conclusion. I had been shamed out of almost everything that could be perceived as queerness. Having been ridiculed for any ounce of femininity, how was I then supposed to wrap my head around the concept of drag? Over time, I began to realise that queerness really is an integral part of our identity – not inherently because of our sexuality or gender identity, but because of the way we are treated.

So many of our lived experiences are intertwined with our

queerness because of the way we're made to feel about it. The options therefore end up being to embrace it or reject it – and I was rejecting it. Why would I want to embrace the very thing that led to the first two decades of my life being full of ridicule? But it's not being queer that leads to ridicule, it's other people's intolerance to difference. The idea that certain people 'give us a bad name' is not the fault of the few but the ignorance of the many. It's people's inability to accept that we are all fundamentally different. Those who berate the LGBTQIA+ community do not need a scapegoat to do so, they will do so regardless. The bigoted do not need a reason to be bigoted. They do not need to be handed ammunition to fire at us, they will simply find it (or make it up).

The idea that the less conforming in our community put a target on all our backs is rooted in internalised homophobia, as we know deep down that to be different automatically means to be cast out. We've all seen first-hand how those who are different are targeted, and we don't want to be next, so we distance ourselves. 'We're no different from anyone else, we're not victims', I often see commented on some of my social media posts. Some of us are so determined to be embraced by the mainstream that we repress any feeling of difference. Because being different is to be wrong. But at its core, difference *isn't* wrong. Starting to truly understand this is one of the first steps in unpacking our internalised homophobia. We do not fear being different; we fear the 'otherness' that comes with being different.

Some people will go through their entire lives never unpacking their unconscious biases. If the impact of it was purely on them, I'd say crack on, it's between them and their therapist. If they want to retain the very prejudices that have kept us underfoot for centuries, let them. But the issue is that internalised homophobia doesn't just stay internal; we often externalise it and project it onto others.

One of the hardest stories was one told to me by Daisy Puller. I'd met Daisy on several occasions as an effervescent drag queen with a quick wit, sparkly outfits, and a smile that lights up a room. But things haven't always been like this for Daisy. She told me of her experience going on holiday with some friends years ago and was at the airport out of drag. The destination was specifically for queer people, and therefore you'd expect it to be queer friendly – which, technically, it was, but only for certain types of queer people.

> 'This group of superhot muscle gays walks past, and the Regina George of the group looks me up and down and goes, "Too tall, too thin, too loud, too gay." He literally hit every chink in the armour, all my insecurities. That little fucking bitch managed to hit the arrow right through my heart. The rest of that holiday, I just felt horrible. Every time we went to the beach, I felt like every single person was looking at me and saying that. Of course, they probably weren't, but I carried that for years and years and years. I could hear that voice from that random person who certainly would never have thought about me twice.'
>
> Daisy Puller (she/they),
> drag queen and HIV activist

Saying something like this is truly unthinkable, let alone to another queer person. But the attitude exhibited here is one born out of internalised homophobia, whether we like to admit it or not. Unfortunately, an experience such as this is all too common, specifically from gay men. We have been so beaten and bruised by society, and in some unfortunate cases literally, that even after coming to terms with our identity, we still feel this urge to put others down to lift ourselves up.

'Too gay', he said to Daisy. My initial reaction was 'What the actual fuck does "too gay" even mean?!' There's no such thing as being too gay or not gay enough. To be anything other than gay would be a different sexual orientation entirely, for starters. But what this man was insinuating was that the way Daisy was expressing herself was too close to the presentation of gay we've been shamed for. Essentially, too feminine. His internalised homophobia was so deep that he felt the need to actively shame another queer person. There are two reasons he would've had this view: either he was personally ridiculed for femininity when he was younger, and therefore he suppressed his own, or he simply witnessed the treatment of other feminine gay men and so his learned behaviour was to do the same.

> **'I think it's usually a bit of privilege as well, because they're usually the people who are the closest in proximity to being heteronormative. There's nothing wrong with being heteronormative, [but] we don't have to put down the ones of us who just naturally aren't, because a lot of us, that's just not in our nature.'**
>
> Charlie Craggs (she/her),
> author and trans+ activist

Often the way gay men idealise a muscular physique stems back to our views around masculinity being superior. 'Too tall' and 'too thin', he said to Daisy in an attempt to belittle them. Muscles and strength are often associated with masculinity, hence why women who are more muscular tend to have their femininity questioned. So, this again was him attempting to diminish Daisy's own masculinity. Daisy was 'too loud', but a specific type of loud – her non-conformity. Like I said, I've met Daisy many times, and she is the life and soul of the party in the *best* possible way. But to some, being flamboyant isn't something to be celebrated, it's something that doesn't align with masculinity. Therefore, it's something to be shamed.

Performing masculinity or femininity is not inherently good or bad. Some people will naturally have more masculine energy in the way they present to the world through expression, fashion, their personality, and overall aesthetic. And this is perfectly okay. Also, this doesn't automatically equal internalised homophobia. I've met plenty of very masculine gay guys who are the loveliest people you've ever met. But that's because they have a stronger sense of self, one that isn't purely held up through attempts at feeling superior. It sounds like a cliche, but the way we see others truly is a reflection of how we see ourselves. So, whilst on the surface the mean gay at the airport may not have appeared to have insecurities about being feminine, he clearly had such deep-rooted fear and shame related to femininity that the only way to experience alleviation of these feelings was to put someone else down for them instead.

'It's just a reflection of the trauma that we've experienced, when you're a young gay person being constantly rejected in school. People actively tell you to your face that you're not enough. So when people treat you like that, you think, "Oh, okay, so I guess it's cool if I do it to other people."'

Romone (they/them),
performance artist

Many of us naturally gravitate to like-minded people, as it can provide a sense of comfort and safety. The issue, however, is that comfort can breed toxicity. As mentioned in the introduction, it's important to surround ourselves with people who have both similar and different experiences from our own. When we associate solely with those of similar or identical viewpoints, we inhibit our ability to grow. If our circle and the media we consume represent only a particular identity and aesthetic, we risk lacking tolerance and understanding for those who are different. But if we make a conscious effort to unpack why we think the way we do and take the time to meet different people and listen to their stories, we may begin to realise there is a whole other world of beautiful queer people out there who we too have overlooked.

Chapter 2

Gender, Sex, and Everything in Between

The topic of gender is one that is both incredibly simple and equally complicated at the same time. To some it's a topic that encourages freedom of expression, self-acceptance, and liberation. To others it prompts frictional debates, segregation, and prejudice. One of the most contentious arguments is one based purely on misunderstanding: the difference between sex and gender. So before delving into this chapter, I want to define some things in case you're new to the topic.

Sex: This is a person's biological makeup, which is determined by anatomy and characteristics such as their genitalia and gonads, as well as hormones and chromosomes. This typically refers to males and females in a very strict binary sense.

Gender: This is a socially constructed idea that determines the roles, behaviours, and expected appearance of men and women. These ideas are pressured onto each of us by society from birth based on a person's biological sex, and gendered labels include 'man' for males and 'woman' for females. The gender assigned by society to each of us from birth often sets the course of our lives. Despite gender being a social construct, it too is often viewed as purely binary and set in stone. This might sound like an abstract concept, but many describe gender as the performance we each take part in alongside the rest of society, from one day to the next. When you think about it like this, the parameters around gender become much more moveable for the rest of us.

Transgender: This is an umbrella term for an individual whose gender identity does not align with the gender they were assigned at birth based on biological sex. This can include a binary trans person, such as a trans man or trans woman, as well as a non-binary individual. Trans+ is the shorthand when referring to the umbrella term, whereas trans is the shorthand for those who transition in a more binary sense or being transgender.

Non-binary: An umbrella term used to describe a person whose identity falls outside of the traditional gender binary. This also falls under the trans+ umbrella, but rather than identifying with one specific gender, they may identify with more than one or none, and this can change over time.

Cisgender: This adjective describes the lived experience of an individual whose gender identity *does* align with the gender they were assigned at birth based on biological sex. For example, I am a cis man because I was born biologically male and as an adult identify as a man.

Intersex: An intersex individual is born with biological primary and/or secondary characteristics such as genitals, reproductive organs, and/or chromosomes that do not align with the binary sex expectations of being male or female. For example, someone can be born with both ovaries and testicles, and sometimes an individual can be born with both typically male and female external genitals. According to the United Nations at the time of writing this, as high as 1.7 per cent of people could be born intersex,[1] meaning although we rarely speak on the naturally occurring variances in biological sex among people, you likely come into contact with intersex people all the time (many of whom could also be unaware they're intersex).

Cishet: A simple abbreviation to describe someone who is both cisgender and heterosexual.

AFAB: Assigned female at birth.

AMAB: Assigned male at birth.

Our genetic makeup determines our biological sex, and our gender is assigned to us by society based on that, which in turn creates a set of rules, boundaries, and expectations for us. Despite often being born perfectly healthy and without complications, if an intersex person is born with visibly ambiguous sex charecteristics, they may be forced to undergo genital 'corrective' surgery often before the age of one, determined by their parents' decision over which gender to raise them as – whilst coincidently, gender-affirming care and surgeries for trans+ adults are often described as 'mutilation' in an attempt to justify transphobic rhetoric. So – *checks notes* – it's 'corrective' when someone decides for us, but is 'mutilation' if it's our own decision? Got it.

Expected conformity to gender roles puts every single one of us in a box that may feel inescapable. When these expectations are upheld on a societal and even governmental level, soon people begin to feel empowered to make decisions over other people's bodily autonomy: the way we dress, the way we act, the way we identify, and even our medical decisions. Not having autonomy over our gender identities and expression can be incredibly detrimental to our self-worth. Like I said in the discussion on internalised homophobia, hiding who we are to any degree only reinforces the shame we're made to feel about who we are; it reminds us that there is something to be ashamed of. This isn't exclusive to sexual orientation; it also very much applies to gender. Shell Rowe opened up in more detail about her experience with losing her hair after her cancer diagnosis and how negative situations can have unexpected, wonderful outcomes. In Shell's case, it was gender euphoria.

'When I was in hospital for treatment, my hair started to fall out. I was just so devastated about it at the time that I went straight from the hospital to the hairdresser's. I had to bite the bullet and just be like,

"Get rid of it." I took my beanie with me, thinking that I was going to walk out of the hairdresser's really embarrassed, really ashamed. And I didn't even wear my beanie. I looked at myself in the mirror and it was this absolute wave of gender euphoria, and it actually makes me emotional, really thinking about staring back in the mirror and just thinking, "I just feel really at home in my skin, and this feels right." And it made me realise that I think I spent my whole life kind of suppressing the way that I wanted to identify and how I wanted to express my gender identity, and just kind of denied those feelings that I probably always had.'

Shell Rowe (she/her),
content creator

Being able to express ourselves in the way that feels most natural to us is crucial to having a strong sense of self and to developing long-term confidence. When we succumb to the pressure to fulfil a certain role or to conform to certain ideals, who we are as a person becomes heavily dependent on how other people view us. For example, when a man feels intense pressure to be strong and masculine, he is unlikely to be able to validate his own masculinity and will instead rely on others to validate it for him. This results in the common chest-thumping and dick-swinging we see a lot of cishet men partake in in order to be seen as a bigger and stronger man, essentially showing off. A man truly comfortable in his own masculinity doesn't feel insecure in his actions, interests, friendships, or any other part of his identity. He doesn't worry about preferring a fruity cocktail over a beer, Disney films over football, or skincare over a seven-in-one shampoo. He feels so secure in his identity and masculinity that the perception of others plays no role in the validation of his sense of self. Those who are insecure in their masculinity will worry about how they present themselves and will in turn likely judge others for their supposed lack of masculinity. These are very specific examples of the pressures of gender roles on a micro level and how, based on our assigned gender, we are expected to only like certain things and act in certain ways. For queer people, the pressure to conform becomes even more apparent as we're even less likely to fit in. That's why figuring out who we truly are often takes us much longer.

> **'What I've learned is whatever feels the most natural, that's who you're meant to be. Don't try and swim against the flow of water.'**
>
> Tyreece (he/she/they),
> fashion creator and performer

To Conform or Not Conform

Two of the most notable contributors to queer culture are drag and ballroom, which both have foundations built on gender non-conformity and self-expression. To some, drag is purely an art form and a way for performers to express themselves creatively, but to others, it can be a form of escape. Being a drag artist quite often makes you the belle of the ball and the most interesting person in the room. When queer people grow up ashamed for who they are, drag can be a way of creating an alter ego to escape the rigid pressures of the gender binary and find more comfort in being a quick-witted entertainer. Yes, non-conformity can put a target on our back (as we've seen with drag bans), but for some it can also be their biggest shield.

> **'You won't find a drag queen out there that's not got some kind of sad story to tell. For me, I was the outcast in school. Then you go out in drag and everybody knows who you are and they want to talk to you. And all of a sudden you're cool, you're everything you always wanted to be.'**
>
> Danny Beard (he/they),
> drag queen and performer

While gender non-conformity is often viewed purely as the way we dress, it also covers how a person's expression *or* behaviour is different from expectations placed upon them from the gender they were assigned at birth. All forms of queerness relate back to gender non-conformity in some way. Even if you feel you present in a conforming way, your role is likely to differ from what is expected of you based on your biological sex.

Heterosexuality is often defaulted as 'the norm' in society, even though same sex attraction can be observed across the animal kingdom. All sexual orientations apart from heterosexuality in some way oppose expectations of our assigned gender identity. A man wanting to have sex with another man does not align with the heteronormative societal expectations for men to marry a woman and have children. More specifically, a man who wants to bottom for another man may be viewed as even less conforming, as men are told to be dominant and assertive, to be the penetrative partner – hence the rife bottom shaming amongst gay men and perception of being 'less than' (but we'll discuss that later). An asexual individual is in some way not conforming to gender expectations, as the overall expectation is that humans are to be sexually attracted to the opposite sex in order to procreate. Whereas an asexual individual experiences little to no sexual attraction at all. Whilst we may not necessarily identify with the concept of gender non-conformity, queer people are all ultimately in one way or another non-conforming to normative gender expectations. The non-conformity for some could be minor, internal, and less easily identifiable, and for others, it could be more overt and expressive. But as a collective we're not conforming to the roles we're told we must play based on our assigned gender. This is why our fights have been so heavily intertwined and why the LGBTQIA+ community was formed. We share the same adversaries and the view that we should have bodily autonomy.

Acceptance of any kind of non-conformity often comes from exposure and representation. Being friends with gender non-conforming people helped me better understand and respect their experiences. Given the queer community's intertwined history with non-conformity, it's surprising that representation of queer people is still often limited to a very binary view, especially when it comes to desirability. Gay men in particular have next to zero representation of femininity as being desirable. In any form of queer media and pornography and in wider society, traditional masculinity is put on a pedestal and seen as the benchmark for a gay man's desirability. This, amongst other things, contributes to the infamous 'no fems' and 'masc4masc' attitudes that have become all too common. Whether people care to admit it or not, this isn't simply a preference, it's internalised homophobia, and it's presented in a way that attempts to devalue femininity.

As queer people, we are so starved of authentic representation and acceptance of who we really are that it determines how we treat others. Because of this, for the first few years after I came out I was plagued with a very shallow and restrictive mindset. Yet today, I wear sparkly earrings, have two nose piercings, have my nails vibrantly painted regularly, and even go through phases of wearing makeup and dresses. My attraction to body types changed, and so did my attraction to different forms of expression. I've been with guys who are incredibly masculine, with guys and non-binary people who are incredibly feminine, and with people in between. In some ways I am now more attracted to someone who appears *more* queer and nonconforming, as it's a sign of being comfortable in who they are and rejecting traditional norms, which makes them less likely to project onto me.

The media representation is still scarce, and we often have to create it ourselves. Poor representation leads to poor self-acceptance, and that leads to poor acceptance of others. With us being given such a limited perception of what queerness can look like in a desirable way, we end up feeling that what we see are truly our only options. Anyone who doesn't fit into the representations we've seen simply isn't seen as an option for us.

Le Fil spent years unpacking his unconscious bias to discover that he in fact is attracted to more than the limited selection the media presents us with, which he said is something that 'loads of the community don't do'. Actively taking the time to expose ourselves to different kinds of people isn't just about understanding others but about understanding ourselves.

> **'One fundamental thing for me was working within the queer community and supporting the queer community. It taught me a lot about myself, and then also moving out gave me that creative freedom to dress and wear what I want.'**
>
> Asad Zafar (they/them),
> queer charity worker

LGB with the T

But what happens when someone is non-conforming in more than just their actions and likes? What happens when their gender identity doesn't align with the gender identity society expects of them based on their biological sex? This is when someone is going to fall under the trans+ umbrella. First and foremost, a person might experience gender dysphoria, which is internal distress and discomfort (at the very least) due to that misalignment of gender. Anyone can experience gender dysphoria, but the level and severity of the dysphoria will indicate whether a person is transgender or not. For trans+ people, gender dysphoria is incredibly intense and one of the driving forces behind their distress and need to socially and/or medically transition. Some trans+ people describe the intensity of dysphoria as having been born into the wrong body. But Maxine Heron, a trans woman, explains this better than I ever could.

> 'For example, if a man was starting from scratch with trying to understand what dysphoria feels like, I think I would ask that person, "What is it that makes you *feel* like a man?" Because it's not what's between your legs. I'd imagine a big part of that feeling of manhood could be that you have assimilated alongside other men, functioning in this gendered world with relative comfort around your maleness. You know that this is the role within society that you feel comfortable in and that your body represents a future that you feel relatively at peace with – in your own comfort, you might not have even given it any thought. You might never have experienced any challenges about that feeling of manhood - that feeling of just being in harmony with exactly what manhood looks like in this gendered world. Now, imagine that you were born with a vagina, and imagine that manhood was not what you were expected to go through, and people around you were forcing you into womanhood instead. Using 'she/her' pronouns and pressuring expectations of femininity onto you from birth. You have a girl's name. You're going to grow boobs

one day, but you still experience this feeling of manhood. The idea of growing up and just having to be a woman is extremely daunting and confronting, because you just know that it's actually just not who you are.'

Maxine Heron (she/her),
writer and trans advocate

Some cis men may feel distress and even slight gender dysphoria over the presence of curves on their body, as it doesn't align with their gender identity or how they believe their body should look. Whilst I don't personally experience gender dysphoria, some trans men and non-binary people have admitted that they find comfort in my body shape. The idealised 'male' body is typically viewed as being muscular, toned, and having a V-shaped torso. Well, that's not me and hasn't been for a *long* time. I'm curvier, specifically around my waist and hips, which are characteristics more commonly associated with women. This is something that can cause trans men or mascs to experience gender dysphoria, as the presence of curves in areas that are associated with women and femininity can cause distress as it doesn't align with their gender identity. But when my body as a cis man isn't representing the typically masculine man or male ideal, some trans+ people have found comfort in understanding that certain body types aren't necessarily restricted to gender identity or sex.

'I've definitely looked at your Instagram and you'll be topless. I'll pause the video, and I'll think, "You can

be masculine, or you can be a man, and you can have a body that looks like this."'

Shiv (they/them),
journalist and broadcaster

Felix Mufti, a trans writer, performer, and activist, noted that hookup apps in particular can contribute to gender dysphoria. He admitted that whilst ordinarily he's not one to compare himself, the bios of some people on hookup apps can make him feel that he *should* be. The very strict representations of masculinity and the 'male' body add pressure to some trans men and mascs to live up to the incredibly high expectations that gay men have set.

But it's not just about how we present ourselves, it's how we're addressed. When we're addressed in a way that aligns with *one* specific gender, it can reduce an individual to that box and the gender expectations that come with it. Using gender-neutral pronouns is a way of fully rejecting the norms and expectations of socially imposed traditional gender roles. One of the funniest arguments against the use of gender-neutral pronouns is that they are grammatically incorrect, which is false. Gender-neutral pronouns are used by everyone every single day when a person's gender simply isn't known. If you speak to a dog owner and aren't sure of the dog's sex, you might ask, 'What's their name?' It's not that the pronouns don't exist or are wrong, it's simply something we're not used to in the context of people. I myself have plenty of friends who use gender-neutral pronouns, and getting used to them wasn't easy. It's not something you become accustomed to overnight, which is also not what people with these pronouns expect. Slipping up is okay and understandable; it simply requires a quick 'sorry' and a correction. People just want to see that you're actively trying. Outright refusing to respect someone's pronouns almost out of spite – that's what people don't like.

For non-binary people, or NBs (sometimes spelled enbies), gender dysphoria is something that seems to be met with even less understanding and has become a point of contention in recent years for those with gender-critical views. Gender-diverse people can experience a range of different and complicated feelings regarding the strict boxes they are put in. For some, it can be more social, such as expression and aesthetic, and for others, it can include an innate need to medically transition. The experiences may be different, but both still fall under the trans+ umbrella.

> **'I am someone who has bottom dysphoria. I'm someone who wants top surgery. But those aren't things that I necessarily talk about too much online. But because I don't talk too much about that online, people then don't see my transness as real.'**
>
> Dee Whitnell (they/them),
> sex educator and trans+ activist

Unfortunately, whilst all queer people are non-conforming to some degree, we see rampant transphobia inside the community from people who see themselves as *more* conforming. The fear being that by associating with trans+ people, their own societal acceptance is in jeopardy. There is often a very specific type of person who upholds prejudices in our spaces, and it is those of privilege. The vast majority of those who wish to denounce any form of queerness bar the 'love is love' slogan are cis, white, and gay or lesbian.

> **'In particular, I see so many white gay men, resting on their laurels. They'll hang out with problematic straight bros, for example, because they are at the top of the queer food chain.'**
>
> Maxine Heron (she/her), writer and trans advocate

A significant and specific form of transphobia comes from a group known as trans-exclusionary radical feminists (TERFs). For the purpose of this book, however, I will be referring to them as gender-critical feminists. Maxine mentioned how she will refer to them as such out of principle, stating that she's 'not trying to be a pick-me or to suck up to them, but it might be the pathway to us existing on the same planet harmoniously one day'. Maxine believes in leading with the same compassion she wants extended to her, and that means respecting the labels they choose to determine themselves with – even if they aren't doing the same. Maxine's sense of self is not compromised by how others speak of her. Yet, if any person says 'refer to me by this', whether gender critical or not, that's how she believes in referring to them. Which is a very diplomatic way of approaching it. Think about any time you've had an argument with a friend or loved one – has hurling insults at each other ever led to a more peaceful exchange? Or did it just rile you both up?

My hope is that if, on the off-chance, a gender-critical feminist picks up and reads this book, they'll see we had enough respect to address them how they wish to be addressed and to show us the same respect by, at least, listening to our point of view before slamming the book shut.

> **'I hope what we'll always do is meet people where they are with the knowledge that they have and take it from there.'**
>
> Dani St James (she/her),
> chief executive of the trans+ charity Not a Phase

Gender-critical feminists often believe that trans women are in fact predatory men disguised as women and are a threat to cis women's safety. They also believe that trans women are in some way taking the rights of cis women away. Yet all these ideas are purely theoretical – there is no data to suggest trans people are a threat to the safety or rights of women. There are no rights being taken away from cis women, and trans women are not a threat. To believe so is to succumb to a fear of fiction. You may as well be a child fearing a monster in your closet. If there were stories of trans women assaulting cis women in restrooms, hospital wings, or changing rooms, they would be all over the news. But they are not. They never happen – statistically, the biggest threat to women is a man they already know, usually a current or former romantic partner.[2] Trans people have been using the restroom that aligns with their gender identity for years, decades even, without incident. Most cis people will have, at some point or another, likely have been in the restroom at the same time as a trans person and not even known, because they're there to use the toilet just like you. I don't think any of us really want to be in a public restroom for longer than necessary.

Maxine opened up about her experience at school, specifically with toilets. Before she transitioned, back in her schools days, if she went into the boys' toilet with her long hair, the boys would mock her and tell her to leave. One option presented to her was to use the teachers' toilets, which, like any student, made her incredibly uncomfortable to be there. Her solution was simply not to use the toilet at school, to the point she wouldn't drink water to reduce the need for her to go to the toilet. The lack of tolerance from her peers was incredibly detrimental to Maxine's school experience. This echoes the experience of trans people who are not at a point of 'passing' in a public setting, and foreshadows trans people's reality should the trans-exclusionary bathroom bills come to pass. Even with such conversations simply taking place, women, including cis women, are having their gender questioned in public bathrooms.

Unlike the make-believe consequences of trans people being allowed to use spaces aligning with their gender, excluding trans people from these spaces has real consequences. At age six, Maxine first put into words that she was a girl, and at age eight, her family were advised by her therapist that she displayed signs of gender dysphoria. Four years later, when she was twelve, Maxine started puberty blockers, which pause the hormonal bodily changes in their tracks and prevent changes such as facial hair, body hair and voice breaking. Puberty blockers were originally developed for what's known as 'precocious puberty', where a young person enters puberty earlier than they should. In cases such as these, kids would be prescribed these exact blockers until they were deemed old enough to go through puberty. In December 2024, the UK government banned blockers both via NHS and private healthcare routes – but only for trans people younger than 18. The exact same drugs are still available to treat certain cancers, endometriosis, and for kids experiencing precocious puberty. With this discriminatory ban implemented for trans people only, by the time a trans person can legally consent to taking puberty blockers, puberty will have already taken hold.

> **'I was afraid of living in a body that no longer belonged to me and instead belonged to that puberty.'**
>
> Maxine Heron (she/her), writer and trans advocate

Maxine recalled seeing her male peers at school going through puberty rapidly: a deepening voice, facial hair, and apparent growth spurts – all things she managed to avoid. The mass hysteria surrounding puberty blockers was primarily around young people's inability to adequately consent to the treatment. Maxine noted the common concern that these treatments were 'being handed out like lollipops', which did not align with her first-hand experience. Few consider the medical and legal hoops a trans person must jump through in order to even be diagnosed with gender dysphoria, let alone be prescribed any treatment. Maxine was monitored by various therapists to assess whether gender dysphoria was consistent through her childhood and teen years, which it was. She recalled one doctor in particular stating that Maxine would 'grow out' of her transness and at one point a different specialist even asked the question 'How's the cross-dressing going?' The idea that trans people are simply able to change their gender with the flick of a switch is an incredibly harmful view that many of the most influential conservative people share. The reason being they do not consult with any trans people. Only 10 per cent of the respondents to the Cass Review, a report commissioned by the National Health Service's public consult on gender identity services, were trans adults. Moreover, fewer than one hundred people were currently being prescribed puberty blockers by the NHS at the time of the ban.[3]

Another focal point for those with gender-critical views is the regret of those who have medically transitioned and wish to detransition. You'd think given the focus on detransitioning that the figure would be dominant, but it's less than 1 per cent of trans people, and one of the main reasons they wish to detransition is due to a lack of social acceptance and the way friends, family, the workplace, and general society treat them post-transition.[4] Regret rates for other consensual surgeries are comparatively much higher. Up to 9 per cent of people regret a breast augmentation, up to 33.3 per cent for body contouring (reshaping) surgeries, and up to 47.1 per cent for breast reconstruction.[5] These are all voluntary surgeries that respectfully do not require anywhere near as many hoops to be jumped through nor cause the pre-op patient as much distress. These are all things that anyone with gender-critical views tends to conveniently miss out on.

'The issue is that it's not about them or what they say. It's who they enable and the actions people take out of the fear that they project. It galvanises fence-sitters into a mindset or sometimes even action.'

Dani St James (she/her),
chief executive of the trans+ charity Not a Phase

Trans+ people are some of the most loving, caring, and vulnerable people in our society and have become a pawn in the games of politics. They've become a football to be kicked about to score political points with the electorate. To quote *Wicked*, 'the best way to bring folks together is to give them a really good enemy'. Political parties live by the motto of a musical villain and create the vision of a false enemy in the heads of the general public just to give them someone to blame or something to be angry about, which distracts them from the genuine issues that need addressing. Nothing gets people out to vote more than a desire for change, and what better change to bring than by finding a vulnerable minority group to blame? If it's not trans+ people, it's gay people, and if it's not gay people, it's immigrants, or it's Muslims, or it's low-income families on government support. On and on the list goes. All to distract us from the real issues that need to be addressed. Why, during a cost-of-living crisis, are some of the biggest talking points about defining what a woman is and where a trans person should be allowed to pee? These are not the groups of people to blame for struggling to pay your rent, for bills going up, for a regression in women's rights, or for not feeling safe walking home alone at night.

> **'On the many occasions men have assaulted me in the past, never once have they counted how many ovaries I have (as a trans woman, the answer is zero). I've been assaulted by men simply on the basis that they perceive me to be a woman, and therefore a target. It's the same when a man assaults any other woman. Trans women are not exempt from misogyny.'**
>
> Maxine Heron (she/her),
> writer and trans advocate

What few seem to acknowledge is the correlation between the progression and regression of the rights of the oppressed. It is not a coincidence that trans women are being targeted at the same time abortion rights are being stripped back. That whilst trans women are being denied healthcare, that Pride parades are being banned in other countries. This concept is known as 'group-focussed enmity' and explains how different prejudices in society aren't isolated and are in fact interconnected by a broader view on inequality. It's no surprise that if someone has prejudice in one form, they likely have it in another.

So despite the views of gender-critical feminists, the oppression and targeting of trans women actually hurts them as well. The UK Supreme Court ruling that defines a woman by biology (sex) and not sociology (gender) puts the entire concept of womanhood and femininity under a microscope. Cis women who are perceived as not being 'feminine' enough have their entire womanhood questioned. This phenomenon has become so common, that it's now been coined as 'transvestigating' (wild, I know). On top of this, the UK Supreme Court's definition also completely ignores the existence and reality of intersex people.

The 2024 Olympics saw Imane Khelif, a cisgender woman, win gold for boxing. The controversy sparked from this put her gender and biological sex into question, with many assuming she was a trans woman because of her more masculine appearance. We saw a number of public figures (I don't need to name who) dogpile and ridicule Khelif's participation purely because their view of womanhood was determined by their perception of acceptable femininity. We've already started to see cis women be asked to show ID or even asked to leave restrooms because they've been falsely perceived as trans due to being more masculine in their appearance. The irony, of course, is that one of the arguments posed by gender-critical feminists is that trans women uphold an 'old-fashioned' perception of femininity, when in reality, it is the gender-critical feminists who are calling into question people's womanhood on the basis of their own views around perceived femininity and western, colonial beauty and bodily standards for womanhood.

Whilst every single ruling regarding transness and gender impacts trans men too, trans women are the public target. The media are making people believe trans women are the threat. Trans women's very existence is debated live on television, whilst trans men aren't even so much as sidelined, as that would imply they were in the room for the debate to begin with. Instead they're left out entirely. Even though there are as many trans men living in the UK as there are trans women. One of the biggest implications of the focus being so heavy on trans women is that the people fighting for trans-exclusionary legislation neglect to consider where trans men come into it. I vividly remember one particular news segment where a commentator's worldview came crumbling down when he realised the bathroom debate would lead to trans men legally needing to use women's bathrooms (and a lot of the trans men I know have thick beards, deep voices, and biceps the size of my head). The change in legislation hasn't been sparked by any singular or recurring instance where trans people have made anyone feel unsafe. The change was brought about by fabricated fear based on misinformation and ignorance.

What many also tend to forget is that for a portion of a trans man's life, they lived as a woman. And for those who transitioned later in life, their experiences as a woman are going to have left an even deeper scar. Many trans men have already been subjected to the same misogyny and sexism as cis women: pay gaps, verbal abuse, harassment, and even sexual assault. I've spoken to trans men who worry about how cis men will treat them in the gym, and who still instinctively hold their keys between their fingers when walking alone at night. Whilst trans men may not be the public's sole focus of transphobia, many will have lifelong experiences of misogyny.

But why are trans women more publicly targeted? The answer is transmisogyny. In a male-centric society, where women are seen as inherently inferior, both transphobia and misogyny intersect. AMAB (assigned male at birth) individuals who transition to women or present more feminine are often viewed more negatively than AFAB individuals who transition to men or are more masculine. Bluntly, those with misogynistic mindsets truly cannot comprehend the idea that someone would want to become the 'inferior' gender. The so-called transgressions of gender or sexual orientation often see AMAB people as the target because they're not just non-conforming, they're doing so in a way that misogyny views as even less than.[6]

> **'When I first started getting involved in media stuff ten years ago now, there was no conversation around trans women versus cis women. Prior to that, we'd only ever been laughed at. We'd never been considered a threat. We were threatened.'**
>
> Charlie Craggs (she/her),
> author and trans+ activist

The biggest irony with the increase in transphobia is its relationship with fetishisation. A fetish is a persistent and sometimes taboo sexual feeling towards an object, body part, or activity and is normally a necessity for the individual to be able to 'get off'. Many fetishes are completely normal and can even be a great way to explore ourselves sexually. But it becomes a problem when the fetish is for a particular type of person or, worse, nonconsensual.

A common and controversial argument against homophobia is that those who preach the most hatred may be closeted themselves. To some this is just a way of clapping back and playing on bigoted people's biggest insecurities, but there is in fact some truth to it. According to the infamous orange porn website, in 2022 porn searches including trans women rose by 75 per cent – it was the third most viewed category in the United States and the seventh most viewed worldwide[7] –

despite trans women making up less than 0.5 per cent of the population. In 2024, the 'trans' category was the fifth most streamed category in the UK alone.[8] Simultaneously, crimes against trans+ people increased by 186 per cent from 2018 to 2023.[9] Maxine believes that the parallel between the rise in fetishisation and transphobia comes from self-hatred. The same people spewing the same transphobic vitriol do so because they hate what trans women bring out of them – simply put, they hate the attraction they feel in response to trans women. Other research found that in the United States, the more 'red' (Republican) a state is, the higher the searches for trans-related porn.[10] The very people voting for the regression of queer and trans rights are the very people who have the biggest fascinations with them. Their internalised transphobia makes them feel so much internal conflict that the only people they feel they can blame are trans women themselves. Sound familiar? It's another clear example of cognitive dissonance.

> 'Many of my trans friends say that in the earliest stages of their transitions, the only place they were correctly gendered was in the bedroom. Conditioned to believe romantic and withstanding love will be gatekept from us, many of the trans women I'm close to, including myself, have tried to subsidise emotional closeness with men with momentary physical closeness instead. Particularly in the current transphobic climate, we're told that's the closest thing that we can get to a consistent connection

from a man - one via our bodies alone, but not our souls. It took time to unlearn this, and decentering men has been key to me enjoying my own long term happiness.'

Maxine Heron (she/her),
writer and trans advocate

Maxine recalled times when cishet men would ask if she was 'pre-op', a question not unfamiliar to trans women. The man asking the question *wants* a trans woman to not have had 'the surgery'. They want the fantasy of what pornography shows them: the ability to experiment with arousal a dick brings them, but for the person attached to it to be a woman.

Le Fil, who is a cis man but presents more feminine, also noted that cishet guys would often show interest in him due to his presentation as feminine. The belief being that having sex with or sexual attraction to a man who presents feminine means that they're straight; likewise, the sexual exploration of penile anatomy without it being attached to a man discredits any belief that they're anything other than heterosexual.

'I've had more than one man say this to me: what's the point in hooking up with a trans woman if she's post-op? I remember one unloading to me via a dating app saying: why would you deal with the societal baggage of hanging out with a trans woman, when you don't even get the exciting porn experience along with it? It's like these men can't believe I chose myself, and not them as complete

strangers on the internet, with the decisions I made for my own body. How selfish of me.'

Maxine Heron (she/her),
writer and trans advocate

Non-Conformity Has Always Existed and Isn't Going Anywhere

Trans+ and gender non-conforming people have been with us for millennia and across cultures. Many of us just didn't have the language for it, or at least not the same language that's used today.

In South Asian culture, predominantly Hindu societies, those who would commonly be referred to as transgender, non-binary, gender non-conforming, or intersex are known as Hijra. The Hijra have been a respected and somewhat divine people in South Asian culture for more than four thousand years. They are commonly born male but present in predominantly feminine ways, and some are born intersex. Most view themselves as neither male nor female but an entirely different gender, often referred to as the 'third gender'.[11]

'There's an erasure of trans history that happens in all cultures, and this view that all these trans people have just popped up out of nowhere is just so false. We've been here all along.'

Dani St James (she/her),
chief executive of the trans+ charity Not a Phase

Whilst the Hijra were traditionally viewed with respect, they are now often subject to marginalisation and prejudice, for which colonisation unsurprisingly played a pivotal role. During the colonisation of South Asian territories by the British, the existence of the Hijra went against the views of our Christian-led empire. In 1871, Hijra were labelled criminals under colonial Christian laws. More than 150 years later and the Hijra have only recently started to regain some of the rights that eluded them for decades. The years of colonial rule led to a once culturally embedded people being seen as outcasts. British colonisers also legislated their views on homosexuality and introduced laws that prohibited 'unnatural sex' between two individuals (i.e., two men or two women).[12] Views on gender non-conforming and queer individuals have been volatile and varied depending on the region, but the majority of laws stem from the colonial era, some of which are still in place to this day.

The reality for a lot of queer people, especially trans women, is that the overt discrimination meant that many of them had to resort to sex work to get by. The most intersectional of queers, such as Sylvia Rivera (a Latina trans woman) and Marsha P. Johnson (a Black trans woman), were so disproportionately impacted that sex work was often the only option. Those who may not have presented in a conforming way, who may have been ousted by their family, who had medical bills to pay, or who simply couldn't get a 'typical' job because of the various odds stacked against them often had no other alternative. The majority of employers were reluctant to hire trans women. The most marginalised in society must often go to more extreme means to earn even a fraction of what their privileged counterparts do, simply because the same opportunities were not presented to them and still aren't to this day. Whilst still subject to discrimination, hiding sexuality would never be as difficult as hiding gender identity. For many queer people throughout history, sex was our shame, joy, escape, and currency simultaneously.

> 'For a lot of my trans friends in sex work, it's a means to an end. I can't speak on their behalf, but men are increasingly interested in trans women, and it's worth noticing the drastic increase in 'trans' porn category streams since the presence of subscription platforms such as OnlyFans. Often, trans women aren't left with many other choices when it comes to generating enough cash to pay for a medical transition. Because how can they do that in a customer-facing job where they might be misgendered, disrespected, or discriminated against? If sex workers feel empowered by their choices and work, I'm here for that—transfer of money is a transfer of power, whatever the work. I worry the increased fetishisation alongside the political smear campaign against trans women will drive us further out of our preferred lines of work we each should be afforded when making decisions about our careers, prospects, and futures. We're more than a category on some dodgy streaming site. We deserve to feel like more than just that.'
>
> Maxine Heron (she/her),
> writer and trans advocate

'Trans people use private healthcare more than any other demographic in the UK. We're a really sparse minority group, and we are being increasingly fetishised and kept in the margins of society, particularly if we sit at any other minority intersections pertaining to our economic status, ethnicity, and whether we have a disability. The harder it is for trans healthcare to obtain, the more that trans people are going to be pushed to jobs where they can accumulate cash to go private, as quickly as they can.'

Maxine Heron (she/her),
writer and trans advocate

Sex work puts many trans women in serious physical danger from both clients and the police, as the police haven't exactly ever been on the side of queer people. The phrase 'walking while trans' was coined by the trans community, as law enforcement would often target trans women on the street over the assumption of them being sex workers.[13] Many were arrested for minimal offences purely due to their trans identity and would even be written up as sex workers despite no evidence of them being so. Trans women, and particularly trans women of colour, are disproportionately affected by acts of assault, be them verbal, physical, and sometimes fatal. Law enforcement is actively part of the problem, not providing any form of support or protection to trans women in danger.

'The queer liberation movement overall, from Stonewall times onwards, was led by Black trans sex workers, and those have always been at the forefront of these fights. It's always people at so many different intersections that are doing the most.'

Maxine Heron (she/her),
writer and trans advocate

As a result of their disproportionately discriminatory treatment, trans+ people have been central to queer rights and liberation movements. The Stonewall Inn was a gay bar in New York City that was frequented by diverse queer people and subject to regular police raids. Up until 1969, queer people were viewed by the public, including police, as being a submissive group who showed little resistance. The Stonewall riots changed this perception when, during one police raid, queer people fought back. The collective frustration reached a boiling point, and queer people, sex workers, trans+ people, and other minorities took the opportunity to show we were no longer going to be society's punching bag. The riots lasted several nights, and Black trans sex workers played a prominent role. Marsha P. Johnson in particular has gone down in history for being the person to 'throw the first brick at Stonewall', igniting the resistance that paved the way for formal queer liberation movements that would actively fight for queer rights.

'A lot of people still want to be accepted by the majority. Because why would you want to distance yourself from a community that has made your ass

legal and more accepted? Because they want to be more conventionally accepted.'

Tyreece (he/she/they),
fashion creator and performer

Despite the pivotal role Black trans women and sex workers played in the progression of all LGBTQIA+ rights, there was an undercurrent of contempt within the community for those whose non-conformity was more apparent. The divisions within queer spaces aren't new. Trans+ people have been subjected to shunning from queer spaces from the beginning of the queer rights movement. We are now just starting to see the transphobia in our community bubble back up to the surface.

'We've been conditioned to believe that there's a table of equality and a table of privilege, and there's a limited number of seats at the table. If someone else comes up and takes a seat, then your seat is at risk. It's simply not true, there's an infinite amount of seats.'

Dani St James (she/her),
chief executive of the trans+ charity Not a Phase

Many activist groups devoted their time primarily to gay men and youths and would actively exclude the transgender movement. So much so that Rivera and Johnson started their own organisation, Street Transvestite Action Revolutionaries (STAR). An infamous example of trans exclusion was on the fourth annual Christopher Street Liberation Day in 1973, named after the street where the Stonewall riots first took place. These were the first organised commemorative days that would go on to become the worldwide Pride celebrations we see today. Rivera was scheduled to speak onstage, and her treatment leading up to and during her speech led to her two-decade hiatus from activism. The transphobia from within the community had become so prevalent that Rivera was mocked on her way to the stage and blocked from getting through. Once she eventually made it onstage, the crowd erupted into collective booing at her presence. Rivera then commenced a speech full of both passion and justifiable anger.

Y'all better quiet down.

I've been trying to get up here all day for your gay brothers and your gay sisters in jail that write me every motherfucking week and ask for your help, and you all don't do a goddamn thing for them.

Have you ever been beaten up and raped in jail? Now think about it. They've been beaten up and raped after they had to spend much of their money in jail to get theirself home and try to get their sex changed.

The women have tried to fight for their sex changes or to become women of the women's liberation, and they write STAR. Not the women's group. They do not write women, they do not write men, they write STAR because we're trying to do something for them.

I have been to jail. I have been raped and beaten many times, by men, heterosexual men that do not belong in the homosexual shelter. But do you do anything for [me]? No. You all tell me go and hide my tail between my legs. I will not, no longer, put up with this shit. I have been beaten. I have had my nose broken. I have been thrown in jail. I have lost my job. I have lost my apartment for gay liberation. And you all treat me this way? What the fuck's wrong with you all? Think about that!

I do not believe in a revolution, but you all do. I believe in the Gay Power. I believe in us getting our rights, or else I would not be out there fighting for our rights. That's all I wanted to say to you all people. If you all want to know about the people that are in jail – and do not forget Bambi L'Amour, Andorra Marks, Kenny Messner, and other gay people in jail, come and see the people at STAR House on Twelfth Street, on 640 East Twelfth Street between B and C, apartment 14.

The people are trying to do something for all of us, and not men and women that belong to a white middle-class white club. And that's what you all belong to!

REVOLUTION NOW! Gimme a G! Gimme an A! Gimme a Y! Gimme a P! Gimme an O! Gimme a W! Gimme an E! Gimme an R! Gay Power! Louder! GAY POWER!

(A video of the speech is available online, and I'd highly recommend watching it in its entirety so you can witness the passion and anger; a transcript doesn't do it justice.)[14]

> **'After the Stonewall riots, when it was one of the first actual Pride marches, they shunned her [Sylvia Rivera] from it, even though she was pivotal in the fucking riots that started Pride.'**
>
> Charlie Craggs (she/her),
> author and trans+ activist

Rivera's speech embodied the frustrations of every trans+ individual who felt the growing distance created by predominantly white gay men. The same arguments that were used to shut trans women out of queer liberation more than fifty years ago are the exact same justifications used to target trans people today. Gay men see trans+ people as posing a threat to the acceptance of gay people in society, purely through association. Trans+ people's role in the progression of queer rights deserves much wider recognition. As a community we need to learn from our history, or we are doomed to repeat it. All LGBTQIA+ people are subject to discrimination in some way or another. Gay men, whilst in a much better position, are still subject to discrimination. From all corners of the community, we know what it feels like to some degree.

Supporting trans+ people is just the right thing to do, but more importantly, we are indebted to them. We would not be where we are today if it wasn't for gender non-conformity. Our rights and our culture would look incredibly different, so supporting trans+ people is something we should feel duty bound to do, if not to make up for the poor treatment by our predecessors at the very least. I used this quote in the introduction, but I'm putting it here again to really hammer it home.

> 'Loving and uplifting gay men has been central to most of our experiences. But we've now reached a point where gay men have been lifted up, and we kind of need you to throw a rope back down for us to get up there with you.'
>
> Dani St James (she/her),
> chief executive of the trans+ charity Not a Phase

And to emphasise the point of this book, empathy is the first step. Empathy without action is still compliance.

What Can We Do to Support Non-Conformity?

Listen

Maxine made me aware of the mantra 'No speaking about us without us'. This has its roots in the disability rights movement but can be applicable to almost any marginalised group. As allies, we shouldn't speak *for* trans+ people but platform them to speak for themselves. When any marginalised person speaks of their experiences, specifically negative ones, we need to listen.

> 'You're fighting for everyone, you're not just fighting for white trans people. You're fighting for trans people of colour, trans people of faith. And sometimes you need to take a step back . . . your voice isn't necessary at this moment, but you can still highlight someone else's.'
>
> Dee Whitnell (they/them),
> sex educator and trans+ activist

> 'In the last census report it was found trans people make up just 0.5 per cent of the UK's population. We don't have power in numbers on our own, so we need our allies on side. A big moment each year is London Trans Pride, where we take to the streets and reclaim them as a space that so often feels unsafe for trans people. Lots of allies that I know

won't free up the time to march with us. I know it's in the summer, I know people are busy, but if you really, really care about my rights, my access to my health care, and my safety, I think it's time to stop finding better plans on that one Saturday each year.'

Maxine Heron (she/her),
writer and trans advocate

Educate Ourselves

This book should not be your primary source of education on trans+ people. There are other incredible books such as *The Transgender Issue* by Shon Faye and *Dear Cisgender People* by Kenny Ethan Jones, to name a few, as well as TV shows like *Pose*. These can help us better understand the trans+ experience and what we can do as allies. Even better, we can go out of our way to find other documentaries, TV shows, and literature that can not only educate us but take the pressure off of trans+ people to do the educating.

'If just trans or non-binary people fight for trans and non-binary issues, then it makes it only a trans and non-binary issue. If gay men, bisexuals, heterosexuals, and all these different communities make it a problem for the government, if everyone's getting involved, that makes it have more weight.'

Tyreece (he/she/they),
fashion creator and performer

'It's about being prepared to be part of changing people's perspectives and not being afraid to

disrupt conversations when you know that they're wrong or that they're harmful to someone. *Never underestimate people's capacity to learn.*'

Maxine Heron (she/her),
writer and trans advocate

Stand Up

This is what's going to make the most difference. As Maxine said, 'Never underestimate people's capacity to learn', and I think that is one of the most poignant quotes in this book. Bringing about change isn't just about legislation and protests. Whilst still important, the role of protests isn't to change people's perspectives but instead to get their attention so we can be listened to. Getting people's attention is the easy part; the next part is about having that difficult conversation. Calling out that joke, educating someone who's misinformed, correcting someone when they misgender someone, and simply having trans+ people's backs when they're not in the room. This isn't speaking for trans+ people; it's not taking up their space – they're not in the room to speak for themselves to begin with. We've seen from recent rhetoric that whilst our rights may be slowly progressing, there are still a lot of people who still view us negatively. Progress cannot be made purely on a macro level; we cannot push for legislation and call it a day. Real change is made when we protest for societal change and have disruptive conversations on an individual basis simultaneously.

'I think holding people accountable and actually taking a moment to show people that this is wrong

is really important, because a lot of the time people who make these transphobic jokes, they don't know why they shouldn't be making that joke, or they don't know the extent of the damage it will cause.'

Dee Whitnell (they/them),
sex educator and trans+ activist

'You may not want to speak up for somebody else because you feel vulnerable. But if you feel vulnerable, imagine just for a second a fraction of what that person is feeling.'

Shiv (they/them),
journalist and broadcaster

Chapter 3

The Alphabet Mafia

'For a community that doesn't want to be labelled, you're obsessed with labels' is a common phrase we as a community are confronted with. But we didn't just create labels for the fun of it. We didn't all sit down one day to plan our 'gay agenda' and say, '*Right,* someone make a spreadsheet, we need to split into teams.' Our identification with labels is a way of finding our own safe space in a society designed to make us feel like outcasts. If you bully people long enough for being different, then they will find their own people and get their own support network. We have created our own little ecosystem with a plethora of identities and labels to help us better understand who we are, explain to others who we are, and find people like us. The many identities we have within the community have always existed, only now we have the language for them.

> 'My mum says that if I were born now she would've known I was trans when I was two, because

the signs were there, she just didn't have the information.'

Dani St James (she/her),
chief executive of the trans+ charity Not a Phase

Over time, more identities have emerged that we get to discover and explore, but now there are also more identities subject to criticism. We're shamed for being different whether we use labels or not. We are constantly put under a microscope for wider society to point out that there's something they don't agree with because it doesn't align with 'traditional' ways of life.

Queer people know better than anyone how it feels to be handed a role in life, a character to play that just doesn't feel natural. Like trying to place a puzzle piece that just doesn't quite fit. For a long time sexual orientation wasn't a concept. Anything other than sex for procreation was viewed as a sexual disorder. Once the concepts of sexual orientation became more widely known, they were still viewed as binary.

'I think these labels were created. I think if you look far back enough in history, you'll find that we would just be.'

Shiv (they/them),
journalist and broadcaster

This became even more complicated for people who not only didn't fit in with what society told them to be but didn't feel they fit within the binary queer boxes either. Terms like *heterosexual* and *homosexual, cisgender* and *transgender,* are all boxes with confines that some may not fit into. Some of us are put into the wrong box entirely, so we create a new one to identify with. This is the exact reason labels exist. Discovering who we really are, what we like, what we don't, who we like, who we don't, and the limitless other factors to our identity takes time.

> 'I think you have to just be accepting that everybody has different ways of living and loving. You can say the same thing for just about anything. Not everybody's two experiences are the same.'
>
> Beth McCarthy (she/they), artist and performer

Discovering our identities is not an A to B process, especially when we have so much societal baggage to unpack through years of conditioning. The idea of 'coming out' implies some form of finish line. We are finally declaring to the world who we truly are. The pressure of this is that this then cannot change, when in reality we are constantly changing. Who I was five years ago doesn't at all resemble myself today and likely will be a distant memory compared with me in the next five years. In a world that tells us who we should and shouldn't be, we have to spend so much of our time exploring what we truly like. Once we discover that, we then have to spend years coming to terms with it internally and accepting the wave of discrimination we are likely to face as a result.

> 'Labels are there to help us. They're not there to hinder us. They're not there to put us in a box. If you

like to use a label to help you personally understand yourself and feel comfortable in your skin, that's fantastic. But if you grow beyond that label, don't feel like you have to hold on to feeling you've got to be perceived in this way and you've got to check all of these boxes. For me, I think it was just about finding the compassion for myself that I know I would have for other people.'

Shell Rowe (she/her),
content creator

Labels or Slurs?

Deviations from heterosexuality and traditional gender norms have been recorded for millennia – these are not new concepts. The idea of same-sex attraction was not only normalised in societies like ancient Greece and the Roman Empire but actively encouraged. Whilst the age discrepancies of coupling in ancient societies were incredibly problematic for both homosexuals and heterosexuals, the notion of same-sex attraction was not something that sparked much debate – so much so that the labelling of such couplings simply did not exist. The concepts of 'heterosexual' or 'homosexual' just weren't a thing.

'People start breaking out of their boxes, and they say, "Well, actually, no, I'm not going to restrict myself to these lines and these boxes that you've created." But because it's what the vast majority of

people are doing, the vast majority of people are in those boxes, [so] you have to have a word for the other.'

Shiv (they/them),
journalist and broadcaster

Since then, the definition of same-sex activity has evolved. Rather than being seen as a sexual orientation, for a time it was referred to as 'sodomy' or engaging in 'unnatural or immoral sexual acts'. The term *homosexual* was first used publicly in 1869 by the Hungarian writer Karl Maria Kertbeny. Living in Germany, he used the words anonymously in two pamphlets criticising the laws against same-sex activity with the aim of moving away from the slurs used to describe those involved, like *sodomite.* A decade later, Kertbeny publicly coined the word *heterosexual* for the first time.[1] This wasn't in replacement for anything, as the concept simply did not exist. There were 'normal' (straight) people, or the various slurs that queer people had hurled at them. Over time, the terms have evolved to the language we use today, including the recently reclaimed *queer*.

Similarly, gender non-conforming people have always existed. Yet there were no clear indicators for their identities, they were merely othered and called slurs by the majority. Slurs being the key word: they were used in an intentionally derogatory way. Following the growing use of the term *transgender,* the term *cissexual* was coined by the German sexologist Volkmar Sigusch in 1991 to describe an individual whose gender identity aligns with their sex assigned at birth. This later evolved to *cisgender,* as it was more closely related to someone's gender than sexual orientation, similar to how *transexual* shifted towards *transgender*.[2] The origins are from the Latin prefixes *cis* and *trans*, which mean 'on the side of' and 'on the other side of', respectively. So these identifiers have no negative or positive connotations, they are just descriptors for what they are.

In the future, the use of labels is something we as a community, and indeed wider society, will hopefully be able to move away from. For now, however, labels have their place and, in a lot of ways, are needed. They help us feel safe and like we're not alone. They help us find our people. They also help us quickly and efficiently explain to others who we are without the confines of 'normal' and 'abnormal'. Labels and other descriptors are used as a way of communicating and identifying each other in all walks of life. If every adult had the exact same body shape, weight, and height, the concepts of thin and fat, tall and short, simply would not exist as these would not be distinguishable characteristics. We've held on to the term *queer* because all of us, every single one of us, in some way differ from the socially constructed 'norm'.

When we don't fit in the box we've been assigned to, society sees it as a problem. We no longer adhere to expectations and we're no longer being kept in our place. It's then that labels can become slurs. These types of labels are used with derogative intent aimed at harming an individual's self-esteem or reputation, and they're mainly used against specific groups of people. Racial slurs tie back to colonial times and were used as a way of asserting dominance and dehumanising slaves. Homophobic slurs tie back to centuries of harassing and discriminating against queer people. We didn't suddenly decide to be offended by language; there is a complex and painful history tied to slurs and the weight that they carry.

Ironically, the majority (cishet white people) are more than content with the creation of labels, until the oppressed create them for themselves. Heterosexual people are happy to label queer people with various slurs and stereotypical descriptors until we create our own labels or flip the script and find something to label them with – even if not in a derogatory manner. As anti-trans rhetoric rises, so does the discourse surrounding the term *cisgender*. Some people, namely those with gender-critical views, have decided that *cisgender* is a slur. What these people don't understand is that you don't get to just suddenly decide if something is a slur. That's not how it works. But that's not an easy concept for them to understand, since these people can't fully comprehend the gravitas of experiencing a slur.

There is zero oppressive or discriminatory history tied to the term *cisgender*. The creation of the term was to help facilitate more constructive conversations around gender by using less abusively motivated terms and to move away from the concepts of 'normal' and 'other', in the same way that *heterosexual* was coined as the antonym of *homosexual*. Much of the reasoning behind the supposed offence taken by the use of *cisgender* comes from people's fear of not being perceived as normal. The concept of 'normal' automatically implies the existence of 'abnormal', and being abnormal gives them power over us. To them, it means that we are the freaks and outcasts, rather than accepting that all humans differ in some way. Those of privilege often don't want that privilege shared, the view being that the sharing of privilege, or what we call equality, will take something away from them. Queer people no longer being seen as 'other' takes only one thing away: their power over us.

We're More Than Gay

When young queer people are coming to terms with the fact they may not be heterosexual, the main alternative that is presented, albeit rarely and seldom positively, is homosexuality. Those who are bisexual may not even know bisexuality is a thing. 'Why does the label matter?' many will think. One of the main reasons is that without it, bisexuals are often stigmatised and erased. An unfortunately common misconception, for example, is that bisexuality doesn't even exist. Some describe it merely as a phase; others describe it as being indecisive, greedy, or simply in denial.

> **'Having had any representation whatsoever of bi people would have allowed me to start figuring that out sooner. Maybe I would still be figuring it out now, but I just think I'd be a bit further along in that journey and wouldn't have had so much shame.'**
>
> Beth McCarthy (she/they),
> artist and performer

In navigating my sexuality, I came out as bisexual first. I knew I was sexually attracted to men but had so much emotional baggage surrounding traditional relationships that I still yearned for that picket-fence life. I truly believed that I wanted a wife, my own kids, and to raise the family I'd been told to aspire to my entire life. I'd been socially conditioned to believe a heterosexual marriage was what I wanted. At the time, the thought of any romance with a man sent shivers down my spine. Even the thought of holding a man's hand in a romantic way was something I simply couldn't comprehend. I soon realised, however, that I didn't experience any sexual *or* romantic attraction to women and I was, in fact, gay. I'd just been raised in a world that didn't show me gay love was even okay, let alone achievable. My entire worldview was shrouded in internalised homophobia. Today, the thought of one day meeting the love of my life at the altar, exchanging vows, and calling him my husband brings me nothing but joy. I am deserving of love, even if it doesn't look *exactly* like the picket-fence life I'd yearned for. I had to spend years unpacking this to get to true acceptance of myself.

But that was *my* personal experience. I truly never felt any sexual or romantic attraction to women, I was just made to feel that's what I should feel. The experience that I had with my sexuality doesn't automatically negate the experiences of others. Just because I navigated my sexual orientation a certain way does not mean every person goes down the exact same path. A binary view of sexual orientation can lead to what's known as 'biphobia', prejudice against bisexuals. Despite the term *bisexual* first being coined in relation to sexual orientation at a similar time to both *homosexual* and *heterosexual*, it didn't become widely used in the UK until the late 1970s. Prior to this, the concept of bisexuality didn't exist.

The Bi Experience

The fights for equality have always had gay people at the forefront, from organisation names to slogans and chants. Yet *gay* and *homosexual* had the distinct understanding of being attracted to the same gender. So when people experienced attraction to both men and women, or more, they were met with confusion and discrimination.

The real consequence? Only 20 per cent of bisexual people report being out to their families, compared with 63 per cent of gay and lesbian people.[3] The discrimination that bisexual people are subjected to comes in various forms. But the harsh reality for bisexuals is that they tend to receive prejudice from both within and outside of the LGBTQIA+ community. This is one of the reasons that, regardless of gender, bisexual people experience higher levels of mental health problems than lesbians, gay men, and straight people.[4] They can be seen as too queer for straight people but not queer enough for queer people, leaving them in a sort of limbo, not knowing where they truly fit in, alongside subsequent poor treatment, which I'll lay out below.

Fetishisation

Bisexuality is commonly fetishised. There is an automatic assumption, specifically for women, that being bi means they'll want to have a threesome with a man and another woman. This fetishising of someone's sexual orientation can create a completely false stereotype. Much like fetishisation of minorities, it's far from flattering and reduces a person down to one specific factor of their identity for sexual gratification.

For bi men, the fetishisation often comes from gay men. I discussed in chapter one how gay men put masculinity on a pedestal, and as a result, some gay men fetishise any man who is closer to the societal norm of masculinity or being a 'real man'.

To some, a bi man is seen as being more masculine, as he also sleeps with women. Not only does this reinforce the idea that being gay is inherently demasculating, but it also reduces bi men to being someone's fetish.

> **'If I go on a date with a straight man who finds out that I'm bi, he'll immediately say, "Let's have a threesome."'**
>
> Shiv (they/them), journalist and broadcaster

Believing They're 'More Likely to Cheat'

Another stereotype is that a bisexual person cannot be wholly sexually satisfied when restricting themselves to a monogamous relationship with one gender. I can understand where this logic comes from: it's fundamentally rooted in fear. The exact same could be said about a heterosexual couple where one person isn't as sexually satisfied in bed because the other isn't keen on taking part in certain sex acts. Or with a homosexual couple with mismatched libidos. But attraction doesn't determine action. All relationships are complicated. They all require compromise and sacrifice. Assuming someone is more likely to cheat because they are bisexual just reaffirms the belief that someone's sexual orientation determines their level of morality, which is a false argument that has plagued queer people for centuries.

Invalidation

Bisexuality is one of the closest sexualities to heterosexuality, in that someone could still end up in a heteronormative relationship. Beth, a cis bisexual woman, explained her personal experience with this and firstly said that she understands some of the privilege of being bisexual. 'I can walk down the street holding hands with my boyfriend and no one bats an eyelid', she admitted, which is something that many queer people do not get to experience. However, what this then leads to is people invalidating bisexuality as not being queer enough, which Beth had to experience from multiple angles. Beth recalled being told that she was 'objectifying women' because she had slept with women but not yet had a relationship with one, when in reality Beth was still exploring her sexuality, which everyone should be graced with the opportunity to do.

> **'I think it comes from a lot of hurt. As a bi person, I get to experience the benefits as a queer person – so I get to write music and get to be championed by queer people – but I also get to live a life in a hetero relationship.'**
>
> Beth McCarthy (she/they),
> artist and performer

When Beth wrote an EP about dating girls, she admitted that during that time in her life she was exploring dating women more and hadn't dated a man for a while. Whilst her queer friends were aware that Beth was bisexual, she was often subjected to subtle jokes at her bisexuality's expense that almost insinuated her being in denial because of her personality and appearance. Whilst these were simply jokes with no ill intent, there was still an element of them that reinforced the invalidation of bisexuality. Having written and released some very queer-centric songs about liking girls, she was met with a lot of negative comments when her relationship with her boyfriend became public. 'Oh, that's a disappointment', she recalled reading. Even though it was meant in a lighthearted way, those types of comments still discredit someone's bisexuality and a very real relationship.

> **'People will just be trying to invalidate their sexuality, saying they feel "betrayed". I think it's so crazy to call it a betrayal or want to withdraw your support from that person or that community. Being part of the queer community is about being accepting, and you're just doing everything that we stand against.'**
>
> Shell Rowe (she/her),
> content creator

One notable stereotype becoming more common is that bisexual women always end up with a boyfriend. Whilst there are many things that determine the partner we end up with, one thing Beth acknowledged was the simple maths of it. Queer people are inherently a minority. So if, as a bisexual person, your dating pool includes heterosexual men, who are an overwhelming majority, and queer people, it is much more likely you're going to find a heterosexual man who actually lives nearby and who you are emotionally compatible with, get along with, and are sexually compatible with. It doesn't necessarily mean a bisexual person has actively chosen a heteronormative relationship over a queer one, it is just mathematically more likely to be possible. Yet, one of the notable criticisms Beth received was 'She's just ended up with a straight white man', to which Beth thought, 'Why are you assuming that he's straight?' Which leads us to the next form of discrimination.

Queerbaiting

Over the last few years we have seen a number of different stories whereby queer people have been forced into a corner and had to out themselves way earlier than they felt comfortable with. The most notable was *Heartstopper*'s Kit Connor. He had not publicly spoken about his sexuality, and at one point he was seen holding hands with a girl. The internet went into a frenzy, claiming that he was in fact queerbaiting. This led to him having to publicly come out as bisexual on Twitter as a direct result of the speculation. We've also seen it with other public figures who are queer but have ended up in a heteronormative relationship; but they are still queer.

> **'Last year, I went through feeling like I did not fit in. I didn't belong. "Maybe I am queerbaiting?" What the fuck?! What do you mean?! Why am I asking myself if I'm queerbaiting when I'm queer?! I'm so proud of it, and it almost pushed me back in the closet to get a partner that was not a girl.'**
>
> Beth McCarthy (she/they),
> artist and performer

The term *queerbait* was originally used to describe when a TV show or film would create characters that would hint at being queer without ever explicitly saying so, essentially as bait to bring in a queer audience, and most of these characters would turn out to just not be gay. In recent years, it has been used to describe when someone actively pretends to be queer and will mimic queerness and take part in the culture to reap its benefits, whilst actually retaining an entirely non-queer identity. Bisexual people are often accused of queerbaiting, predominantly on the internet. The difficulty with the assumption of queerbaiting is that it plays into the stereotype of someone having to be perceived as queer or queer enough. We don't owe people the appearance of perceived queerness. No one owes anyone a 'coming out' story either. We know how complicated it is trying to navigate and come to terms with our identities. We know what it's like to have people speculate about our sexuality at school and make assumptions, so we need to show the same patience to other queer people.

> **'People can't comprehend that there's anything other than straight or gay. You can still like girls and celebrate liking girls, even though you also like everybody else.'**
>
> Beth McCarthy (she/they), artist and performer

Rejection

Bisexual people can also experience rejection based on their sexual orientation. Beth was also subject to some critiques from lesbians and queer women who actively did not want to date a bisexual who had 'touched men'. She recalled one girl saying to her that she understands if you've gone through a phase of dating men before you realise you like girls and that you're a lesbian, but once you've started dating girls you can't go back. Beth then dedicated a lot of time diving deeper into queer culture and found that some of that mentality may stem from past experiences with bisexuals. And for some it can even be the general dislike of men. Studies have shown that bi women quite frequently experience rejection from lesbians for a multitude of reasons, one being the idea of 'sleeping with the enemy' (men). Don't get me wrong, even I struggle with men and I'm literally gay, but feeling negatively towards men should not be taken out on bisexuals.

As a result, some lesbians have a tendency to view bisexual women more negatively than gay men view bisexual men.[5] This is a topic of conversation that stirred up quite a bit of controversy when I addressed it online, as some believed I was singling lesbians out. Naturally and obviously this isn't *all* lesbians. But prejudice does not justify prejudice. A person's experience can be used to explain their behaviour and thought processes and help us better understand why they may feel and act the way they do. But it does not justify their actions. Explanation and justification are not synonymous.

Explanation can instead help us unpack our unconscious bias, as some of the prejudice may in fact come from past experiences with another bisexual. It's normal for our past experiences to impact our future feelings. But an experience with one individual does not determine our experience with another. Explanations can prompt a more constructive conversation, but justification deflects from accountability and in turn halts progress.

Accused of Being 'In Denial'

The study cited above also brought up a theory known as the 'Androcentric Desire Hypothesis', which discusses the perception that bisexuals (*perception* being the key word) are inherently more attracted to men than to women. A common stigma (and delusion) is that bi women are secretly heterosexual or just experimenting, which devalues them on both sides: they are not queer enough for queer spaces and just a fetish to explore in heterosexual spaces. Another common misconception is that bisexual men are in denial and are secretly just gay. Navigating bisexuality can be incredibly difficult because of the stigma from all angles, especially when society is still trying to push us into a box of liking one gender or the other. A bi person can have a 50–50 attraction to genders, and another bi person can have a 95–5 attraction – both people are still bisexual.

> **'The whole point is we all sit here and are all happy in our queerness and say, "You can't choose it. You can't choose who you love." But then, apparently, when you're bisexual, you should.'**
>
> Beth McCarthy (she/her),
> artist and performer

Pansexuality, similar to bisexuality, is another identity that is often misunderstood and invalidated. The term was coined later than other sexual orientations and has, like other sexual orientations, varied in meaning. The modern usage of the term describes someone who is attracted to people *regardless* of their gender identity, meaning gender does not play a key role in attraction for them. This is often conflated with bisexuality, with some claiming there is no difference or simply not understanding the difference. It even took me a while to learn the difference. But they are indeed different, and that difference is important.

Pansexuality was something I wanted to cover because of its conflation with bisexuality. I did my research, read various accounts of pansexuality, and now have a much better understanding of what it is. Bisexuality is the attraction to *two or more* genders, meaning gender plays an active role in attraction, as a bisexual person may not necessarily be attracted to *all* genders. Pansexuality is attraction regardless of gender, as gender plays little to no part in attraction to a person. That's it. This may be easy to understand, it may take a couple of reads, or you still may not fully grasp it. That's okay. What matters is accepting and respecting that someone may identify differently from how others do.

Labels are a shorthand way of communicating who we are to others, often as a direct result of misunderstanding and stigma. Given the vast array of stereotypes that bisexual and pansexual people are subjected to, having a label for them is a clear way of declaring that they're not 'in a phase' and bisexuality, pansexuality and all other sexual orientations are just as valid. Not respecting or acknowledging someone's sexual orientation or identity will not change it; the only thing it will change is how they feel about themselves. It will not change who they find attractive; instead it will just add to the shame they feel about it, which is the very thing every queer person can relate to.

No one is saying you must understand every single identity

on an intrinsic level. We do not have to fully understand someone to respect them. Just because I don't experience something does not mean it doesn't exist.

The *L* Comes First

With representation and advocacy mainly focusing on gay men, lesbians are often left behind. All queer people are subjected to their own unique stigmas within society, and historically gay men have been worse off, from the AIDS crisis to laws aimed specifically at male-male sex and other forms of persecution. Gay men have been uplifted by the community for generations, especially by lesbians, because of the more apparent negative treatment gay men were subjected to.

> 'It's *L* first [in LGBTQIA+] because lesbians stepped up in a time when the gay community was experiencing lots of grief and lots of trauma through the AIDS crisis. The lesbian community said, "Well, hold on a minute. We're all one family, and we're going to stand up for you and stick with you."'
>
> Shiv (they/them),
> journalist and broadcaster

The original acronym actually used to be GLBT, but it was later changed to honour the bravery and courage shown by lesbians and queer women during the AIDS crisis, as they stood by the bedsides of gay men, and for their pivotal role in the progression of queer rights. It was also an attempt to bring greater awareness to the wider community, rather than focus purely on gay men. Lesbians and gay men were also known to have 'lavender marriages' to help protect each other from discrimination. The intense pressure to have a traditional life, to marry, and to start a family meant that many queer people were at risk of being found out if they didn't follow this path. So lesbians and gay men could form a sort of platonic alliance whereby they could keep up appearances by being legally married. This then helped them protect each other and to still be able to pursue queer feelings.

Yet despite the faultless allyship lesbians have shown to gay men, lesbian erasure was and is still a prominent issue within queer spaces, and that's if the spaces exist. Lesbian erasure and misogyny often go hand in hand in queer spaces. In chapter one, I discussed the ways in which lesbians often feel unwelcome in queer venues. The existence of safe spaces is a direct result of exclusion, discrimination, and poor treatment in mainstream venues. But as stated, gay men are not exempt from misogyny. Lesbians were often ejected or refused entry to gay bars, as many of the gay bars were strictly men only.

> 'It's important for any community to have a space where they feel completely safe to be who they are. Just because we're all in the queer community doesn't mean that we don't have individual needs and differences as well. Yes, we have the umbrella, but there are things in the gay community that I can't understand, that you might not be able to understand about the lesbian community. If we've

got so many queer spaces that are male dominated, we should have spaces that are female dominated.'

Shell Rowe (she/her),
content creator

Lesbians are subjected to this misogyny within queer spaces, whilst still having to deal with straight men. Shell worried that non-conformity would make her more of a target, and once she embraced having short hair (which looks amazing, I might add), that fear did unfortunately become a reality. But now, Shell is so comfortable in who she is that embracing her authentic self outweighs the ridicule she gets.

'I never, ever received the comments I do now when I had long hair, when I was more feminine. And now the most heinous things will be said to me, and I know it's because people look at me and they go, "Lesbian." It's so important to note that when people want to say, "Oh, we don't need Pride in this country, it's so much better", not everyone is having the experience that you are having.'

Shell Rowe (she/her),
content creator

Lesbians in particular are subjected to two different types of treatment based purely on how much they conform: prejudice and fetishisation. Shell recalled a time when she was in a club with her girlfriend. Whilst dancing and kissing, they both opened their eyes to see a group of men had encircled them to watch. Later that night, two of the men followed Shell and her girlfriend home and asked to 'rent the lesbians'. This is something that gay men do not experience, or at least nowhere near the same level. Shell puts it well: 'Not everyone is having the experience that you are having.' Being the same sexual orientation or gender doesn't automatically mean our experiences are parallel. Our treatment runs much deeper than how we identify.

Sex Isn't Everything

'I'll have people say, "Queerness is about sex, so where does asexuality fit?" It's actually kind of sad that you think queerness is entirely about sex.'

Yasmin Benoit (she/her),
model and asexual activist

Queerness is such an incredible spectrum of different identities, and both aromanticism and asexuality are just as valid as any other. So let me clarify what they mean:

Aromanticism

Aromanticism means having little to no *romantic* attraction. People who are aromantic may not get the traditional romantic 'spark' or 'butterflies' that most people do when feeling romantically attracted to someone. Imagine a time you may have been sexually attracted to someone and maybe even had sex with them but did not have a desire to pursue a romantic relationship with them. Aromantic individuals can also date, maybe just not for the same reasons as other people do, such as for companionship, physical intimacy, and emotional support. Aromantic people may not automatically be asexual either; they can experience a sexual attraction, just not a romantic one.

Asexuality

Asexuality means having little to no *sexual* attraction. This is often confused as not wanting or enjoying sex, which isn't the case. Yes, some asexual people are sex negative, meaning they don't experience the attraction and also do not like sex. But some asexuals are sex favourable, meaning that they do actually enjoy the act of sex itself but don't necessarily experience sexual attraction to people. And some are sex neutral, basically meaning they can take it or leave it (sometimes literally).

A few years ago, I saw a video online by an asexual person explaining the concept of asexuality. The video itself was harmless and even a little funny, but the comment section was full of discourse from allosexual individuals (people who *do* experience sexual attraction). In those comments, there were two common 'solutions' to navigating dating an asexual: open the relationship or simply break up. Like I said, asexual people can still very much enjoy sex; they may just lack the specific urge many of us feel to have sex with a specific person. Essentially, they can still get horny and experience arousal, but not necessarily at the thought of a specific individual. Opening the relationship, whilst it may be a solution for some, should not be assumed as the ultimate solution to avoid a breakup. Relationships in general are about compromise, mutual understanding, and communication. Expecting a partner to fulfil your absolute and every need is not realistic, not to mention putting an overwhelming amount of pressure on your partner.

> 'I was at a conference recently, and they were talking about how they don't like peas. And so they don't really spend their time thinking about peas. I also don't like peas, but I do spend my time thinking about how much I don't eat peas, because in the British society, we put peas in everything. And consequently, it actually comes up a lot how much I don't eat peas, even though it probably shouldn't. And then I realised that asexuality is actually very similar to that.'
>
> Yasmin Benoit (she/her),
> model and asexual activist

> 'When we talk about conversion therapy and how trans people weren't protected by the ban, I definitely saw the community rally around, raise awareness, and make sure that that's an issue that's highlighted. Asexual people were never included, and no one cared.'
>
> Yasmin Benoit (she/her),
> model and asexual activist

Some research suggests the number of asexual people could be between 1 and 2 per cent of the population, but there are medical professionals who see asexuality merely as a problem to fix. Sound familiar? It should: it's alarmingly close to the history of homosexuality and transgenderism. Asexuality gets immensely little media coverage, and as a result, asexuals are 10 per cent more likely to be offered or undergo conversion therapy than other sexual orientations.[6] The majority of those identifying as asexual are women and non-binary, and Yasmin Benoit, an asexual activist, noted how this leads some people to seeing a medical professional for a medical diagnosis rather than exploring the possibility of asexuality. Some have even gone to a medical practice for an unrelated problem, and upon being asked if they were sexually active and responding no, the entire focus was shifted to their lack of sexual activity rather than the problem they initially went in for. They may have their hormones tested or undergo a forced genital examination, or even be investigated for the possibility that they have a problem with men in particular, making the entire process incredibly straight oriented. In one particular case, the endometriosis an individual went to see a doctor for was left completely neglected for over a year due to the doctor's fixation on 'curing' their asexuality. This led to irreparable muscle damage and seriously affected their internal organs.

> 'The reason everything's under the same umbrella [queer/LGBTQIA+] is because the issues that everyone's facing all stem from the same things and all relate to each other. Asexuality isn't under there by fluke; it's under there because it is a queer experience.'
>
> Yasmin Benoit (she/her),
> model and asexual activist

Like the other identities in our community, asexuality is one that helps people realise that they're not broken. Yasmin recalled assumptions of her being sick or traumatised because of her lack of interest in sex on top of the various other things you have to deal with at fifteen years old. Representation of asexuality will help people realise that it's okay and that they're not broken, like representation does for any identity. Bigotry affects all queer people, discrimination affects all queer people, and most importantly, conversion therapy affects all queer people.

***

There are of course way more identities in the community than have been discussed in this chapter that are just as valid. But it was more important to discuss fewer topics in great depth than every topic at a surface level. We are all different, and that's what's important to acknowledge. I want to bring us back to the image I described in the introduction, the queer iceberg. Just because one identity is less represented doesn't make it less real, and just because we don't relate to an experience doesn't mean it's not valid. Just because we don't understand someone doesn't mean we can't empathise with them. We're more than just gay: we are a community of different kinds of people from all different backgrounds. And taking the time to learn about how different kinds of people are treated is vital in developing empathy.

Chapter 4

Preference or Prejudice?

The title of this book is actually only half the story – it's missing two other prejudices that are unfortunately (and commonly) seen on dating profiles: 'No Blacks, no Asians'. Obviously, as a white man, I am not going to boldly write those two on the cover of my book. To do so probably would be career suicide and certainly wouldn't have gotten any backing from publishing houses. Even the title I went with was rejected by more than thirty publishers before my agent secured a deal, in fear of it not being palatable. But the conversation around race and culture within queer spaces is one that I knew needed to be highlighted and needed to be done right. So, most of this chapter will be platforming the experiences of the many incredible queer people of colour I have interviewed, as well as academic research to emphasise the real impact of prejudices within our spaces.

I want to start by addressing the white readers of this book, specifically the white queer readers: You may not have hate in your heart, but you can still unknowingly be part of the problem.

Racism is one of the most prevalent issues in queer spaces, yet the one that seems to be discussed the least. While internalised racism is something that a lot of people have, the consequences are felt only by racial minorities. In Western and white majority societies, the impact of racial prejudices will go mostly unnoticed, because they just don't impact white people. When Black Lives Matter came to prominence in the media in 2020, one thing I heard repeatedly was 'I didn't realise it was still an issue!' If you are a white individual with a predominantly white circle around you, then you wouldn't. It's not something we think about, it's not something we face, it's something that rarely enters our immediate field of vision – including myself.

In school, we are not taught about the atrocities committed during colonial times. We are not taught about our role in the slave trade and the long-lasting systemic impacts this has had on Black people for generations. It literally is not mentioned. We are not taught about the indisputable, overt evidence of Winston Churchill's racism; instead we are taught only that he was a war hero . Western society has a consistent pattern of portraying itself as the hero whilst attempting to kick our rampant atrocities throughout history under the carpet.

Because of this, most white people grow up with absolutely no knowledge of our ancestors' horrific part in history. One thing we hear often from people of privilege when any minorities discuss their oppression is 'You've got your rights, what more do you want?' Many seem to think that one simple legislation will just erase however many centuries of racist treatment and the generational trauma that it's left. Only in 1964 was segregation officially outlawed in the United States, and today, fights for an end to police brutality still take place. Yet, an astounding number of people will still reject the very notion that racism exists, purely because the 'law' says otherwise.

For some, their racism is a lot more active. It's not purely down to lack of education or representation but instead the result of systemic views based entirely in prejudice. Their views have been passed from generation to generation and are something they refuse to so much as acknowledge, let alone work on. Despite many people not realising racism is 'still a thing', it very much is, and the queer community is no exception.

I vividly remember when the first progressive pride flag came to prominence. My first thought upon seeing it was 'But sexuality isn't about race? The pride flag includes *all* LGBTQIA+ people, so why make it about race?'. I'd just come out, and I'd not really had the concept of racism enter my sphere before, let alone racism within queer spaces. So, I truly didn't understand the reasoning behind the new design. It was only by surrounding myself with different people from different backgrounds that I gradually became more educated on the subject. Having grown up in my small, conservative, and very white town with absolutely zero education on our colonial history, I was blissfully unaware.

'Intersectional representation matters because our stories are not monolithic. We need to show that queerness exists across cultures, religions, abilities, and experiences so no one feels like they have to choose between their identities.'

Ryan Lanji (he/him),
cultural producer

Being narrow-minded to begin with often isn't our fault. It's a result of our upbringing, our environment, who we associate ourselves with, and any media we consume. Nobody is born with a prejudice, it's a direct result of two things: 1) not being shown that there are various types of people that exist, and 2) not being actively taught about embracing those who are different. It's not enough to simply cast someone of a minority in a TV show. Active work needs to take place early on to encourage young people to embrace those who are different and to learn about different cultures and backgrounds.

> **'I saw a lot of stuff about Black love online, and I was looking more into it, and I was like, "Do you know what? It would actually be really nice to take away certain things that I would have to explain about myself to other people, that if I was with a Black person, they would just get."'**
>
> Char Ellesse (she/her),
> founder and content creator

Phrases such as 'I don't see colour', whilst there being no ill intent, still pose one significant problem: they don't acknowledge the vast differences in people's cultures. Being different isn't a bad thing. We *are* different and that is the beauty of diversity. It's about embracing and celebrating our differences, not ignoring them or, worse, using those differences as a reason to discriminate. Taking the time to fully comprehend another person's lived experience isn't easy. It requires taking a step back and, rather than viewing society through our own lens, looking at society through an objective lens.

Take Pride, for example. Whilst Pride claims to be for everyone, in a lot of places it can still be culturally monolithic, with little focus on the cultures of queer people of colour. This is when movements such as Black Pride and Trans+ Pride were founded as a way of creating a dedicated space for marginalised people who are further marginalised within their own community. The majority of representation for the entire spectrum of queerness has often been reduced down to white gay men. Yes, white gay men still need support, and we are of course still fighting a battle. But when thinking back to privilege, if someone is gay, Black, feminine, and plus size, for example, their discrimination is likely to be tripled through their intersectional identity and the prejudices they will face from more than one angle.

> **'The only time I feel seen at a Pride is at Black Pride. It [Pride] isn't designed for us. I think it's a place for white queers to be around other white queers.'**
>
> Romone (they/them),
> performance artist

The irony, of course, is that much of queer culture that we embody and celebrate today has its roots in the Black ballroom scene, which was frequented by many queer minorities who were subjected to overt racism and femphobia, predominantly by white gay men. Much of what we see on popular shows like *RuPaul's Drag Race* is from the ballroom scene: walks, vernacular, voguing, realness, etc. In fact, the first-ever recorded drag queen, titled the 'queen of drag', was William Dorsey Swann, a formerly enslaved Black gay man. The general concept of drag or cross-dressing has been known to occur throughout history. However, Swann was the first person recorded using variations of *queen* and *drag* to describe himself and the gatherings of predominantly formally enslaved Black gay men. The same premise used during Swann's gatherings would develop into the ballroom scene and wider drag culture itself, with many of the same principles still in place.[1]

> **'Whiteness just overwrites everything. The entitlement of being white overrides being gay in a lot of gay men, to the point where there's not even any recognition or appreciation of why you are able to be gay in the first place. Because it was Black people and trans+ people. Why do you think you're even able to be out here holding your man's hand?'**
>
> Char Ellesse (she/her),
> founder and content creator

Queer culture is inherently intertwined with Black queers. So much of the culture is celebrated and appropriated without credit for its origins, all whilst upholding racial prejudice for the same people who were emboldened enough to resist. As I discussed in chapter two, Marsha P. Johnson and Sylvia Rivera, who both played such pivotal roles in American gay and transgender liberation movements, were subsequently shunned from the table by white gay men due to being perceived as less palatable. Those who experience the most injustice are the ones who fight the hardest against it. Queer people, white queers in particular, have a duty to learn about our history and give queer POCs the credit they are long overdue.

Desirability Politics

> 'There's just different levels of beauty standards wherever you go, period. When I went to New Orleans, I felt way hotter than I feel here, because I know that they have a different beauty standard, and it's all to do with the beauty standards of where you are.'
>
> Char Ellesse (she/her),
> founder and content creator

Dating is hard enough in general. When you're queer, the dating pool is then even smaller. 'Are they even queer? If so, are they into mascs or fems?' are just a couple of questions we have to ask ourselves. For queer people of colour, this becomes even more difficult. Char noted how her dating experience often depends on whether a person dates Black women to begin with, before even considering the standard forms of compatibility when looking for a partner.

> 'This actually physically makes me feel sick to say. I used to always say to my girls, "Yeah, I'm gonna have my white husband", blah blah blah. That's where I was. I used to be a white man's whore. I've

unlearned a lot of internalised racism within myself, even for my own people. I think that's the legacy of colonialism, that we're meant to look up to the white man.'

Asad Zafar (they/them),
queer charity worker

Desirability politics for people of colour is already difficult in a society with white beauty standards. The hierarchy that's created means that certain attributes have more perceived value than others, with whiteness often holding the most 'value'. One study has shown that white individuals in particular have a stronger 'preference' for other white individuals, and even when minorities have a preference to date *outside* of their race, there is an overwhelming preference for a white partner than of any other race.[2]

'In *Sex Education*, we have Eric [played by Ncuti Gatwa] who dated the Arabic French guy that really cared about them, and then they fucked off the Arabic guy to be with the white boy that was fucking bullying them. Like that does not help.'

Romone (they/them),
performance artist

Romone, a Black and more fem-presenting performance artist, commented on how Black feminine men and NBs generally do not fit into tribe culture or into (white) society's ideal of what Black men should present. Thus, dating and intimacy can become increasingly difficult to navigate. What Romone noticed, however, is that a lot of the desirability they do experience actually comes from older white men.

Romone subsequently sent me an interesting study that explains why this could be the case. Older white men, be it consciously or subconsciously, can use their race to their advantage to date a younger partner. Youth is often seen as one of the biggest indicators of attractiveness amongst gay men, especially when desirability representation is often of those with youth. A lot of older gay men then favour a younger partner, despite it being more difficult to attract one when their age puts them outside of the beauty standard – meaning that some older men feel they are less likely to attract a younger white partner and therefore use their 'race status' to their advantage, as a way to attract a young minority partner.[3]

> **'White men are at the top. Even though the optics are different because it's a marginalised community, in that marginalised community there's still a hierarchy, and the white man will always come out on top.'**
>
> Char Ellesse (she/her),
> founder and content creator

Whether this mentality is conscious or not is not discussed within the study. But as we've already established, our unconscious bias can be working overtime behind the scenes based on the way we've been conditioned to think. Racial bias runs so deeply within queer spaces that desirability of the white beauty standard is something that queer people of colour have to face at almost every turn when dating.

It's Not a Preference, It's Racist

The defence used by those bluntly declaring 'No Blacks, no Asians' on their profiles is again that it's 'just a preference', when in reality it is outright racism whether they want to admit it or not. The definition of a preference is to have 'a greater liking for one alternative than another'. If you actively dislike vanilla ice cream and love strawberry, you wouldn't say you 'preferred' strawberry, because that would imply that vanilla was at least an option for you. When it comes to some gay men's 'preference' in sexual partners, what they claim to 'prefer' isn't actually a preference, it's a created standard that will not be deviated from. Claiming something is just a preference attempts to soften the blow of rejection, which doesn't work for two reasons.

Firstly, there should be very few scenarios during rejection when you need to specifically disclose you have a 'preference' for something the person you are rejecting does not have. This makes it personal, especially when the so-called preferences are often regarding body image, disability, race, or gender expression (masculine or feminine).

Secondly, and more simply, rejection is completely transparent. Rejection does not take place over a mere preference; it takes place because of an aversion to something. The way we view other people's expressions, race, and body images is incredibly complicated and something few want to acknowledge. But claiming it's because of a preference is a way of relinquishing responsibility. If you tell yourself that it's just a preference, in your head it diminishes it to the equivalent of preferring different ice cream flavours, and therefore you don't have to think about why your 'preference' exists to begin with.

> **'They would blatantly say, "You're pretty for a Black boy but not my type."'**
>
> Tyreece (he/she/they),
> fashion creator and performer

Those who demonstrate the most prejudice are often the ones who get most offended when accused of it. 'It's just my opinion', 'It's just a preference', and 'You can't say anything these days' are all common things we hear in someone's defence of saying or doing something they shouldn't, as it's a way of psychologically reducing its severity. Few people want to proudly proclaim they are racist, so sidestepping it entirely and labelling their prejudice as a preference is more self-preservation than anything. It means they won't have to take a step back to reflect and understand why their mind works that way.

Racism has also become more covert through fear of being held accountable and the consequences that come with it, rather than understanding it just makes you a dick. Some may even claim *reverse* racism when similar views are expressed towards white people, but reverse racism is a myth. It does not exist. Racism is upheld by the systemic imbalance of power held by white people over minority groups, meaning that white people do not experience *any* systemic discrimination or prejudice purely for being white.

But why do these 'preferences' exist to begin with? Racism is fundamentally systemic and, in today's so-called progressive society, stems from a fear of the unknown and lack of understanding – leaving us with a narrow-minded approach to anyone who is different from us.

> 'There are regional gays that grew up in a white town, and you're the first Black person they've ever met in their fucking life. They're not going to be into you, and they've been taught not to be into you. They've been taught not to see you as a romantic or sexual person, because all the representation that we see in the media is you being the funny best friend. It's queer media's responsibility to highlight different people in a romantic and sexual capacity.'
>
> Romone (they/them),
> performance artist

As discussed in chapter one, poor representation may not only mean a lack of understanding for those who are different, but also influence who we find attractive. As Romone put it, 'They've been taught not to see you as a romantic or sexual person'. For Le Fil, who is of Chinese heritage, the impact of poor representation was evident to him.

> 'For a long time, I thought I never fancied Asian people, Chinese people like myself. And that was when I was a teenager living up north, and there were no Chinese people around me. And then I went

to Hong Kong when I was seventeen or eighteen, and I was like, "Oh my god, I fancy everyone." I never thought why. And then I came back [to the UK], and I realised that it was because I never saw them on TV. I never saw them in the newspaper. I never saw them in the top ten hunks of *Heat* magazine. I never saw them in adverts topless. I never saw Asian men being put on a pedestal as desirable. And that really impacts our understanding of what we find desirable.'

Le Fil (he/they),
artist and drag performer

When we are fed only one standard of beauty, that becomes the standard we uphold. Asad, who is Pakistani, admitted something similar. When one of their friends started listening to the music genre K-pop, Asad admitted that initially they didn't find any of the men attractive. What Asad did next was something that unfortunately a lot of people with racial bias do not do: unpack the reasons as to why.

'I had to have that chat with myself. I was like, "Is this internal? This is internalised racism within me that I need to unpack, because why am I not seeing people from this race as an option?" I wasn't consuming media that highlighted East Asian people, different kinds of people, or just saw them represented at all.'

Asad Zafar (they/them),
queer charity worker

Fetishising Is Not a Compliment

I touched on fetishisation earlier in the book with trans women as well as bisexuals, but some will even fetishise a person's race. Quite often when minorities are represented, it is in a very specific way that plays into sexual stereotypes. Some people will then begin to fetishise minorities based on the stereotypes they see, only through a sexual lens and nothing else. For example, one stereotype that fetishises POCs is dick size: some demographics on average have bigger or smaller dicks (and, by the way, natural size will still vary regardless of who you are). People will then assume these sizes affect the role they'll play in the bedroom, as well as the type of sex they'll have (but more on this later). As a result, some might shut themselves off to an entire race based on a stereotype. Again, this will likely be an unconscious bias and a more reflex assumption. But when you take a step back and consider the belief that a specific race is assumed to automatically take a specific role in the bedroom, you realise it is an incredibly damaging stereotype. You may also be missing out on some great sex in the process.

One of the biggest contributors to this mindset, specifically in the gay community, is porn. In the next chapter, I'll discuss the way gay porn categories are structured and how the tribes we've created can be problematic. But for now, it's just important to note that the representation of 'desirability' is largely of white men. For Black men in particular, their representation in porn is often based on racial stereotypes: being aggressive, well built, or well endowed. When this is the only representation people get of a Black man in a desirable way, soon these stereotypes become internalised, and people begin to navigate approaching Black men in real life with what they've been conditioned to believe in fabricated scenarios. You will often find people (usually non-Black people) brazenly include 'seeking BBC [big Black cock]' in their bio because of the stereotypes they have in their mind about dick size and the type of sex they've seen only in porn.

> 'The whole premise of it is "being the Black thug with their big Black cock, fucks little white boy". A lot of mainstream porn is created through the lens of whiteness. So then you have these white producers that produce porn just actively perpetuating those stereotypes. It's exhausting, because a lot of people are learning about sex through watching porn, they're approaching you with what they've seen, which isn't even fucking real.'
>
> Romone (they/them),
> performance artist

Uzo, who is a tall, gay Black man, said in our interview that because he is Black *and* tall, he often feels 'typecast', based on racial stereotypes people are fed, as being the 'solely dominant figure in the bedroom', when in reality, he really enjoys both. The added pressure for Black men is that they are often assumed not only to have bigger dicks but also to automatically be the top and to be dominant.

Romone and I had a similar conversation about the way

Black men are expected to perform hypermasculinity in a way that aligns with people's stereotypes and expectations. Romone's treatment on dating apps depends on the way they present themselves, meaning a topless photo looking slightly more masculine garners them a lot more attention. Conforming to the racial stereotype leads to greater sexual gratification. Romone even noted, 'You see the Black guys on Grindr that have, "BBC for now", and it's like they're prepared to objectify themselves to get any form of gratification from white men.'

> **'Facing fetishisation based on racial stereotypes has taught me to seek connections where I'm valued for all the layers of who I am.'**
>
> Ryan Lanji (he/him),
> cultural producer

There is a huge difference between genuine desire and the fetishisation of a minority. Genuine desire is about seeing a person for who they truly are and desiring them for those existing qualities, whilst fetishisation involves a distorted perception of an individual based on preconceived ideas of their identity, often based on specific physical characteristics. Queer men of colour can then become seen more as an object of desire based on fabricated ideals, rather than as an individual to be valued on a personal level. Having a fetish in general is often perfectly normal and completely okay. But much like how trans women are often fetishised by closeted or 'curious' men, fetishisation of a *person* is not a compliment.

Queers of Faith Exist

One specific and often stigmatised topic within queer spaces is that of queerness and religion. Representation of intersectional queers is already scarce, let alone the additional layer of being of faith. Asad opened up to me about their experience navigating being a Muslim alongside their queerness. They admitted that there's a bit of a double-edged sword when being a queer person of faith. Asad will get non-queer Muslims online criticising them and proclaiming that they will 'go to hell' for being gay. Simultaneously, they will have queer ex-Muslims message them asking, 'How the fuck could you say you're queer and Muslim?!' based on their personal experiences with the religion. All whilst many queers, who have never been of faith, simply cannot wrap their head around someone being both queer and of faith. Asad recognises that everyone's experience of faith is different and that their experience of Islam may differ from those who renounced their faith, but surely Asad deserves the same understanding back?

> 'It took time to reshape what my faith meant to me. I'm still a Muslim. I believe in Islam. I practise Islam, I pray, I make dua, I give to charity, I participate in Ramadan, I do everything that Muslims do. I'm just a raging faggot at the same time.'
>
> Asad Zafar (they/them),
> queer charity worker

Queer people who don't understand someone being queer and of faith simultaneously often comes from misunderstanding, poor media representation, and generalisations, particularly by those who have never been of faith. People cannot wrap their head around two supposedly conflicting beliefs existing simultaneously, bringing us back to 'cognitive dissonance'. There's a bit of a recurring theme with queers experiencing cognitive dissonance in this book.

A particular example of this cognitive dissonance was a topic that dominated the media from October 2023: Palestine. 'Why would I support a country that would throw me off a roof for being gay?' is a comment I've seen over and over again. This is a response often used as a way of coping with cognitive dissonance, because there is no logical or moral justification for genocide. People have also developed this mindset that if it doesn't affect them directly, then why should they care? But despite the anti-LGBTQIA+ laws, queer people still live in Palestine. People like you and me who feel the same things we do, who are currently living under discriminatory laws as well as missile strikes. If you or I were in Palestine, we'd be more likely to be killed by a missile than being 'thrown off a roof for being gay'. Asad, who is a strong advocate for a free Palestine, words it better than I ever could:

> 'Queer people grow up in a world that doesn't accept them, and when you see other minorities or groups that are going through injustice, of course we're going to feel strongly towards that. I'm going to show up for them because until we're all free, none of us are free.'

Asad Zafar (they/them),
queer charity worker

My unconscious bias with religion is something I want to be honest about. Having spent time with someone who is queer and also Muslim meant that I saw first-hand how practising faith and queerness can be done simultaneously. If I were to come across someone who's Muslim on a dating app, I wouldn't bat an eyelid. Yet, my growing up in a predominantly white country with its primary religion (and ideologies) being rooted in Christianity meant that the majority of religious-based homophobia I was subjected to was from Christians who were often also conservative voters. This led to an unconscious bias towards those of Christian faith, more specifically Christian queers. The idea of dating someone who was queer and Muslim created no internal conflicts for myself, yet the idea of dating someone who was queer and Christian did. If I saw that someone's dating app bio said they were Christian, it would create cognitive dissonance. This was something I had to unpack and understand that, like Asad, being queer and of faith (any faith) can both be equally true. It was only because of the society I had grown up in, as well as my personal experience with non-queer Christians, that I had formed the unconscious bias that both identities could not exist harmoniously. Fundamentally, this is not the case.

One of my best friends in the world is Christian, and she is one of the most liberal, progressive, and understanding people I've ever met. Even the church she had her wedding in (where I was a bridesman and got to walk down the aisle) celebrates Pride and embraces the LGBTQIA+ community. I've also since heard stories about how some queer people were wholeheartedly accepted by their Christian family and their local church. An experience with one individual or idea does not automatically determine the experience with another. It is through taking the time to meet, listen to, and understand those who are different from us that we can have a greater level of empathy for our fellow queers.

Of course, these experiences are not the case for everyone. There are some queer people who are shunned from their family homes due to their family's homophobia under the guise of a religious belief. The trauma something like this creates is not one I have first-hand experience with, and I am not about to tell a queer person who renounced their faith how to feel about their past religion. But for those who are queer and still of faith, Asad gave some beautiful insight into how they reshaped what their religion meant to them and how both parts of their identity remain intrinsic to who they are.

> 'Meet other queer people belonging to a faith, who practise their faith; run in those circles, because that is what helped me, knowing that I wasn't alone. When you grow up feeling very isolated and very alone, it's just important to know you're not alone and that you're not the only one.'
>
> Asad Zafar (they/them),
> queer charity worker

Safe Spaces Matter (Not Just for Slim White Gays)

'Just create your own spaces!' is often a response given to intersectional queers feeling uncomfortable and unseen in larger queer venues. The creation of safe spaces means people of similar culture are able to feel seen for more of their identity, as well as shielded from prejudice. White people do not need a safe haven based on our race, as almost every space is for us. This is where the argument, used predominantly by white people, 'not every space has to be for you' comes crumbling down, because more often than not the people saying so have access to a lot more spaces than the person they're saying it to.

> **'Not everything needs to be body positive'**, says the person with the societally ideal body type that is accepted and praised in almost every space.

> **'Not everything needs to be about race'**, says the white person whose race has never made their life more difficult to navigate.

> **'Not everything needs to be about sexuality!'** says the cis-het person who's never so much as blinked at the thought of holding their partner's hand in public for fear of verbal or physical assault.

These mindsets don't always come from a place of intentional malice. They're often a combination of unawareness of privilege and a lack of empathy. When we take a step back and look objectively at our own privilege, we can start to see that whilst life may not have been easy for us personally, it may not have been as difficult as someone else's. The very least we can do is not actively make things even harder.

Romone helped me navigate queer raves and other dedicated queer events for the first time. What became quickly apparent, however, was how white-centric these events could be. Let's just say the dance floor had a very *distinct* colour palette.

When I first started experiencing these spaces, it simply wasn't something that crossed my mind. Naturally it wouldn't have, growing up white in a white town; looking around a room of people with the same race as me had been second nature for so long.

The more we attended these events, the more Romone would mention the emotional exhaustion they felt the next day. When a space is filled with people who look identical, someone who doesn't fit the same aesthetic is not going to feel that they fit in, and that can take a mental toll. Especially when one of the sole drivers for the event is for people to feel desirable, which is what much of queer nightlife is. Sure, some of the spaces we went to would celebrate the big boys, but overwhelmingly the *white* big boys. When an event caters to a very specific demographic under the guise of inclusivity, is it truly inclusive?

> **'We need spaces where intersectionality isn't an afterthought but the foundation.'**
>
> Ryan Lanji (he/him),
> cultural producer

Shortly after, we started looking for other queer nights we could attend that would be more inclusive and would likely make us both feel completely at home, and this was not easy. There was only a handful of queer nights, but they were truly some of the most inclusive spaces I have ever been in. People of all backgrounds, orientations, genders, races, and body types, all in one place. Multiple rooms that focussed on celebrating music from different cultures and creating a space where everyone felt welcome and at home. But we came to understand that different events often cater to different demographics, and events that wholeheartedly celebrate every corner of queer culture are few and far between.

> **'It's hard to even get into some of the spaces, realistically. Think back to the last awards show you were at or something. How many people did you see that looked like me in that room? How many Black women did you see in that room?'**
>
> Yasmin Benoit (she/her),
> model and asexual activist

Thinking about the queer awards shows I have been to, I realised there were very few people of colour at most of them. And the more events I attended, the more apparent it became. This is something that I, as a white person, previously wouldn't have even noticed. But by listening to the experiences of others, the diversity of a space (or lack thereof) is now something I will notice straightaway. Of the few POCs who were there, the vast majority of them were part of the catering staff and waiting on tables. Yasmin admitted that multiple times, she too has been mistaken for catering staff at events, rather than being seen as a guest.

It's a direct result of this that many queer minorities have to find or create their own spaces in a world where queer spaces are often seen as white spaces. In some online discourse I've seen recently, there were discussions around non-queer people frequenting queer venues and treating them like their own, when in reality non-queer people have their own spaces. One of the counterpoints that was interesting to read was 'What spaces are dedicated for straight people then?' You read that right, and I hope your jaw dropped as quickly as mine did. It took me a minute to comprehend what I was reading before realising this comment was coming from a place of immense privilege. Spaces are not labelled as 'straight venues' because it is assumed. Every venue is a straight venue, because you will not walk in feeling any unease at being ridiculed purely for the fact you are straight. You are automatically welcomed, as you are seen as the norm and statistically make up an overwhelming majority of the population. Queer people create their own spaces as a way of feeling safe from ridicule from the majority. Queer spaces are a result of discrimination and prejudice; they're a result of how straight people treat us.

> **'I love going into a night that's more focussed around Black queers, or even going to Black Pride and getting to dance to my cultural music with people that look like me. I don't get that often.'**
>
> Romone (they/them),
> performance artist

The exact same logic applies to spaces created for queer people of colour. Venues that are strictly for *white gay men* do not exist anymore, or at least not said with full chest. Yet at most queer venues, this will likely be the majority of the clientele. Naturally, with the strict white-centric beauty standards, and people of colour frequently being subjected to prejudice or fetishisation, entering such spaces isn't likely to make them feel completely at home. The purpose is then to create a space where minorities do feel at home, contrary to the majority of 'queer friendly' spaces.

Ryan Lanji, for example, started the first UK LGBTQIA+ Bollywood club night. Being from South Asian heritage, he 'needed a space where I didn't have to leave parts of myself at the door'. The vast majority of queer spaces focus on embracing queerness purely through a white lens, meaning that white queer individuals can often enter and embrace these spaces without feeling the need to hold back any parts of their identity. For intersectional queer people, a huge part of their culture is often left behind. And whilst we may have some shared experiences as queer people, cultural and ethnic differences means that a big part of their lived experience is not one that can be shared by others.

Something I have seen become more common in recent years in response to social discourse is the phrase 'it's not that deep' or 'not everything needs to be analysed'. This again is a way of reducing a topic's severity and relinquishing responsibility. Stating that something 'isn't that deep' more often than not means that there is little if any impact from the topic being discussed on the person responding as such, much like when I didn't understand the need for the progressive pride flag: 'Why make it about race?' I admitted to thinking. I wasn't impacted by it directly, so I didn't understand its importance.

But as I've learned, and as I mentioned in the introduction, just because something doesn't impact you directly does not mean it doesn't impact others. It may not exist in your world, but it exists in others'. This is where queer empathy comes into play and understanding that not all our experiences are the same. The existence of one struggle does not invalidate another. The absence of a specific struggle for one individual does not mean it ceases to exist in its entirety. Understanding this is an important step in having more empathy overall, specifically for queer people and intersectional minorities.

But understanding on its own will not bring about change unless it coincides with action. This is the point I mentioned where you might be thinking "well, what now?", and you're right to be thinking that. Right now we're working on understanding the prejudices that exist and the impact they have. This chapter aims to have achieved just that, and so do the next few chapters. It's in the final chapters that we'll get into turning awareness into action. It is there that we will take the understandings we have learned, and use them to bring about change.

Chapter 5

The Body Image Crisis

This is the chapter I was dreading writing because I knew it was going to require some of the rawest honesty from myself. I didn't want to write this as a motivational piece or as 'inspiration porn', as that's not what this book is. I want to call *all* of us into a much-needed conversation about the way we treat each other. Body insecurity is something that every single person can relate to in some capacity, especially queer people. This chapter will explain the relationships queer people have with their bodies and why these relationships exist. There is no doubt that almost every issue within queer spaces has trickled down from wider society. Our bodies aren't viewed as the biological phenomenon that carries us through life and are instead frequently seen as mere objects of desire and as social currency determining our 'value'.

Before I get started, I want to remind you of something I mentioned in the introduction: it may not be about you. Quite often when discussing body image standards amongst queer men and the reasons they exist, I'm just met with 'But I don't work out for these! I do so for X, Y, Z, blah blah blah.' Evidently, if your reasons for working out aren't discussed here and focus more on physical health, enjoyment, or mental health, then these conversations may not apply to you (so long as you're not projecting these standards onto others either). So, when reading this chapter, I want you to keep in mind that this is not automatically accusing you of anything, rather bringing these very real issues to your attention whether they apply to you or not.

Anyway, now that the T & C's are out of the way, let's crack on. Body image is a set of socially constructed ideas that plague modern society and fluctuate like trends in fashion. We went from idealising extreme thinness in women, dubbed 'heroine chic', to the Kardashian-esque curvaceous BBL aesthetic in less than twenty years. So-called role models in the media tell us how we should look and who we should find desirable, and we have almost no say in it. We are fed the new ideal body over and over again until we feel we are no longer enough. Our overall aesthetic is the first thing people notice: the way we dress, the way we style our hair, our smiles, our eyes, our hand gestures, and our bodies.

As humans we are constantly evaluating our surroundings, often without even realising it. We take note of what we see in someone and our brain makes a quick judgement before we've even had a chance to think. Our unconscious bias is like a reflex. The second our brain receives the information of what we've just visually observed, our unconscious bias jumps up to take centre stage. This isn't something I want anyone to beat themselves up over. Unconscious bias isn't our fault, but it's our responsibility to do something about it.

'I moved to Manchester because I knew it was so queer. I wanted to move here because I felt like that's where I'll fit in. And then I turned up here overweight, not conventionally very good-looking, and I didn't fit in, and I was quite gutted.'

Danny Beard (he/they),
drag queen and performer

I want you to be honest with yourself here, and I'll be honest too. At any point in your life, whether it's recently, as a teenager, or even as a child, have you ever made a snap judgement about someone's appearance? More specifically, have you made a snap judgement about someone's body image or weight? Have you seen a plus-size person walking down the street, in the gym, or in a club and your brain has instantly fed you a harsh critique? Not one you necessarily verbalised or that even prompted so much as a facial expression, but the thought just popped into your head without any hesitation. The likely answer is yes. I'm ashamed to admit that I've been very guilty of this in the past, especially when I was struggling with my own body. It's also something that from time to time I still have to pull myself up on – not even just about body image but any form of judgement.

There are a number of reasons harsh judgement can be a reflex response to what we see. We may have such a deep-rooted aversion to the idea of being fat, plus size, or even remotely distant from the thin ideal that our aversion is then projected onto others. Those who are most judgemental are often the most insecure. Insecurity doesn't have to be as severe as looking in the mirror and 'hating' what you see; it can be as simple as micro-critiquing ourselves. It doesn't have to be as severe as 'hating' fat people; it can be as simple as micro-critiquing them.

When we discussed privilege, I mentioned how those made aware of it often see it as a personal attack. The same applies to fatphobia, which is the unreasonable dislike or unfair treatment of people because they are fat.[1] Many will take the definition at face value and assume that if they are accused of a fatphobic mindset or comment, they are instead being accused of either A) actively disliking anyone who is fat or they may view as fat, or B) actively treating the same people unfairly, neither of which is necessarily the case, but it can manifest in smaller ways known as microaggressions. Often unintentional, and as a result of our unconscious bias or stereotypes, microaggressions are smaller, more subtle words or actions that can cause harm, normally to marginalized groups. The prime example being the dirty looks fat queer people can be subjected to in queer spaces simply for being there and looking a certain way (not built like an Olympic diver, for example).

We've all likely heard someone say at some point, 'They shouldn't be wearing that', or 'They can't pull that off!' in reference to a particular type of person wearing a perfectly normal item of clothing. This is our unconscious bias making a judgement based on never being shown that body type wearing a certain item. Instead, we've only seen that body type be the butt of someone's joke, something to be ridiculed or just the side character to someone more 'conventionally' attractive.

'If you want to buy a jock[strap] or something, you just see muscle maries in a jock, or on the off-

> **chance you'll see a slightly bigger guy, he's also white or very fair skinned. Even the belly and the love handles are a certain type that's acceptable. Because they're like, "Yeah, see, inclusive!" but there's only a level of fat that they'll allow.'**
>
> Asad Zafar (they/them),
> queer charity worker

Ultimately this comes back to seeing difference as something to be shamed and not celebrated. Different body types exist, they've always existed, and that is not about to change. Despite this, our brains are often full of preconceived stereotypes and judgements of those who are different from us or just different from the beauty standard, which can lead to fatphobia. Even fat people themselves can be victims of internalised fatphobia, which can create a lot of conflicting feelings. One of the most common examples I see is that some guys will *love* a thicc boy. They'll be attracted to a big hairy belly, love handles, and all the things we're told not to like. But they won't like having the body themselves. 'I love this body type on others but not on me' is an all-too-common thing I hear. We are often our worst critics. Even if we are sexually attracted to a bigger body and believe that they're more than enough for us (pun intended), our internalised fatphobia can still make us believe that *we* aren't enough. We can feel that what we find desirable is not representative of wider society. We may be attracted to bigger bodies, but we struggle to believe anyone else is. Given that representation heavily focusses on the idealised body type, which is inundated with praise, this is hardly a surprise.

Some people's desire for a muscular partner isn't born out of a malleable 'preference' for that body type; instead it is born out of an aversion to bodies that do not meet a set of rigid standards or are perceived as being subpar. I know this is going to sound like a personal attack, but it is not. Having an aversion to bodies that deviate from the beauty standard is not your fault. The important thing is to acknowledge it and to call it what it is. To deny the presence of a body image crisis would be to ignore the copious amounts of research that proves otherwise, which I'm about to share with you. We have a duty to the community to unpack our prejudices and understand why they exist, with the hope being that it will lead to greater acceptance of ourselves and, in turn, others.

> 'I can't tell you how many times I've been getting ready to go out with my friends, [and] I just look at myself, and I'm like, "Yeah, I'm not going." I would just cancel forty minutes before and get in bed and feel really shit about myself. Because I know I'm going to be looked at in a way that I'm just not meant to be in some spaces or that I look too weird or that I'm not being in those spaces for desirability. I want to have fun with my friends, but I don't want any [dirty] looks from skinny or muscular guys.'
>
> Asad Zafar (they/them),
> queer charity worker

Most of us knowingly joke and make reference to the body standards within the community and the damage they have.

Despite the very real consequences they pose, many of us feel all we can do is simply shrug it off with a 'that's just how it is' mentality. Those who are on the more privileged side may deny the issue even exists. But the below statistic shows us the real psychological impacts and that we really do need to work to change.

> **Gay and bisexual men are more than ten times more likely to be diagnosed with an eating disorder or show symptoms of disordered eating than straight men.[2]**

Ten times more likely. This isn't just a little bit more likely, it's a truly insane disparity and is only the tip of the iceberg. The reason the term *disordered eating* is used is because not every person who shows symptoms of disordered eating will be formally diagnosed with an eating disorder. One is less severe than the other, but the consequences, both physical and psychological, can still be incredibly damaging. Not only are gay and bi men more likely to engage in thinness-oriented disordered eating, but they are also more likely to develop muscle dysmorphia.[3] Gay and bi men can become obsessed with the idea that their body is 'too small' or not muscular enough, from thinking their arms are slightly too skinny to overly criticising their body daily until they truly believe, no matter how much muscle they gain, that they're not enough.

> 'When people tell me, "Romone if you were more muscly I'd be super into it", that causes the feeling

of "If I was bigger, would I have a better time dating?" I mean, I'd still be a fucking faggot. But people would be more willing to give me a chance based on how my body looks.'

Romone (they/them),
performance artist

When we're relentlessly exposed to the ideals of gay male beauty, it's quickly understood that one of the best chances to find a partner is to be more muscular. However, few understand the severity of muscle dysmorphia, sometimes known as 'reverse anorexia', and the impact it has on gay men. Whilst muscle dysmorphia itself is not an eating disorder, those who experience muscle dysmorphia are also more likely to display symptoms of disordered eating as well as exercise addiction.[4,5] Some may push their bodies to extremes simply to be seen as more desirable or valued within queer circles and become addicted to it without even realising. But because we're told that exercise and 'clean' eating are automatically healthy, disordered eating in more muscular physiques is often overlooked. What many see as being lean and healthy can instead be the result of an incredibly complex and even harmful state of mind. We then end up with a vacuum of insecurity that few can escape, an endless cycle of judgement, desire, and competition that continues to uphold the toxic body standards we felt we had no choice but to accept – including myself.

'We're all fighting to be in this middle point. There's fat people who are trying to lose weight to get

in. Then there's really slender guys who can't gain weight. They would just never feel enough if they are not what they see on the cover of a gay magazine.'

Uzo Emenike (he/she/they), musician

'You've Stopped Looking After Your Body . . .'

For those of you who have seen my social media, me talking about body image will not be anything new to you. A big part of the conversations I try to have online are about normalizing different body types, particularly amongst gay men. On a couple of occasions I've briefly explained why this is, but now I want to tell you the full story.

I spent most of my teenage years feeling like I had to hold my breath. Before I even started experiencing confusing sexual feelings, I was already being ridiculed for being feminine. I felt like my every move was being watched, like being onstage and playing the role of someone completely different from myself and with the whole school waiting for me to slip up. By my mid-teens I had started watching some gay YouTubers who helped me realise that life as a gay man might actually be okay. The only issue (which I didn't realise till later in life) was that they were all white, muscular, and pretty masc presenting. I didn't know that queerness could look like anything else. I didn't know you could be a hairier gay guy with a belly, I didn't know you could experiment with fashion and makeup. Not only did this dictate who I thought I had to be; it also dictated who I thought others had to be. I didn't see trans+ people, I didn't see Black queers, I didn't see queers of faith, I didn't see disabled queers. I didn't see most of the people who gave us the rights we have today – all I saw was white gay men. This, paired with the shame brought on by years of ridicule for being effeminate, resulted in someone with a pretty narrow mind and decades of therapy ahead of him.

In my late teens, I developed a very particular aversion to love handles, or body fat on the lower back around the waist, and this was born entirely out of the representation I was exposed to of the ideal body. I remember occasionally seeing some of the YouTubers I watched in Speedos in some of their videos. I'd see how their firm butts were perfectly hugged and held up by the swimwear. I'd see how their lower backs and V-lines would blend seamlessly into the tops of the trunks. This was the only type of person I ever saw wearing a Speedo, that and Olympic divers. On one occasion, one of their friends was wearing a Speedo in a video, and his body was different from what I'd seen. The Speedo didn't perfectly hold up his butt and his back didn't seamlessly blend. He was the first person I saw with love handles wearing a Speedo. My unconscious bias jumped straight into action and made a snap judgement: 'That's wrong. He shouldn't look like that, or if he does, he should wear something else.'

> **'As I've gotten older, I've realised I actually don't fancy the body type we've been fed. I was just being told that, and it was perpetuated everywhere.'**
>
> Tyreece (he/she/they),
> fashion creator and performer

My own judgement, caused by my unconscious bias, then birthed a whole new insecurity for me that I'd not once in the past paid any attention to: love handles. I remember constantly looking in the mirror to see if I could feel even the slightest bit of body fat around my waist. I started doing half an hour of ab workouts every single day for more than a year. This was all after an hourlong intense heavy-lifting gym session, twenty minutes on the treadmill, and a five-mile walk to and from my gym, as well as running five kilometres three days a week. All to get home and eat my carefully calorie-counted meal with as little fat or carbs as possible. I was literally scared of having body fat or being perceived as fat. This was internalised fatphobia. I wasn't at all thinking about my health; my only priority was how I looked. I remember talking to my mum about it when she saw me scrutinising myself in the mirror. Despite my repulsion at seeing body fat on me, my mum didn't see a thing. She truly didn't see what I was talking about. She tried to talk me down and explain that I had nothing to worry about, but my brain was so hardwired to fear body fat that I simply wouldn't listen. One of my best friends had to give me a serious talking-to at one point, because I would cancel plans with her to go work out. I'd gone to the gym every day for as long as I could remember, but I couldn't go to the cinema with her that evening because I hadn't been to the gym yet that day. She saw how it was consuming my entire life, and not for the right reasons.

A few years passed, and I was the leanest and most muscular I'd ever been, or as some would describe me, a 'twunk' (more on that later). By this point, I had determined the only way to get the validation I yearned for was through my body.

Suddenly having a six-pack and not an ounce of body fat made me worth people's time and attention. The more I worked out and posed online, the more validation I would get. It was an endless spiral that I couldn't just end, because the validation was so short-lived that in order to feed the dependence on it I had developed, I had to keep working out.

I then had my first ever seminude photoshoot that was entirely focussed on my body. I had been working hard and was so excited to show off my progress. When I say I'd been working hard, I mean I was eating zero carbs and working out every single day with no rest. I will never take away from the hard work it takes to craft your body, but the issue is the mindset. With the shoot being body focussed, I needed to be oiled up and do forty press-ups between photos, and I was even offered a cock ring to make my dick look bigger – all the things to make the photos as unrealistic as possible, and that's before Photoshop.

A few weeks passed and I finally got the photos back. In one of them I had a full six-pack! Now let me tell you, we took five hundred photos, and I'd managed to get a perfect six-pack in *one* of them. I had to tense in a very particular way and lean back slightly, they had to adjust the lighting, and *boom*... washboard abs. I'm genuinely surprised I didn't burst a blood vessel (or something else) tensing that hard. I was *so* thrilled that I sent this photo over to a guy I had been talking to. He was a handsome American man with a cheeky smile and the body of a Greek god. When he opened it, he simply responded, 'Wait one sec, I'm doing something, hopefully you'll think it's funny.' Whilst I waited, I sat and admired my physique in the mirror beside my bed and analysed every fine detail, looking for perfection (or imperfection). I was anticipating maybe a funny filter or a doodle on there, but no, what I got back was shocking. 'Here you go', he messaged, alongside a highly photoshopped image. He'd taken the photo I'd sent him and made my shoulders, pecs, and arms bigger and my hips smaller. Not my waist, my hips. Honey, that is *bone*. That's not even physically possible to change. This wasn't done in an unrealistic and humorous way – you know, when people massively overedit their photos as a joke to look 'skinny'. He was being deadly serious. He followed this with 'Just something to aim towards!' I was speechless. I had a photoshoot that took ridiculous prep, years of exercise, and a lot of confidence, just to be met with 'something to aim towards'. At this point in my life I was pure muscle and didn't have an ounce of body fat on me, and it still wasn't enough. Unfortunately, I was still in a very image-focussed mindset, so I simply shrugged it off and thanked him. (Yes, I thanked him. If I met younger me today he would be getting a slap.) I internalised what he said to me. 'I'm still not enough', I thought as I got ready to go back to the gym. I began treating others the way I had been treated. I spent the next few years still focusing on achieving the unrealistic 'perfect' body, whilst simultaneously expecting others to do the same.

Despite having a twenty-eight-inch waist, visible abs, and V-lines, I still edited my photos to make my waist smaller, my biceps bigger, and my shoulders broader. This was at my leanest and most muscular, and I still wasn't happy. My mindset wasn't being proud of my progress and continuing to work hard; it was that I hadn't worked hard enough. I even refused to ever upload a photo without heavily editing my face. I made my eyes brighter, my jawline sharper, and my beard thicker and removed anything else I saw as an imperfection. The person I created online was a complete facade. I had no idea how to exist as a gay man in the twenty-first century, so the only thing I could do was follow the very limited example I had been set – this example being: beauty is our ultimate currency. We have to look and act a certain way in order to be desirable, successful, and, most importantly, validated.

A couple more years and hours upon hours in the gym passed, and the unthinkable happened. We were hit with a global pandemic. This historical event paused the world, but in many ways helped a lot of people. Being forced to focus on ourselves gave us the time to figure out who we really were. The day lockdown started, I began taking my first ever anti-depressants, which are known to cause weight gain. Gyms were closed, and I was comfort eating. So, you know, a really good time for me mentally. Like most people during Covid, my body started to change, and people who followed me online began to notice. My muscles slowly started to fade, and very small pockets of body fat began to build (mind you, I was still seven stone lighter than I am now). I started being criticised for no longer having abs, and as my muscle mass faded, so did my confidence. My boyfriend at the time comforted me as I tried to navigate this new wave of invalidation and ridicule from people who once supported me. I soon realised that any confidence I had built over the last few years was held up entirely by this brittle facade. My 'perfect' body was the only thing giving me confidence. Once that was taken away, I didn't know who I was.

Over time, I realised that I didn't want to live life like that.

I didn't want my entire self-esteem to be held up by the validation I desperately fought to receive from strangers. This makes us incredibly susceptible to being validation fiends. We crave it. The only way we feel worthy, or even just a fraction of the worth that heterosexuals do, is to work twice as hard to *prove* our worthiness. And this is what I was doing with my body. I never felt like I was enough, but when I started working on my body I experienced this unfamiliar feeling of validation – and I became addicted to it. I finally felt worth something, but in reality what I was feeling was the fleeting satisfaction that comes with all external validation. It is temporary and not at all sustainable. So I decided to shift to working on myself mentally and to become truly content and confident in who I was and what I could offer to the world, rather than what my body could. This is where my work today comes from. I didn't want to be the curated, pristine and very limited representation I had of gay men growing up. I wanted to be the very thing that was missing – someone who helped queer men feel like they're enough.

Then things became even more . . . fun (sense the tone). After a couple of years, I had to have a difficult conversation about my body with the same boyfriend who comforted me when it was changing. When the relationship started, I was both lean and muscular. But thanks to the pandemic, my body began to change: my stomach was no longer flat, and my abs were starting to be hidden by a little belly. Unpacking my body image issues was already difficult with the various expectations from other gay men and the criticism I was receiving online. But what I didn't expect was for those very expectations to be upheld by my partner. I was being looked dead in the eye whilst

I was sat on the bed in nothing but my underwear as the words 'you've stopped looking after your body' trembled from his lips. In that very moment, my world shattered. Those feelings of shame came rushing back, and the invalidation washed over me like a tsunami. I was still relatively slim at this point, but the sight of me having a bit of a belly was off-putting enough for the last ten months of our relationship to be completely sexless. Even to this day, dating someone is where I feel at my most fragile. I do not feel insecure in my body during casual sex, but as soon as I start dating someone my anxiety creeps up and makes me fear that I'll be left if my body changes. This damage is something for me alone to work through. But this is the reality that harsh body image expectations can leave us with.

Despite the way I was made to feel, I am and always have been empathetic to his reasoning, just like I have been this entire book. I understand where the mindset came from, and even he admitted a great deal of shame for feeling the way he did. This didn't take away from the hurt it caused me, but it was important in helping me realise that it was less about me and more about him.

One thing we talked about was preferences (a topic that keeps popping up in this book). He knew I liked big arms. It wasn't anything major or something I actively sought in a partner; they were more of a turn-on if they were there. One day he paused and asked me, 'What's the difference between you liking bigger arms and me liking a flat stomach?', which, to be fair, is a perfectly valid thing to ask, but there was one fundamental difference: bigger arms for me were like a small bonus, not a necessity. That's a huge difference. If the person I was dating suddenly lost loads of weight and became really slim, I would still want him. If they suddenly gained a bigger belly, I would still want him. I'm not saying this just because I can. I am saying this because I know it's true. I have worked to unpack the previous fatphobic mindsets I had and no longer have an aversion to different types of bodies. I've enjoyed sex with hairy six-foot-eight Olympic lifters, petite five-foot-six feminine guys with very little body hair, guys with a big belly and little muscle definition, and *many* other different types of men.

I have no shame in saying that I've been, well, 'busy'. But what I would have shame for is making someone feel less than because they don't reach an unrealistic societal beauty standard. I've been with so many different body types, and they have all been beautiful. Sure, some of them I may enjoy a little more than others, and that's completely natural and okay. *That* is what a preference is, the greater enjoyment of one thing over another. It's not the outright aversion to someone being slim, or having a belly, or being feminine, or being a person of colour, or having body hair, or any of the other various 'preferences' gay men like to declare.

But this is just my story. What I went through won't be everyone's experience with body image, but that despair and frustration I felt might feel familiar to you. You might have read this and felt like it's your own biography, you may have felt my story is just a fraction of what you've had to endure, you may have become aware of some of the harm you personally may have caused others, or felt you did not relate at all. But this chapter isn't all about me, it's about the body image crisis at large. For me personally, a lot of my body image struggles come down to poor and inauthentic representation. But this is just one of many reasons for the incredibly intense body image pressures gay and bi men experience.

Masculinity versus Femininity

Many gay men's deep-rooted shame and frequent ridicule over our femininity at a younger age can lead to our desire to overcompensate by achieving an overtly 'masculine' physique through being more muscular. That's not to say muscularity equals masculinity, but there are many who perceive this as such. It's a perpetual cycle: the very pressure we had put on us to be masculine at a younger age is then internalised, and we continue to place this pressure on ourselves long after coming out. We in turn put the same pressure on potential partners by expecting them to uphold the same ideals we were shamed into upholding. As a result, gay men are more likely than straight women to put pressure on their partners to be muscular.[6] We're at constant loggerheads with each other, feeling the intense pressure to achieve the perfect physique whilst simultaneously expecting the same of others.

> **'We're fickle fuckers, and we hate to be judged but judge so harshly.'**
>
> Danny Beard (he/they),
> drag queen and performer

This one is likely to be hard to digest and will require a lot of psychological digging. The pressure and expectation for gay masculinity didn't just appear out of thin air, it was created as a direct result of our mistreatment throughout our younger years into adulthood. The pressure of masculinity versus femininity can also create body image issues, depending on how we present, as often our gender expression and body image are heavily interlinked – especially when certain body types are often perceived as being one or the other. Shell Rowe, a cis woman and lesbian, admitted that when she began presenting in a more masculine way, she no longer felt entitled to her physical femininity. Whereas Uzo, a plus-size Black cis gay man, admitted to being ridiculed at school for having what was seen as a more 'feminine' figure.

> 'I certainly have become a lot more conscious of my body since presenting more masc. I've got curves, I've got bigger boobs, I could be more feminine if I wanted to. When my hair fell out, I didn't really feel entitled to that femininity anymore. For a while I stopped wearing makeup and felt I needed to wear a sports bra instead of normal underwear. I thought if I was going to be masculine, I had to be a masculine stereotype. I still had to go on that journey of understanding I don't have to fit into either box. Gender is not a binary, and now I feel a lot more comfortable.'
>
> Shell Rowe (she/her),
> content creator

> 'I've always had wider hips and a bigger bum, I was ridiculed in school for that and always made fun of

because it was seen as a more feminine figure than it would be a masculine figure.'

Uzo Emenike (he/she/they), musician

The perceived femininity of larger, curvier, and fat bodies adds to the pressure to achieve a more muscular physique. For some gay men it's not just about needing to appear overtly masculine, it's also about avoiding all perceptions of femininity. Gay men who were less conforming as a child by expressing more femininity tend to have *more* body image issues as adults, compared with gay men who were more conforming as a child and therefore more masculine.[7] This isn't to say that inherently masculine gay men don't experience difficulties with their body image, but their reduced or lack of ridicule over their masculinity growing up means they can feel less of a need to overcompensate with masculinity by striving for a more muscular physique. In fact, heterosexual men who displayed more femininity growing up admitted the same, so this isn't just for queer people. The pressure of masculinity stems fundamentally from the patriarchy and society's desire to create some form of pecking order. But gay men end up in a sort of traumatising whirlpool where our expectations for masculinity become exacerbated and create their own hierarchy and body image expectations.

'The pressure for a muscular body stems from misogyny and the valuing of masculinity. Masculinity is something that is praised so much in our society, often to the detriment of women. The more you

strive for that pinnacle of masculinity, the more you have access to things.'

Romone (they/them),
performance artist

This hierarchy also makes us believe that masculinity determines perceived strength. We live in a patriarchal and misogynistic society, where femininity in any form is seen as inferior, particularly by men. Femininity has also long been associated with queerness and being submissive. Queer people who are more feminine in their expression are more likely to be perceived as queer and therefore more of a target. All nonconformity makes us a target – people fear what they don't understand and those who are different – but a homophobic man is less likely to provoke a six-foot-four guy built like Popeye, as his aim is to feel superior, which he likely won't if he picks on someone much bigger and stronger than him.

Now, brace yourself for this one. Many cis men also associate having a larger dick with strength, dominance, and masculinity. One study showed that 38 per cent of gay men feel anxiety about the size of their dick, which doesn't mean occasionally thinking, 'Ah, it would be great if it was a little bigger' (I think most of us have had that thought cross our mind at least once). It means that for 38 per cent of gay men, their dick size causes them active and noticeable anxiety.[8]

A common stereotype is that dick size, and its perceived masculinity, contributes to the role someone plays in the bedroom: a bigger dick means being a top or more dominant, and a smaller dick means being a bottom or more submissive. Men with a bigger size may naturally have more confidence in their topping abilities, as their size is likely to mirror what has been seen in pornography. When the only representation we see of topping is normally a guy hung like a horse, you're likely going to think that's a key requirement to doing it well. On the flip side, if you believe that you have a smaller size, then it may fill you with more confidence to remove it from the equation altogether and strictly bottom – not just because you worry your size won't fulfil (or fully fill) in the way you believe it should, but also because of the associated femininity that comes with being smaller. That's just, again, unconscious bias showing.

Whilst I'm sure you're sick of talking about preferences, and trust me, so am I, we're going to talk about them again anyway. For some, a muscular physique may be a genuine preference. This means that if given the option, then a muscular physique would be the body you'd be more likely to choose. But a preference does not mean you automatically reject those who do not fit that bill (*cough* 'no fats' *cough*). A preference, for example, can be likened to someone who has a type; there may be an image in your head of who you'd want as a partner, but your actual partner may not match that. But as it is merely a preference, your partner was not ruled out.

For me, I like someone who's taller. I find it attractive and would say it's a preference. But I have never rejected someone for being the same height or shorter than me, and I still find guys shorter than me attractive (some of the best tops I've been with have been short kings, FYI). So whilst I may go a little weak at the knees talking to someone taller than me, it does not make everyone else invisible to me. But I often see gay men actually mocking the idea of a tall bottom. God forbid someone be submissive but also be six foot three. The standard for bottoms is often to be shorter, more petite, and potentially more feminine ('within reason', unfortunately). Height is something that is literally beyond our control, yet we may reject a potential partner under the guise of a height 'preference' because they don't fit the standard of what we expect them to be.

Bedroom roles that are based purely on the stereotypes we are fed doesn't automatically make for a fulfilling sexual experience. Sex is a lot more than masculinity, height and dick size. It's a lot more than who's the top and who's the bottom, who's the giver and who's the receiver. Being masculine, tall, muscular, and 'hung' doesn't automatically make you a good top. Just like being feminine, slim, and short doesn't automatically make you a good bottom. They may be fitting the ideals of what you've come to believe should be adhered to, but it may also mean you're missing out on some great sex by sticking to them.

Don't get me wrong, it is okay to have a preference. Just make sure that's what it actually is. You're allowed to like a bigger dick, a muscular physique, someone tall, someone masculine. But gay men have become so well acquainted with our 'preferences' that we use them more like a tick list of requirements for a job interview candidate. The more we learn to unpack why we are wired the way we are, the more accustomed we will become to life rooted in connection, empathy, and acceptance. One that does not strive merely for perfection but for happiness.

'There's muscle gays who are only around other muscle gays and wouldn't be seen dead with a fat

person. It just wouldn't make sense of their aesthetic or their lifestyle.'

Uzo Emenike (he/she/they), musician

Objectification

Now I want to introduce you to objectification theory. This is where we are exposed to ideals within the media that can, over time, determine the way we view ourselves. Primarily this theory is used to discuss how when women are viewed as just sexual 'objects', they can then internalise their objectification and put the same pressure on themselves, on top of the external objectification. This has been extended to gay men, where the objectification normally experienced by women from men becomes experienced by men from men. Gay men in turn begin to feel reduced to their appearance and sexual ability.[9] We objectify and are objectified.

Gay men experience a double-edged sword of expectations – being men *and* being attracted to men. All you need to do is look at the comment section of a fat or even just less-toned man looking happy in his body; you'll see nothing but praise from women and body shaming from men. Whilst for most people, physical attractiveness is at least somewhat important, research has shown that both heterosexual and gay men tend to place a higher level of importance on physical attractiveness than women.[10] Meaning that the dual presence of men in a relationship can make the pressure of body image feel almost inescapable. Gay men therefore become quite literally their own worst enemy.

'There's been so many times I've dated bigger guys, and they've said, "Oh, do you mind that I'm big?" I'm like, "Why is it shocking to you that I would find you attractive?"'

Romone (they/them),
artist

When we're shown only a specific body type, on top of everything else, it only intensifies the vacuum of insecurity that many gay and bi men become trapped in. This becomes heightened by the way less represented body types are only ever shown as playing a side character: the funny one, the kind one, or sometimes even the villain. Bigger bodies are never shown as being the desirable character.

'Representation does matter. But whenever I did see big Black men on television, they were seen as the funny best friend. If they get a kiss from someone, it was like this lucky moment or something. I never got to see that as sexy or attractive in that way until I was older. I'd grown up absorbing it. I grew up being told that's how a big Black person was supposed to get by. They're supposed to be funny, charismatic, whatever, and I tried to bank on that growing up.'

Uzo Emenike (he/she/they),
musician

More specifically, when we see bodies that only fit the gay ideal of being slim and muscular in porn, we very quickly internalise this as being the only desirable body type. If we're seeing only a certain body in a sexual scenario being lusted over, it's easy to look at ourselves and think, 'But that's not me, I must not be desirable.' Even today, if I'm watching porn, I often struggle to enjoy the majority of videos available, as they simply do not represent me. I cannot see myself in them (pun not intended). I cannot feel aroused watching two ripped masculine men going at it, because it doesn't make me feel sexy. I and many others prefer consuming content that makes us feel seen and feel sexy, yet content that represents anything other than the ideal is few and far between.

> 'How often do you see a curvy guy on a club poster, even on *Drag Race*? It was the biggest thing in the world when a random-ass franchise had [one] – "Oh, they've got a chubby guy!" – when even then he just didn't have a six pack.'
>
> Danny Beard (he/they),
> drag queen and performer

One of the reasons the pressure to have the 'perfect body' is amplified is that gay and bi men experience a dual pressure of both the muscular *and* the thin ideal.[11,12] Women tend to experience more pressure over the thin ideal (by men), and men are more pressured over the muscular ideal (again, by men). Meaning that gay and bi men are often pressured over both simultaneously. The contradiction between these idealised bodies makes for a more specific body type that is even harder to achieve.

Some may be surprised to learn that some of the pressure to have the 'perfect body' actually stems from the AIDS crisis. It's a pivotal part of our history that still echoes here, more than forty years since it began, and is something that many readers of this book are fortunate enough to have not had to endure. In 1981, the first AIDS cases were reported in both the UK and the United States. HIV would spread through minority communities like wildfire, with the vast majority of those infected being gay men. HIV would then develop into AIDS (now known as 'late-stage HIV'), which would lead to various health complications caused by a reduced and sometimes ineffective immune system.

It wasn't until 1996 that an effective treatment was finally discovered, which would transform the lives of millions living with HIV. Up until this point, the extremely thin bodies of queer men was a common sight. The most notable symptom of HIV and AIDS-related illnesses was a loss in overall weight and muscle mass. The thin male body then became an image of illness as gay men were disproportionally affected. Dismissive governments did next to nothing to help and saw it as no more than nature taking its course on our community. Naturally, many gay men were terrified of this image, let alone of experiencing it.

Whilst body image was the least of our concerns with HIV on the rise, being thin wasn't just seen as less desirable but now something to be feared. This inadvertently added to the way in which queers with disabilities were viewed, and are often still viewed today. With many who had late-stage HIV (AIDS) becoming disabled in one way or another, disabilities in general had an extra layer of stigma added. The solution for many gay men was to work on achieving a more muscular physique, as this was seen as being healthy, strong, and HIV negative. The muscular physique therefore became even more prominent and seen as the peak of desirability. This then likely contributed to the dual conflict of thinness and muscularity. With body fat being off-putting and overt thinness signifying illness, many gay men strived for lean muscle, as it balanced both ideals.[13]

> **'The reality is that we are in a community where you are visible if you are handsome, if you are young, and if your body is beautiful.'**
>
> Ignacio Labayen de Inza (he/him), founder of the charity Controlling Chemsex

For older queers, the reality of our intense beauty standards can be even harder to navigate when ageism comes into play. Youth implies beauty, and beauty is our priority. This, paired with men caring more about the physical attractiveness of their partners than women, can make men even more likely to want a younger partner. The difference between gay and straight men, however, is that gay men are more likely to *act* on wanting a younger partner. Since we've become so accustomed to both declaring and acting on our 'preferences' in desirability, it's no surprise that the same applies to the age of our partners.[14] Too often do we see men lusting over those who are younger whilst refusing to date anyone their own age, let alone older than them. Too often do we see gay men obsessed with the idea of youth and repulsed at the thought of aging. There is nothing wrong with wanting to date around your age, and there's also nothing wrong with having an age gap. But many of us who feel insecure in ourselves are still expecting the world from others.

Ignacio, who's fifty-five, admitted that he used to be 'terrified' of aging. Not just the general fear of getting older, but because he had witnessed first-hand how older gay men were treated. He even recalled someone saying, 'That guy should be in a home' upon seeing an older gay man in a club. Ignacio came out at the age of twenty-seven, when slight wrinkles and grey hairs started to appear. Being new to the gay scene, and seeing the way older gay men were treated, he started to cover up the grey hairs, received botox, and did all he could to avoid aging, no matter the cost. But these things never made him happy. They didn't cure insecurity or magically create confidence, as these were still dependent on validation for Ignacio. Any form of rejection he experienced was traumatic for him. He'd look in the mirror and think, 'It's because of this, it's because of that', as he had attached so much of his self-worth to being valued and validated by others. This is the reality of forcing ourselves to meet the standards that we've set. The confidence we think we have is not held up by us as people but instead held up by the validation we get from looking a certain way.

Ignacio isn't alone in this feeling. With aging being seen as the end of the (gay) world, and both youth and beauty going hand in hand, gay men are up to four times more likely to undergo cosmetic surgery than heterosexual men.[15] Now I'm not here to shame cosmetic procedures; your body, your choice. Instead, I urge us to consider the implications our insanely high standards are having on us as a community and the lengths we go to adhere to them.

At the end of the day, aging is an inevitability. But it's not viewed as something natural or just a part of life for gay men, it's often seen as shameful and something to truly be terrified of. The beauty and body standards have become such a focal point that we end up fighting the inevitable, which Ignacio said only made him 'miserable'. Aging is something that every single one of us will have to face during our lifetime, and the way we are treating older queers is exactly how we are going to be treated if the standards aren't addressed.

The level of pressure created by these standards aren't just felt differently based on age but also by gender and sexual orientation. In a lot of ways, both gay men and straight women tend to have similar behaviours and mindsets when it comes to body image, lesbians less so, and straight men being the least affected.[16] And that's all because of the male gaze. Men fundamentally set the standard to which the rest of society falls in line, and queer people are no exception to this rule. With this in mind, the more involved in the community gay men are the more likely they are to desire a muscular physique, as it can just be lots of men all treating each other the same way that straight men treat women. The pressure is amplified.[17] And whilst lesbians can still struggle with their body image, it's not necessarily to the same extent that both straight women and gay men do, as men play no part in their perceived desirability.[18]

But that doesn't mean that queer women automatically have no shit to deal with – the patriarchy still plays its role. Objectification theory asserts that women have been subjected to objectification for most of their lives, even at a young age, and have always seen other women be objectified. The blueprint for treating women has been set by society, by men.

> 'I thought it would feel more welcoming. And then I started to realise, wait, there's still crazy dynamics going on that are affecting my body issues, and that's fucked up.'
>
> Char Ellesse (she/her),
> founder and content creator

Char, who identifies as queer and is open to dating men, women, and anyone in between, talked about how she experienced body image pressure prior to queer dating. Like many of us, she expected to feel welcomed and accepted in a community that claims to provide just that. The reality was a harsh truth she quickly had to learn: that the issue persists even in queer spaces. Char still noticed this objectification even when exploring queer dating, only this time the objectification was from women.

> 'I'm noticing similar answers to literal men in what they find attractive. They want femininity and someone that "looks after themselves", or "I want to feel more masculine, so they need to be small" and things like that. They sound like a man, and that's

really triggering. They act like a man in what they want, but then they're like, "But I'm not a man, I'm a woman, and I deserve this." But they're literally moving like a man.'

Char Ellesse (she/her),
founder and content creator

We can become so focussed on sex that, as a by-product, our bodies become our currency. Simultaneously, we can become so focussed on our bodies as a determinant factor of our worth that our anxieties around our bodies can make us feel insecure and inadequate in bed. And here's the proof: gay men are up to twice as likely to hide part of their body during sex than heterosexual men, whereas lesbians are slightly less likely to do so than straight women.[19] There's one clear common denominator here: men. When people jokingly (or not so jokingly) blame men for everything, they're kind of right. Objectification very much comes back to men. The entire concept becomes an endless cycle; if not broken, we truly begin to believe that in order to attract sexual partners our bodies need to be as near as possible to perfection – something that no one can achieve. Rejection is never nice, no matter the reason. But when it happens constantly for not presenting the ideal body type, it begins to take its toll. We truly begin to believe that our supposed undesirability as a sexual partner is our doing. In reality, it's far from it. We are all desirable in some capacity, and someone's ability to find you desirable is a reflection of their ideals and not at all of your worth.

Competitiveness

As we've already established, gay men have succeeded in creating a strict hierarchy in our spaces. We may feel the need to overcompensate with perfectionism because we're constantly reminded of our shortcomings, the main one being our sexuality. What better way to overcompensate than to be 'better' than our fellow queers? Men in general have a tendency to compete with their fellow men, often due to the *perceived* sexual benefits that come with a higher status. Unsurprisingly, gay and bisexual men are even more likely to experience this. Sexual field theory suggests that our stress over competing is even higher because we can 'size ourselves up' against our potential partners due to being the same gender.[20] Dual presence isn't just the expectations we put on each other; it's also being able to directly compare ourselves with our partners using these expectations, which is something heterosexual couples don't have to navigate.

When we consume queer media, go to queer events, and use queer dating and hookup apps, we soon begin to realise the strict entry requirements for acceptance and validation. Dating, sex, representation, financial status, job role, and of course body image are all categories we use to be perceived as 'better' than our peers in order to receive the validation we crave. For some it can be as simple as this: if you don't enter the competition, then you can't win the prize, which is validation and a seat at the top of the queer hierarchy. So many of us feel there is no choice other than to compete.

'We live in a society where it's impossible to achieve perfection. And there comes a point where you realise that maybe before doing work on your physical outside appearance, that that work needs to come from within first, especially when it comes to confidence.'

Shiv (they/them),
journalist and broadcaster

Queer people grow up constantly being told that we're not enough in one way or another, and that feeling becomes internalised until we truly believe it. Even years after coming to terms with who we truly are, *gay shame* persists. This is a concept Alan Downs, PhD, wrote about in his widely recognised book *The Velvet Rage*. Our shame leads to us feeling a subconscious need to overcompensate and to prove our worth. One way in which we do this is through our bodies. For gay men in particular, our bodies are a way of overcompensating for perceived femininity, but they're also a way of compensating for our perceived overall value. We feel that by achieving and maintaining the 'perfect' body that we will in some way feel more valuable. We feel it may help us not only feel more valid amongst queer people but also in society in general.

'When our identities are being categorised by our physicality on a greater level, I guess it makes sense that the physical attributes of that become the currency, become the focus, become the most important thing.'

Daisy Puller (she/they),
drag queen and HIV activist

As a result (and this is the really sad part), gay and bi teenagers are up to six times more likely to use anabolic steroids than straight teenagers. More specifically, they are more likely to use steroids with the sole motivation to 'improve' their appearance.[21] The very standards we set for ourselves and are committed to upholding don't just affect us as adults but also the future generation of queer men. Ignacio, who will speak a lot more in the next chapter about substances, opened up in our interview about why he used steroids in his past as an adult.

> **'Why did I first use steroids? Because I wanted to be visible. If these are the standards, these are the standards. And ultimately, I wanted to be loved. I wanted to find someone.'**
>
> Ignacio Labayen de Inza (he/him),
> founder of the charity Controlling Chemsex

This is a heartbreaking yet all-too-common reason for gay and bi men to start steroids. One consequence Ignacio mentioned was that whilst to begin with it was about being seen and finding love, once his body edged closer to the expected standard, he began experiencing greater levels of validation. Like his experience with aging, his self-worth was dependent on validation from others. Having a more muscular physique didn't make him happier – in fact it was the opposite. He just received more short-lived validation, which he needed to be continually fed. Soon it was no longer about love, it became more about sex, it became about instant gratification.

'I was absolutely obsessed and miserable. My self-esteem was so low. I became obsessed with "I'm fat, I'm fat!" and "I need to have a liposuction." I visited private doctors, and most of them said to me, "What you need is a psychologist, you don't have any fat." I have pictures, and I had a great body. But it was never enough.'

Ignacio Labayen de Inza (he/him),
founder of the charity Controlling Chemsex

I'm not going to sit here and shame the use of steroids, but anabolic steroids are known to have a wide range of serious health risks like any other substance. Now, many organisations focus more on risk mitigation and harm reduction techniques than instilling fear to discourage their use. Harm reduction is often a controversial technique, as some view it as encouragement, when in reality it's understanding that, regardless of any advice we provide, we cannot control someone's actions.

'Strict parents raise sneaky kids, whereas I think firm parents raise children who feel comfortable enough to ask questions.'

Asad Zafar (they/them),
queer charity worker

Providing a teenager with a strict curfew and never remotely discussing alcohol consumption makes them more likely to sneak out of their bedroom window at night and drink vodka in a field. Promoting abstinence in schools as a means of preventing teen pregnancies only leads to more pregnancies, since teenagers are not being educated on how to have safe sex. Instilling shame as a means of preventing steroid use doesn't do what's intended. Instead, steroids are still likely to be used, only in the least safe way possible. Harm reduction instead aims to ensure that if people are going to partake regardless of whether they're told not to, they do so in the least harmful way possible.

> 'I'm a bit more aware that I'm doing it and that everyone's doing it. Probably everyone is feeling horrible about themselves in one way or another, and they're just faking it till they make it too. I think it sort of takes that pressure off.'
>
> Daisy Puller (she/they),
> drag queen and HIV activist

There's a reason gay men are often seen as having perfect bodies, the best apartments, the prettiest boyfriends, the nicest clothes, successful careers, etc. It's compensating for gay shame. Whilst attaining the ideal body might provide some temporary and surface-level relief, it doesn't work to solve the problem at its core. The shame of not feeling enough will lie dormant and can rear its ugly head at any given moment, most likely when we feel invalidated: maybe a setback at work, or someone we find attractive rejecting us, or a critique of our body and so on. Quickly the perfect life we feel we've curated doesn't feel quite so perfect, and one small thing can bring all those feelings of shame rushing back.

Too often as a society do we focus on a short-term bandage

rather than long-term healing. Whilst steroids pose their risks, they are not an isolated issue. They are one of the many consequences of the unrealistic body standards that gay and bi men are measured against. The competitiveness we feel forced to take part in contributes to the vacuum of insecurity many of us are trapped in. We aspire to have another's body to be validated, and in turn others aspire to ours. We compete with others to be valued, and others compete with us. Ultimately, we're all battling some form of insecurity that others don't see, and often those who feel the strongest need to compete end up battling with the most insecurity.

Sex and Pleasure

For many queer people, when first starting to discover and experiment with sexuality, it is almost impossible to form romantic relationships. Not only does everything feel delayed because of shame, but it is also done in secret. As a result, many skip dating altogether and go straight to sex – not through choice but through necessity. This is still a common occurrence as we learn to be a more accepting society. For many, queerness in any form was ridiculed growing up. Maybe we had some more support from teachers or the occasional queer poster in our school, but the mocking from other kids was still likely to occur. Thus, coming to terms with sexuality is still an ongoing battle.

With the normalisation of hookup culture and the prioritisation of sex over dating, being physically attractive has become more important. The unfortunate consequence is that 42 per cent of gay men feel that their body image is detrimental to their sex life. Now you'd think that this would be a pretty common figure amongst most people, as we all have insecurities. Well, it looks much worse when I tell you this is more than both straight women and lesbians, and even twice as much as straight men.[22] Can you see a theme developing here? The more men that are involved, the worse body image issues become.

> **'If someone doesn't want to have sex with you because you've got body fat in places, then you don't want to have sex with them anyway.'**
>
> Felix Mufti (he/they), writer, performer, and activist

For cis gay and bi men in particular, there is another very specific dual presence that can cause anxiety. Yes, I'm going to talk about dicks again. So, lesbians, feel free to tune out (I'm kidding, you might find this interesting). Gay men will encounter more dicks than straight men. They are often (sometimes literally) a big part of our sexual experience, and so many of us tend to get up close and personal on the regular. This means we have way more opportunity to compare ourselves with others. This is a more specific example of sexual field theory, where we can 'size ourselves up' against each other in a more literal sense.[23] For heterosexual men, whilst they may see dicks in porn, they're unlikely to see one up close (unless they're 'straight'). When a cisgender heterosexual couple have sex, they aren't going to be comparing their partner's body with their own, as they will be anatomically completely different. Any anxieties they may have are more likely going to be as a result of porn and representation, as well as maybe past partners. Queer people experience all of that, plus potentially comparing our body with what we see in front of us. People joke that gay men give better head because we know exactly what a guy wants, and I wouldn't be surprised if that's true. But it also means we may know more about what men want in terms of desire and expectations. So, it's very easy, when we're naked and at our most vulnerable, to compare ourselves with who we are with.

Now buckle in for some statistics to ground us in reality. The average erect dick size in the UK is between 5.1 – 5.5 inches, with less than 15 per cent being bigger than 6 inches, only 1 per cent being between 7 and 8 inches, and 0.6 per cent being 9 inches. Anything over and above is seen in only two in one thousand (0.2 per cent cis men. Yet, all we see in pornography are sizes that less than 1 per cent of cis men have.[24] The size that is glamourised in porn, specifically gay porn, is an incredibly small minority. But it's easy to believe that it's way more common than it actually is. If we internalise this (as many cis men do), we begin to experience anxiety about our own size and can perceive it as 'small' when it may be perfectly average or even bigger. Given the dual presence, we can also begin to have unrealistic expectations of what our partner's dick should look like and how big it should be.

One of the most common things I still see on hookup apps is 'hung only' or 'hung4hung'. Sometimes that is *all* a profile will have. No face, no name, no information, simply leading with their best foot forward, so to speak. For some men it simply is about pleasure. One thing few people note when discussing the pressure gay men experience about dick size is the difference between anal and vaginal sex. Now I'm not about to justify being a size queen but instead explain one of the reasons some cis gay men tend to put more of a focus on dick size. The vagina is a finite space that ends when you reach the cervix – the small canal that connects the vagina to the uterus. This area *cannot* be penetrated, and it can be painful if something starts smashing up against it. The average vagina can expand in length to about four to eight inches when aroused, so it is possible to accommodate larger dicks, but only to a certain extent. This is likely why 84 per cent of women say they are happy with the size of their partner's dick, as the more common sizes are going to fit more naturally into the vagina.

But anal sex is a different story, as you can experiment more with the size of what's going in (with a lot of practise and patience). The anatomy of your butt means that most dicks will only go as far as the rectum. But once around six to eight inches inside, you reach the sigmoid colon. This is where poop is stored before you need to go to the toilet. Have you ever heard of a guy talking about reaching the 'second hole'? This is the area they're referring to. Speaking from experience (and practice), this can feel great, whereas reaching that deep into a vagina can instead hit the cervix, which does not. But less than 1 per cent of cis men will have a dick eight inches or bigger, so reaching the second hole will be impossible for most without the use of toys. Disappointment over the size of your partner's dick isn't because they're not big enough but because your expectations are unrealistic.

Sex is also way more than penetration; there are so many different things we can explore, and this is something that some tend to forget. The prostate itself (the male G-spot) is only 2.5 inches inside the anal canal, and the vast majority of dick owners will be able to reach it and adequately stimulate it with fingers alone. In my experience, those who *don't* whip out an elephant trunk can often be even better in bed, because they're not relying purely on their size to determine their performance. Too often do I hear stories of guys who have a big dick and a body made of steel, but their performance is meh. Some will feel that having the ideal body (in all areas) will mean that sexual attraction is enough to make the sex good. News flash, it's not.

Gay men are already a minority. If you then expect your partner to have an incredible physique and a giant dick, be single and emotionally available, and find *you* attractive and actually get it on with you, you are going to be looking for a needle in a haystack. This isn't about 'settling'; it's about being realistic and not letting the expectations set by porn or our need for perfection shroud our view of potential partners. Plus, expecting your partner to automatically be good in bed for having a big dick can lead to disappointment, *trust me*. It's not the size; it's how you use it.

We're Tribal

The result of the various body expectations and hierarchies gay and bi men have been subjected to has been the creation of tribe culture. Tribes are various groups we can fit into based almost entirely on our physical appearance. They are most notable amongst gay men but are also seen in the lesbian community, albeit less rigidly enforced. Before I go into more detail, I want to define some of the most common and notable tribes amongst gay men:

Otter: Often a slim, athletic, or average build with a lot of body hair.

Wolf: Slim to muscular with an average amount of hair.

Bear: Larger build, often with a belly, with a lot of hair and usually very masculine.

Cub: A younger-looking version of a bear. Often less masculine and the submissive partner.

Chub: Very large build with not a lot of hair.

Pup: Slender with little to no hair, potentially the early stage of an otter.

Twink: Slender with no hair, young, often seen as submissive or fem.

Twunk: A more muscular twink but still relatively slender.

Jock: Muscular and masculine (basically every underwear model).

Daddy: An older father figure, often with hair, but no specified body type.

You might already know a great deal about tribes, or you might know nothing at all. Tribes are often predetermined for us based on our body type, hairiness, and gender expression. Some see tribes as no more than a humorous label, whilst others feel their identity is heavily intertwined with this culture and they host/attend dedicated events for them. Some even centre their entire friendship group around their shared aesthetic. Having dedicated spaces for identities isn't inherently bad, and in some ways they can be beautiful, especially if such events are committed to inclusivity and diversity (e.g., events for bigger boys, for trans+ people, and for people of colour). It becomes an issue when segregation is masked as community and creates clear divides and hierarchies within our spaces, when inclusion becomes exclusion. Many times you'll see photos of the people attending a club night and there is not a single belly in sight. Everyone has a six-pack, and even though that particular body type is in the minority, if you walked in looking like anything less than a Greek god, *you* end up feeling like the odd one out.

> **'I told my mate I was gay, and the instant response was "So, you know you're a bear, right?" And I was like, "Babe, what the fuck is a bear?"'**
>
> Asad Zafar (they/them),
> queer charity worker

To many, this entire concept may seem bizarre. But it didn't just come out of nowhere; culturally, tribes have played a big part in our history and there's a reason they exist. As many queer people couldn't date publicly, our only guide for a compatible partner was sexual attraction. It would be as simple as slightly prolonged eye contact, a little smile, and a nod. Next thing you know, our bodies were intertwined in a fleeting moment of connection that we had to cherish before retreating behind the facade we had created to protect us from not only judgement but even being arrested.

Back in the '70s and '80s, queerness was so widely shamed that femininity in men was far from celebrated and masculinity was very much the pinnacle of desirability. This in turn led to the development of a hierarchy of bodies and perceived masculinity by excluding those who were felt to be less than, birthing the entire concept of 'no fats, no fems'.

> **'I feel like everything can be sexualised when it comes to bodies. You can be muscular and built, but what else is being offered other than that? There's nothing wrong with liking those bodies, I like those bodies, but there's just more than that in our community.'**
>
> Ady Del Valle (he/she),
> plus-size model and advocate

We didn't have hookup apps or easily accessible queer venues, so cruising was our lifeline. Mainly used by gay men, this is the process of subtly loitering in the hope of meeting other gay men in public spaces for sex. One of the most notable ways we could identify our 'tribes' whilst cruising, or just about anywhere, was using what's known as the 'Hanky Code'. This came to prominence in the '70s and continued into the '80s and was a covert way of identifying other queer people and their desires. This code was genius. The varying colours of handkerchief indicated which sexual act the individual was interested in. Then, having the handkerchief in the left back pocket indicated they were the active person in the action (the giver) and the right back pocket indicated they were the passive person in the action (the receiver). So, for example, a navy-blue handkerchief indicated anal, with the left pocket being the top and the right pocket being the bottom. As we had almost no other way of identifying each other and openly communicating, this is what we had to do. The Hanky Code made this process quicker and simpler. You have to hand it to us: the queers are nothing if not creative.

The code itself was incredibly vast, with some sources suggesting that there were more than seventy-five different meanings through varying handkerchief shades and materials. But it wasn't just about what position people took. Within the code there were patterns that would indicate wanting a man of a certain race with a certain body type, a certain kink, and so on. I highly recommend looking it up, it's fascinating and kind of wild at the same time. This is where our attitude towards 'preferences' originated, and it contributed to the existence of the tribes we see today.

Jocks, Twinks, Bears . . .

But why specifically did tribes formulate? Essentially, exclusion breeds exclusion. The bear tribe has been described as 'a sanctuary from the greater gay male community, in which "fat abuse" was described as a frequent occurrence'.[25] The creation and celebration of this tribe can be seen as a direct response to the unrealistic body standards within the community. With muscles and masculinity being seen as the peak of desirability, anyone who didn't fit the bill was often left out or shamed. As someone who is slightly bigger, I absolutely feel more comfortable, welcome, and even celebrated in bear spaces than I do at circuit parties. We want to go where we'll feel good about ourselves, where we'll feel validated and confident. In a space that embraces having a belly and body hair, we can feel a lot more confident walking around with our top off knowing that all of us there have likely experienced similar ridicule but are coming together in a big cuddly bundle of celebration. The bear tribe has been described as one of the friendliest spaces and focusses on embracing those who do not fit the societal ideal of 'sexy'.

> **'I think it's important for people's own mental health, within a community that is so judgemental, to find another subsection of that community where they say, "Look at us. We all stick together."'**
>
> Danny Beard (he/they), drag queen and performer

Tribe culture and subcommunities are a beautiful way for us to feel a greater level of connection to those whose experiences are even closer to ours. Surrounding ourselves with a group of people who make us feel good is the very least we deserve in a world that tells us we shouldn't.

> **'I feel these subcommunities, being part of the bear community or the twink community, that's where**

it might be helpful for people, because that allows you to manoeuvre and navigate sex and sexual interaction and hooking up with people in a space where you don't feel judged.'

Danny Beard (he/they),
drag queen and performer

But that doesn't make it a perfect system. Tribe culture can be a place for us to find our people and at last feel safe, but this isn't the case for everyone. When these subcommunities are created as a direct result of being ostracised by others through fatphobia, femphobia, racism, transphobia, misogyny, classism, and many of the other prejudices that plague us, sometimes subcommunities and tribe culture can also cause harm.

Fit In, Stay In

Once we've found our home in a tribe, often after not being accepted in another, we want to hold on to that feeling. We can feel that in order to remain part of our new chosen family, we also have to remain exactly as we are. Tribe culture can actually lead to varying eating disorders due to the strict body ideals within each tribe.[26] Bears are expected to be larger and can often choose to remain larger to stay valid and included within that tribe. Twinks have to remain slender to avoid going through what's jokingly referred to as 'twink death'. Jocks have to remain muscular in order to avoid being seen as 'letting go' or 'giving up'. It then doesn't come as a surprise that statistically those who identify with tribes tend to experience much greater psychological stress than those who don't.[27] Tribe culture can be a beautiful thing that helps us find people who like us and accept us for who we are. But to what extent are people actually accepting us for who we are? Are we being accepted only in *that* moment and in *that* state? Will the acceptance remain if we change? It can on occasion resemble being back at school and wanting to fit in with friends. We may develop new interests, want to dress differently, and just organically change, but will we still be accepted and celebrated by our friends and in those spaces if we do?

> **'Tribe culture can feel like being handed a preassembled IKEA identity you didn't choose.'**
>
> Ryan Lanji (he/him),
> cultural producer

I went on a date with a really sweet guy a few years ago, and he opened up to me about the pressures he felt with his body around his friends. We were on our second date and naturally got on the topic of body image because of my work. He seemed very kind natured and had the type of face that lit up a room when he smiled. But I could also tell from the way he spoke that he was very caught up in the importance of appearance, and he clearly worked very hard on his body. 'I know my friends would judge me if my body wasn't like theirs', he admitted with a sigh. 'They're lovely people, but I know that this is what they're like.'

It took me a moment to process what I was hearing. I could not believe friends would judge someone they cared about for the way their body looked. I could just see the pressure he felt, but didn't judge him for it. He couldn't help the way his mind worked. Even if he didn't self-identify with a tribe, the whole conversation was thought-provoking and just made me even more aware of the pressures we feel about our appearance in modern queer culture.

> **'Be around people who accept you 100 per cent I don't have a lot of friends, but I've made a good small circle that've motivated me but also accepted me completely.'**
>
> Ady Del Valle (he/she),
> plus-size model and advocate

I myself don't even know what tribe I would fit into. I'm not big enough to be a bear, I'm not slim enough to be a twink, I'm not muscular enough to be a jock, I'm not hairy enough to be an otter. So when tribes are so engrained within our culture, there is immense pressure to fit into one of these boxes. Even when someone says they want a 'big boy', quite often they have a specific body type in mind: a bigger chest, a big yet firm belly, and bigger arms. But everyone's journey with their body is different. If you are someone whose body has been through a lot of changes, whilst you may still be larger, you may have slightly looser skin and a belly that isn't as firm. Your arms may not be as big despite having an overall larger frame, or whilst having a bigger chest, it may not be as muscular. This is then the type of body or 'bear' that some people won't have in mind. Even now I'll see someone online saying, 'Ugh, I love dad bods', and it's about a photo of someone who visibly works out a lot but had a pizza at the weekend. Some want a big boy, but only the right type of big boy. This is where tribe culture can become a double-edged sword: to some it is a beautiful way of finding our people and feeling included, and to others it's just a pinball machine of rejection after rejection from tribe to tribe, unless we choose to conform to the specific entry criteria.

Once the ridicule of me gaining weight had died down and I was friends with (and followed by) the right people, I started being showered with praise for it. 'Being bigger really suits you' or 'You look so good bigger' were things I started to become used to hearing, and they made me feel good. I liked the feeling of people complimenting this new version of me, but this new praise still made me uneasy. Once we have learned to accept our body in one state, often through just time and age our body will change again. Then we have to accept this new version of our body, and on and on it goes. The unease I was feeling was the fear of change. My body and weight fluctuate a lot; I look like a different person every year. We are constantly changing and evolving, but in tribe culture this can be a hard thing to accept. My fear was no longer about gaining weight, it was about losing it. 'What if I become slimmer again and am less attractive?' I started thinking, to the point where although I wanted to focus more on some cardio workouts to improve my, erm, stamina, I was worried to do so in case I became smaller. As queer people, we often have a void of validation in our lives. When we get a taste of it, we will cling to it no matter the cost, whether because we like the way people lust over our bodies, idealise our beautifully decorated homes, compliment our gorgeous partner, or so many of the other perfectly curated aspects of our lives.

Learning to accept the impermanence of body image will unearth a whole new realm of self-acceptance. This means attaching less of our self-worth to our image, so if our body changes for reasons beyond our control, our mind remains strong and our confidence intact. This, however, is one thing I have yet to master. This isn't, of course, a nirvana state where you never feel insecure again – you likely will. But it may be easier to navigate if your body changes.

Be This, Not That

There are two responses to feeling othered: to accept and include all who are different or to band together with your own group, which in turn perpetuates exclusionary practices in queer spaces. Some from the bear tribe, because of their frequent mistreatment, have deliberately gone over and above to distance themselves from the twink aesthetic due to their stereotypical views of them being 'feminine'. Jocks and bears both often focus on masculinity but with different approaches. Jocks focus more on the definition of a man's physique whilst also likely having less body hair. Bears, however, tend to lean more into the hairy, rugged 'dad bod' aesthetic, which can unfortunately pave the way for even greater femphobia.

> **'I would say it's almost cliquey. The reason why all of these categories came to be was because some gay people didn't feel they had a place, so they fucking made one. Which is great, but you don't get to co-opt it.'**
>
> Andrew Gurza (he/they),
> disability awareness consultant

My friend Asad is six foot three, very broad, and incredibly hairy. Like, beautifully hairy. Whilst aesthetically often fitting into the bear tribe, they're also non-binary and often play around with gender expression. We've been to events where they've been rocking a cute short black dress and talons for nails, and they look incredible. The difficulty arises when we attend more bear or 'masculine'-oriented events together. Whilst Asad is someone who will be very much celebrated for their body hair, beard, height, and broad shoulders, they sometimes feel limited in their overall gender expression, as others assume, based on their more physical characteristics, that their personality and expression will follow suit.

> 'When I started getting [my nails] done, they were much smaller. I started with nail polish. And when I was in a club and a guy would see my nails, I would see the visible disgust on his face. There was this guy who started dancing with me, and we got really close. It's like we were about to make out, and he saw my nails and was like, "Hmmmmm", and drifted away. Then I'd stop getting them done.'
>
> Asad Zafar (they/them),
> queer charity worker

There are few if any tribes that openly celebrate femininity. Even if they do, it's a certain type of femininity. It's palatable femininity. The main tribe that may have less gatekeeping on femininity is the twink tribe, and this is only because the body type is closer to the societal ideal of femininity by being slim, hairless, and having little to no visible muscle. Even now on hookup apps, when you see people are exclusively looking for 'fems', the majority of the time they are blank down low profiles. They're almost always seeking trans women or twinks, as for them it's experimenting with the fantasy of queerness whilst the individual still presents as feminine, therefore reducing their own perceived queerness by being closer to heteronormativity. Yet, the queer men who come out about their sexual orientation tend to go in the opposite direction. Femininity in men is then seen as the epitome of queerness and is therefore distanced. Femininity is often lusted after in secret and shamed in public.

> 'The less fem I was, and the more "boy" I was, I actually had more [dating] potential. But I was unhappier because it wasn't how I wanted to express myself or live creatively.'
>
> Le Fil (he/they),
> artist and drag performer

Oops, All White

Think back to the list of tribes for gay men I mentioned earlier. You likely had a pretty clear image of what people within each of these tribes looked like. Even when you google these tribes, a very particular type of person comes up, and I'm not writing this to judge; we all have our unconscious bias that, until recognised, is completely out of our control. But I'm going to assume that when imagining each of these tribes, the person that came to mind was white. We are not only accustomed to our media being white-centric but our culture too (even though some of the most notable parts of queer culture are in fact from Black queers). Now this isn't saying that tribe culture is completely POC exclusionary, but it was created from a white man's perspective. The importance of representation is that it determines not only how we see ourselves but also how we see other people.

> **'Tribes are very much coming from a white man's perspective, because if someone asked me what tribe I follow, I couldn't tell them, because show me a picture on Google of all of them [different tribes]. You know what we're going to see.'**
>
> Uzo Emenike (he/she/they), musician

For the majority of us growing up, we didn't have any mainstream representation, and so our first experiences viewing queer people was in porn. The extent of porn categories that exists feels almost unquantifiable, but there are boxes and lists for almost everything. I want you to have a look at a gay porn site. Have a look at the twink category, the bear category, and the jock category. Notice anything? Or should I say, notice *anyone* who's missing? People of colour. Even if not, I'm curious how far you had to scroll. This sets a very early precedent in our young queer minds for when we enter the real world and experience the reality of tribe culture. Our unconscious bias begins developing in the background, and we begin to automatically see tribe culture through a white lens. Often the only time we see people of colour in porn is if they are searched for specifically. Even then, the categories of porn for people of colour, specifically Black queers, are often limited to very specific stereotypes.

> 'I feel like there's different tribes for everybody, other than Black fems. The Black masculine guys get to be jocks or they get to be bears.'
>
> Romone (they/them), performance artist

With twinks presented as almost exclusively white and Black men often presented in a stereotypically masculine way in pornography, Romone feels there is no place for Black fems within tribe culture. Whenever they have posted a topless photo on a hookup app and has focussed more on flexing to appear more muscular, or at least less feminine, their phone has blown up. Guys are suddenly interested because Romone is playing closer to the stereotype we are presented.

Tribe culture, whilst not inherently POC exclusionary, can become so because we are taught to view it as such. Tribe culture is often most apparent in our nightlife, where the events we attend are normally for a very specific queer demographic. With privilege comes easier access to more spaces than those lower down the 'hierarchy'. Sure, we can all technically attend pretty much any event we want to, but when the other attendees of many of the events make us feel actively unwelcome, we may as well not have been let in.

> 'I'm skinny and I'm athletic. There's always a certain level of acceptability. However, my plus-size Black

friends – diabolical, dia-fucking-bolical. I could be out with Uzo, [and] we'll get dirty looks in the club just for being there.'

Romone (they/them),
performance artist

As discussed in chapter four, we end up with spaces where many people won't feel comfortable. The spaces where Romone may feel more comfortable in regard to diversity in race, may not be in regard to body image. The spaces that solely celebrate bigger bodies like mine are often white-centric due to tribe culture. Don't get me wrong, we've always had a great time when we've gone out; they've been my ride-or-die for a long time now. But tribe culture means that there are few queer nights where both of us feel truly at home.

The argument is then presented: Do we conform in order to feel desired but inauthentic, or do we focus on authenticity and only experience fleeting moments of desirability? Oftentimes, the scarcity of feeling desired means we're more likely to accept it from whoever we can get it from. Some form of intimacy can feel better than no intimacy at all. This is why many will choose inauthenticity. In a world that's already judgemental, the queer community can be more so. We already have a target on our backs from society, so naturally we want to avoid having another one from those within the community too. But Ady Del Valle, a plus size model, approaches this differently, in a way that can "open the door for others".

'Being in certain spaces, I stick out. But by being in those [spaces] looking how I do, it kind of opens up

the door for others that look like me to come in and join in! Just by showing up, you're breaking that stereotype in bodies that we have.'

Ady Del Valle (he/she),
plus-size model and advocate

"We're Inclusive! . . . if you're able-bodied"

In all forms of porn (and most queer media, to be blunt) there is one particular representation that is almost completely absent: disability. Disability is yet another example where tribe culture can be exclusionary, particularly since it focusses so heavily on body image.

Before I delve further into this topic I want to define a key term: ableism. Quite simply, this is a set of beliefs and/or behaviours that actively discriminate against disabled people. These can be conscious and overt where someone genuinely views a disabled person negatively, and their behaviour reflects that. But it can also be unconscious, known as internalised ableism. This is similar to the various other internalised prejudices discussed throughout this book, where our views on disability have been shaped by an ableist society, determining an unconscious bias towards disabled people. Internalised ableism often manifests in microaggressions, where the intent is not to cause any harm or offence, but the outcome is exactly that.

An individual with a disability is almost instantly desexualised for a number of reasons, one of them being the conversations about consent. Whilst yes, there are some who will not have the capacity to consent, the overall assumption is that disabled people automatically cannot consent, which is not true.

This leads to disabled people virtually never represented as having the capacity for romance or sex. Andrew Gurza, who has cerebral palsy, has urges and desires like everyone else. Yet navigating sex isn't exactly easy for them, especially with gay men. They recall the various times they've been at a bar and been met with a sympathetic "Good for you for being here and getting out of the house", or something to that effect. Andrew, however, is there, like everyone else, hoping to meet a guy. Because of the poor representations around sex and disability, Andrew isn't viewed by the other patrons in a sexual manner. But Andrew discussed how they don't necessarily want to be in a space where they're being judged purely for their 'fuckability' – which is unfortunately what tribe culture often is.

There have been occasions where Andrew *has* met a guy and they've gotten on well and gone back to Andrew's place. With Andrew's disability, getting into bed requires certain lifts and aids, which the guy he's taken home will need to help with. Despite the guy claiming to be fully comfortable with this and being happy to go home with Andrew, upon seeing the equipment, some men have suddenly made up an excuse to leave. Andrew admits to spending a lot of their time having to comfort a guy over their discomfort over Andrew's disability rather than the guy making sure Andrew was okay.

> **'I remember watching [porn] and getting turned on, but thinking, "This isn't for me, because where's the representation for me?"'**
>
> Andrew Gurza (he/they),
> disability awareness consultant

Some people who are not usually around those with disabilities may experience discomfort simply not knowing what to do, how to act, and just generally how to navigate someone with a disability. Since for most gay men our only reference for desirability is pornography, Andrew made the brilliant decision to star in their own porn film. Andrew spent a lot of time discussing with their scene partner how they wanted it to look, and they specifically wanted to include certain elements of their disability beyond just being a disabled person in a porn film. Andrew was adamant that they wanted some of the film to be shot in their wheelchair, where the scene partner was sat in Andrew's lap whilst they made out. 'I want people to see that in my chair that they're so afraid of, that I can receive and give someone pleasure', they admitted. They wanted the scene to represent disabled people's sexuality but also to normalise the use of some of the necessary equipment for it and make it sexy.

> 'There's a scene where he's putting me in bed using my special lift and all the things that I normally use to get in and out of bed, but doing so in a sexy context. And so that was really powerful for me. At one point when I was eating my scene partner out, he grabbed on to the lift . . . and hoisted his ass up so I could reach better.'
>
> Andrew Gurza (he/they),
> disability awareness consultant

The main intent was for disabled people to see themselves represented, but also for able-bodied people to see that whilst the experience may look and feel different from what we've been shown, pleasure is still a valid thing for everyone to experience. By representing different bodies in a desirable way, it normalises the conversation, normalises seeing it, and even helps us better understand our capacity for sexual attraction.

The lack of inclusion isn't just in queer media, but our spaces too. Even when queer spaces claim to be truly inclusive, many neglect to include disabled queers. There are, of course, some disabilities that are invisible or won't have the same impact as others. But Andrew mentioned how they don't tend to go on nights out anymore because navigating the accessibility of queer venues is hard enough, and they only feel disheartened by the behaviour of others if they do manage to get in. With so many queer events being subject to unspoken segregation and limited accessibility, our community, which speaks often of uplifting the unheard, still remains exclusionary to many. Not to mention that a vast majority of venues claiming to be queer inclusive don't so much as have a ramp at the entrance to make it accessible for disabled queers to begin with.

> **'We're not at a place yet in queer spaces where somebody like me with a severe disability, who rolls up in my power chair, is given the same kind of weight as someone else. So when I come in, I'm still seen as the alien person that no one knows how to navigate.'**
>
> Andrew Gurza (he/they),
> disability awareness consultant

This doesn't even begin to scratch the surface of the experiences a queer disabled person will be faced with. Directly listening to queer disabled people will truly open your eyes to the day-to-day ableism they are subjected to in our so-called "inclusive" community. Andrew's book, *Notes from a Queer Cripple: How to Cultivate Queer Disabled Joy (and Be Hot While Doing It!)*, is a great place to start. I actually read it myself alongside writing this book. Not only did it highlight the personal impact of ableism, but it also helped me reflect on the ways in which I may contribute to it, which is something as a community we *all* need to take the time to unpack.

Lipstick or Chapstick?

Whilst a lot of the focus on tribe culture tends to be on gay men, an equivalent to tribes also exists for the lesbian community. But the reason this is less spoken about is because it's navigated slightly differently (as well as queer conversations often focusing on gay men). First, here are some of the most notable lesbian types:

Lipstick: Hyperfeminine, often associated with makeup and feminine clothing and presenting overly feminine.

Fem: More conventional and passive femininity in personality and demeanour, but not necessarily in appearance.

Stud: A race-specific term for a Black masculine lesbian that celebrates them and usually has a particular aesthetic and fashion sense.

Butch: A lesbian who encapsulates masculinity in almost every way.

Chapstick: A mixture of both a butch and a fem, more androgynous.

There is a clear and noticeable difference between these tribes and gay men's tribes: body image. Whilst the appearance of masc or fem can be influenced by body image, that is not the sole focus for lesbians. They focus a lot more heavily on energy, personality, and sense of style. So whilst lesbians may still have a type, they seem to be much less body image focussed than gay men. When we remember the higher level of importance *all* men place on physical attractiveness than women, it helps to explain even further why lesbians build strong emotional connections. They don't put the same immense pressure on physical attractiveness in the way gay men do.

> 'I think with women, perhaps the labels aren't as important. I think women just connect emotionally very strongly. I was not my girlfriend's type at all when we first started dating. You could say you have a type, but I think within the lesbian community it's who you emotionally have a connection with, and maybe that's why we're less dependent on those labels and those boxes a lot of the time.'
>
> Shell Rowe (she/her), content creator

***

I hope after reading this chapter you can begin to understand that the nature of queer body standards is incredibly complex and has numerous moving parts. It is not a result of one wrong-doing or mindset. It's the result of various complicated attitudes and stigmas that are all intrinsically linked to create the shit-show that is our body image crisis. Surrounding ourselves with different types of people, listening to different stories, and acknowledging other people's experiences are all important steps in starting to understand and empathise with those at a disadvantage. Given the real consequences of the body standards within the community, we have a duty to unpack and unlearn them – if not for yourself, then for the betterment of others.

> 'If someone gave you a plate of food that you never tried before and there were only two items, and then someone gave you a full platter, then obviously you're more likely to find out what you actually like from the full platter than if you only had the two options in front of you.'
>
> Char Ellesse (she/her),
> founder and content creator

Chapter 6

Slutty or Liberated? (Probably Both)

Despite being the reason we all exist and an activity that the majority of humans naturally crave, sex is often still viewed as something to be ashamed of by most of society. Even those who do not identify with a specific faith will still unknowingly hold beliefs that were either introduced or heavily reinforced by religions. No sex before marriage, no sex with anyone other than your spouse, and no sexual 'aberrations' or anything seen as beyond the norm. But marriage itself hasn't always been a religious proceeding, and early reports of marriage predate religions like Christianity by thousands of years. The introduction of modern religions soon saw marriage become binding spiritually as well as legally. Breaking the rules of marriage was no longer just about the law but also about sin. It was the pursuit of the unnatural.

'Romans didn't care about who they shagged; they didn't have labels for it. It was just what people did. But as that started intersecting with religion, and as religion emphasised this idea of purity, it created these boxes and these lines that shouldn't be crossed. Desire itself was seen as impure, so desire needs to stop. [Sex] should just be for procreation. Then within all of that mess, you get the idea that homosexual relationships are impure and unnecessary, because they don't lead to the end goal of procreation and continuing this religion. Any other reason for sex is for desire and therefore impure.'

Shiv (they/them),
journalist and broadcaster

Think about the law against acts of 'sodomy'. Whilst this has various meanings, at its core it refers to any nonreproductive sexual activity, hence its common association with homosexuality. The law itself, however, referred to a multitude of sexual activities, including oral sex and anal sex, between heterosexuals. It also included bestiality or any other form of sex seen as being unnatural. Yes, historically a man getting a blow job (from anyone) was on the same level as engaging in sexual acts with an animal. Wild, I know. Whilst the vast majority of us can distinguish which of these are morally sound and which are *absolutely not*, colonial and religious societies lumped them all together.

And yet, same-sex couplings and sexual relationships have been observed in more than 1,500 different species. For some, such as dolphins and apes, same-sex couplings are frequent in both males and females. Both species are known for pursuing sex for pleasure and even affection.[1] There are also a number of species of birds, including swans, who have homosexual couplings, but for the purpose of courtship and raising their young together. Male Black swans in particular can form lifelong bonded pairings where they will raise an egg donated by a female (adorable, I know) and even have a much higher success rate of the young surviving.[2]

Looking for a Third

The irony is that in a biological sense, humans are not monogamous in the same way some animals are. Some species will have young with only one lifelong partner, but humans are often described as being socially monogamous, meaning we tend to form long-term bonds and raise children with one partner, but the partnership isn't often lifelong. Humans also have a rich history of being a lot more sexually free than what's expected of us today. Humans are considered to be sexually nonmonogamous, meaning that socially we may have the desire to have one primary partner, but having multiple sexual partners comes naturally to us. Whilst human monogamy is difficult to analyse in ancient history, religion itself is often the driving force behind our social norms.[3]

Sexual monogamy seems to be something we have been more socially conditioned to believe in. Before you think I'm denouncing monogamy, I also class myself as monogamous at this moment in my life. Personally, I'd love a husband to live with peacefully in the woods and away from all the chaos. But having a better understanding of human nature and religion's impact on our societies can help us be more open-minded overall. No, that's not me asking you to open your relationship; that's me asking you to be more understanding of those who do.

Non-monogamy itself encompasses any relationship that involves more than two people, sexually or romantically. Polyamory and open relationships are both types of non-monogamy. Polyamory is the formation of more than one sexual and romantic relationship, often described as having a 'primary' partner as well as others, whereas open relationships tend to be more about sexual freedom, with the rules being specific to each relationship. Non-monogamy is significantly growing in popularity in society and is especially common amongst gay men.[4] Quite regularly I see the discourse surrounding monogamy and non-monogamy pop up on my social media feed, which results in an instant eyeroll from me. Monogamists criticise open relationships and their participants for being greedy or promiscuous and simply claim the relationships won't survive. Simultaneously, there will be non-monogamists declaring that monogamy is against human nature, restrictive of our freedom, and heteronormative. Time and time again we will witness the two seemingly opposing sides at loggerheads over which relationship type is more valid and the correct route to take.

But neither ideology is correct nor incorrect. One person's relationship has zero impact on another's life, and it's none of anyone's business. Biologically, humans may not be monogamous beings, but it doesn't mean we can't be. Whilst marriage in modern society is deemed as being a solely religious proceeding, it doesn't mean it has to be. It fundamentally comes down to individual choice and how a person's brain is wired. The only things that need to be considered is if a relationship is becoming non-monogamous for the right reasons and if the participants are in a good headspace, with consistent, open communication. By 'right reasons', I mean you have to want it. Entering an open relationship purely because your partner wants it or to 'save' a relationship is not a good idea, much like having kids to save a marriage. It needs to be something you're ready for.

On the flip side, being in a monogamous relationship does not also need to be critiqued. Some queer people love the idea of one day getting married and raising a family, whilst some have no interest in the idea of a legal union or having kids. And for those who still argue that monogamy and marriage are heteronormative: I hate to break it to you, but whilst heteronormativity as a blanket concept is damaging, adhering to *some* heteronormative ideals isn't inherently wrong (emphasis on *some*), so long as there aren't any problematic intents or consequences. If a queer couple does desire a more traditional life, such as a closed marriage with kids, so long as they're not projecting those ideals onto others and believing less heteronormative relationships are wrong or abnormal, then they're well within their rights to do so. Relationship styles do not need to be a war of opposing sides. The issue isn't being monogamous or non-monogamous, wanting or not wanting kids—it's the attitudes people have towards them and believing your way of life is the *only* correct one. Fundamentally we all just want to be happy, and if we're in a relationship style that works for us and our partner(s), then that's all that matters.

Where's Your Shame?

Queer people are often labelled as promiscuous as a result of our sex-positive attitude. But many neglect to consider the harsh truth of our reality: sex was literally all we had, not only as our only form of connection but also our main source of escape. The one thing that our bodies craved most was also the main thing that would allow us to pause the world and let us get off (in more ways than one), even for just a moment. Sex became a way of reclaiming control of our bodies and embracing the autonomy we were denied by society.

> **'For a lot of queer and trans+ individuals, our bodies can become our enemy. And in the way I reclaim my body through tattoos and piercings, people can reclaim it through sex.'**
>
> Dee Whitnell (they/them),
> sex educator and trans+ activist

Promiscuity itself is defined as having many *transient* relationships, meaning short-lived or impermanent. Stating that someone in an open relationship is promiscuous may actually be correct in some cases. Saying that any person is promiscuous for having multiple casual sex encounters is technically correct. The issue isn't being labelled as promiscuous; it's seeing promiscuity as inherently negative. Two consenting adults who wish to explore a purely physical connection with each other is perfectly okay. If a couple want to head out to sleep with different people, separately or as a couple, that is perfectly okay.

If you wish to engage in consensual, casual sex to sate a desire, that is okay.

> 'Maybe they're not sexually liberating themselves. Maybe they're sexually repressed. Maybe they've never had the opportunity to explore themselves, feel sexy and feel good.'
>
> Felix Mufti (he/they), writer, performer, and activist

And if we're going to talk about sexual exploits, we have to acknowledge the biology behind it. Both males and females produce testosterone in some capacity, but most cis men naturally produce more. Testosterone is the driving force behind a person's sexual desire and is often why cis men who are experiencing a low sex drive may have their testosterone levels tested. Trans men also often report increased sexual desire once starting on testosterone for this same reason. However, cis women's primary sex hormone is estrogen rather than testosterone, and their sex drive tends to fluctuate depending on their menstrual cycle. So when you get two individuals whose dominant hormone is testosterone, sexual desire can be more prominent and easier to access. Of course, sex drive overall varies from person to person, but science indicates that without the influence of any other factors, those with higher testosterone tend to experience a heightened sex drive.

> 'They have the internalised view that being sexually liberated is something that should be reserved

for marriage. "What would your future husband think?" Well, I hope he'd be on board with it, or I've married some boring c*nt.'

Felix Mufti (he/they),
writer, performer, and activist

Social stigma for perceived promiscuity is again often rooted in religious ideas, specifically the idea that premarital sex or sex with anyone other than your spouse is 'sinful'. Even the sex education we receive in school is never about pleasure or enjoyment. It's always fearmongering. Sex is seen as an awkward topic of conversation and inherently shameful, and those who outwardly embrace it are often subject to ridicule. You're entitled to disagree with these sentiments and have your own opinions on promiscuity, but to deny the religious roots would deny the existence of any social conditioning in society.

'People literally say, "Where's your shame?" As if everyone should have loads of shame attached to themselves and sex.'

Felix Mufti (he/they),
writer, performer, and activist

Shame itself is the feeling of embarrassment and a bruise to our pride over perceived foolish or 'wrong' actions. At the core of shame is concern for the opinions of others. Would embarrassment or pride exist if we're never perceived by other people? We are socially conditioned to believe some things are inherently shameful and others are worthy of praise. We are made to believe that judgement by others is one of the biggest things we have to fear. But why is being sexually liberated or promiscuous something to be shamed? What about these are 'wrong'? Because religion has told us so. It is no coincidence that sexism, queerphobia, and sex-negative views are rife in modern societies in a way that align with traditional religious values. Even amongst those who are not of faith, the values persist. Much of society is built on religion, and so even without practising a faith, many of our so-called morals and ideals yield to one without us even knowing it.

Sexual Liberation = Queer Liberation

Most queer people didn't get to start our romantic life with a first date, holding hands in the park, or a shy kiss in the cinema. Dating wasn't something that could be done publicly with ease. Even with many Western nations having 'equal rights' for queer people, the long-lasting stigma of our existence means that the mistreatment still occurs as well as our fear of experiencing it. So, whilst modern queerness has certainly come a long way, a need for subtlety, anonymity, and emotional avoidance is still very much engrained in our culture.

Queer people tending to be more sexually liberated is ironic because of the centuries of shame and ridicule homosexuality has been subject to. In historic law, the majority of legislation focussed on male-male sexual relationships, mainly anal intercourse. Rarely was lesbianism mentioned, mainly because women weren't meant to experience sexual desire, but instead be the subject of it (by men). Gay men were subjected to imprisonment, and any women showing sexual desire were put in an asylum for "hypersexuality" (just being horny). Such social stigmas meant we operated in the shadows and often had to skip emotional connection altogether. This meant we would act on our most primal instincts, and sometimes still do even to this day.

Even after the decriminalisation of homosexual acts, social stigma remained, and homosexual acts were still a very taboo subject. Queer people were shamed and told that what we did in bed was wrong, but we did it anyway. Queer sex became our protest. So what was the harm in a little extra experimentation? Sex was shrouded in shame, and queer sex even more so. We lived in that shame, so adding some new activities wasn't going to make it any worse. As a community, we created safe spaces where non-conformity in both sexuality and expression could thrive safely, and this included kinks and fetishes. Doing things that were taboo or beyond the norm became our home, so we made the most of it.

Our sexual liberation as a community paved the way for the rejection of many social norms and has encouraged much of wider society to follow suit. Queer people tend to be more sexually adventurous and kink positive; we became so used to living in shame that engaging in even more taboo activities just added to the thrill. Our very existence goes against what so much of society tells us, so we feel many of the religious, heteronormative, and colonial rules simply do not apply to us. We can't be told that our very existence is wrong but still be expected to follow the same rules as our heterosexual counterparts.

Yet shame around kinks and fetishes still exists. I defined a fetish earlier in the book and how, if focussed on a person (especially non-consensually), it can be very problematic. A kink is still a less conventional sexual interest but can involve a wider range of things and normally isn't a necessity in order for someone to 'get off', whereas with a fetish it often *is* a necessity. Think of it like a less intense version of a fetish. More importantly, not all fetishes or kinks are problematic; in fact they can be a *lot* of fun (speaking from experience).

Considering how society treats queer people, you'd think one queer shaming another for having a foot fetish wouldn't exactly be a priority. Despite feet being one of the most mocked fetishes, it's also one of the most common, with almost one-fifth of all men admitting to having one and the number being even higher for gay men.[5] One of the reasons the number may be higher for gay men is simply that we're less sexually repressed, but still repressed enough to kink shame. The origin of fetishes is still researched and debated to this day, and many are considered to be learned behaviours, but the bottom line is that we have no right to pass judgement if a kink or fetish has no moral implications, is consensual, and puts no one's health at risk. I personally don't dislike feet but don't have a fetish for them either. To me, they simply exist just like my hands do. But to others, feet could be the only thing to make them orgasm.

Another prominent example is that of pup-play, which is often widely misunderstood. Pup-play is in fact a form of BDSM, as one of its main elements is power play – dominance versus obedience. The controversy for many stems from the belief that it's related to bestiality, which is false. Like most BDSM practices, one of the main driving forces is escapism and taking on the form of an 'alter' in a form of role play.[6] It's not related to any sexual interest in animals, but instead mimicking the power dynamic that comes with being trained, being rewarded, and being obedient – like a trainer and a dog. It can also be about experimenting with other kinks simultaneously (such as leather). Whilst classified as a kink, a lot of pup-play activities don't actually involve sexual activity; it can be about community and friendship, as well as embracing playfulness and feeling more free. It can also be about overcoming anxieties around body image, as taking on the role of the pup (known as the pup headspace) can mean the person is less preoccupied and more focussed on the role play.

Like pretty much everything else discussed in this book so far, the stigma around pup-play comes from lack of understanding. I do not have any sexual interest in pup-play, but that doesn't mean others can't enjoy it. I can almost guarantee that anyone who makes a snap judgement about this particular kink has not read up on its history nor spoken to anyone who takes part. So if this is you . . . guess what I'm going to suggest you do.

Kink shaming simply upholds the shame of queer sex. It encourages people to mock and ridicule those who take part in sex acts that are deemed 'weird' or 'unnatural', despite there being no moral implications. Bluntly put, what consequences arise from someone being sexually aroused by their partner's feet? What part of that requires any form of conversation when it does not involve yourself? If you do not find enjoyment in particular kinks and fetishes, that is completely okay, but you shouldn't deprive others from enjoyment.

'I think it's so important that we do talk to young people about it [kinks] and that having kinks is okay, and how to navigate that safely, both legally and also consensually.'

Dee Whitnell (they/them),
sex educator and trans+ activist

Some queer people will shame more than just kinks or fetishes, so let's talk about bottom shaming. Some see bottoming as the feminine role in a heteronormative sense, for being the passive partner. There's also often a lot more slut shaming experienced by bottoms than tops. Bottoms may be subject to ridicule over their number of sexual partners, whereas a top is more likely to be praised.[7] Sound familiar? It's very similar to the way heterosexual men and women are viewed when it comes to sex. This can be traced as far back as ancient Greece, when husbands were allowed to have sex with as many other people as they liked, whilst wives were restricted to the household and were not allowed to have sex with anyone else. Today, straight women are shamed for sex, whilst men are often praised for their 'conquests'. Even in same-sex relationships, we seem to uphold the same misogynistic values. More than this, it's almost identical to the way male-male sex was viewed in ancient Greece: being the penetrative partner was seen as being of high social standing and dominant, and being the receptive partner was for the lower born or apprentices. Men weren't criticised for fucking other men; instead, they were criticised if they bottomed. So believe it or not, bottom shaming isn't a new concept. In fact it's older than Christianity.

> 'When you talk to the boys about pornography, they share their opinions. They tell you what they've seen, they tell you what they've heard. Girls are completely silent because of how society tells them they should act and react to conversations around sex or around porn.'
>
> Dee Whitnell (they/them),
> sex educator and trans+ activist

Shame around kinks, fetishes, and sex overall leads to one thing in particular: silence. People don't talk, they don't communicate, which means they don't learn. Sex is the most physically intimate thing you can do with someone, and a lot of the time we have to figure it out for ourselves. We have no form of comprehensive sex education, and almost everything we know comes from pornography, forums, or even during sex itself. Here's why all three are an issue:

Pornography is not a reliable source of information. It can be fabricated, staged, edited, and fundamentally not based on real life. It often represents an unrealistic body standard and creates incredibly unrealistic expectations around what to expect from sex. The editing frequently cuts out any conversations around consent. Even when the disclaimer at the beginning of the video states all acts are consensual, let's be honest: No one reads that. No one's reading the thirty-page T & Cs from a phone contract. So when you're young, uneducated, impressionable, and horny, it's easy to take what you see online at face value. Porn can also glorify unrealistic scenarios and nonconsensual acts. The idea that you can grab the plumber's ass when he's bent over fixing the kitchen sink, that you can flash a stranger and they'll just go along with it, or that you can come to an 'arrangement' by providing sex instead of payment – many of us know these are fictional scenarios. But on a grander scale, they enforce the idea that consent is an optional extra rather than a necessity. Consent is non-negotiable in every scenario, regardless of how much you've had to drink, what you're wearing, who you're with, where you are, or any other factor. Consent needs to be obtained. Yes, that includes slapping someone on the ass in a club. You may think it's a joke or light-hearted, but it's putting your hands on someone in an inappropriate sexual way without their consent, no matter how you try to frame it.

> 'Your hypersexual desires are totally fine, if you've got someone who is matching that and is welcome to receiving it, particularly sexual comments or images or advances. But I think so often, and I don't think this is just an issue with the queer community, people don't necessarily check to see if those advances are welcome from that person at that point in time.'
>
> Shiv (they/them),
> journalist and broadcaster

Forums may not be regulated enough to be a reliable source of information. Some people can comfortably speak from experience and provide advice, but it's still not going to be the same as getting information from a professional who has a greater understanding of intimate health and safety. Forums may also be a place for misinformation and problematic viewpoints. You just need to have a look at the rise of incel content and its followers to understand the implications.

Sex itself should not be where we learn about sex. It is the natural place to experiment, figure out what we do and do not like, and potentially learn about ourselves. But it shouldn't be where we learn crucial information. A top shouldn't learn that he needs to go in slow when doing anal only after the bottom yells out in pain because he slammed it straight in. Consent can be an issue here too: you should not have to discover that you may be into spit because someone randomly spat on your face during sex without asking first. Anything you want to try in bed needs to be discussed prior. A question that gets mixed feedback on hookup apps is 'What're you into?' Some feel it's putting pressure on the recipient to reel off a list. It's okay not to have any kinks, but regardless of the motive behind the question, they assess what someone's boundaries and limits are to ensure everyone is on the same page when you get down to it.

'I'm always saying "you're probably going to do this once in your life. You're going to navigate this space once in your life. That's okay. Here's how to do it safely". Because if you tell young people, "Don't do

> **this. If you do this, these bad things will happen", young people are more likely to do it to test your authority.'**
>
> Dee Whitnell (they/them),
> sex educator and trans+ activist

Hookup Culture Isn't Going Anywhere

In chapter five I discussed the history of the Hanky Code and how this was gay men's way of identifying each other in secret. While this was an integral and necessary part of queer history, it doesn't mean that the same method needs to be used in modern society. Today, rather than wearing a hanky in our back pocket to indicate our sexuality, we open a hookup app and simply write exactly what we're looking for and what we're into.

The impact of dating (or hookup) apps cannot be denied. We're smacked in the face with an easily accessible bundle of profiles all with a tick list of our preferred 'criteria'. But when it comes to hookup culture, we have become so well acquainted with our 'preferences' that we've forgotten to treat people like, well, people. Profiles stating 'no fats, no fems, no Asians, no Blacks, no this, no that', over and over again, just perpetuates the prejudices within queer spaces. These issues existed long before the invention of the apps, but these platforms have acted like a can of gasoline being flung onto the fire.[8]

To most people, a hookup is transactional. It's not emotional, it's just sex. We have an itch to scratch, and someone who fits the bill is willing to scratch it. There is nothing inherently wrong with hookup culture. In a lot of ways, it can be great. I have a lot of emotional damage to heal from (most of us do), and so most of the time I am not in the right headspace to give my all to a relationship – but a boy has needs. So hookup culture can be a really great way of having an outlet whilst not requiring emotional connection. But it has to be done right, and this is what I mean by right:

Don't hook up for validation. It is simply not sustainable to use hookup culture as a means to feel better about yourself and your body. Sex is physically the closest we can ever feel to someone and it's also where we will feel most desired, and so to want sex as a form of validation is understandable. But the issue is that we will need to keep having sex to continue feeling desired and validated. External validation is like a cup with a hole in the bottom: you need to continually fill it up or it will run out. In the long term, you won't feel any better about yourself. Internal validation, or actually fixing the cup to prevent any water leaking out, means you don't need to keep topping it up. You won't need hookups to feel valued, because you'll feel valued enough by yourself. But we'll talk more about self-worth in the next chapter.

Be considerate of people's heath (and your own). This means that you are being regularly tested for STIs and taking the necessary precautions to prevent their spread. There shouldn't be any shame in getting an STI – sometimes they happen and that's okay – just make sure you're being safe. It also means that you are mindful of other potential dangers of hookups, so make sure a friend knows where you are.

Communicate openly and honestly. If both of you are on the same page with it being more of a physical transaction and at peace with that, no one will walk away scathed. If, however, one individual lies about their intentions and claims to want more but really doesn't, or claims to just want to hook up but secretly wants more, then one of you runs the risk of being hurt. Being open and honest means that you both fully accept the interaction for what it is. Sometimes (albeit rarely) both of you only want something casual but can unintentionally fall for each other, which is great! But don't go into the interaction in the hope of that happening.

Don't use hooking up for emotional regulation. This is one I used to unknowingly engage in myself, which I'll go into later. This is where we use sex as a means of escape and as a coping mechanism in order to regulate our emotions. Sex is something that feels good both mentally and physically, and so it is naturally something we may want to do in order to alleviate any negative emotions we may be experiencing. The issue arises when we form a habit of using sex as a means of avoiding any negative feelings, known as a 'behavioural' or 'process' addiction. Our instant response to a negative emotion is to find someone to have sex with, almost like a reflex. This means we are not adequately processing our emotions but instead avoiding them entirely. This also leads to the development of an unhealthy relationship with sex, where it's no longer seen as something to do for joy and pleasure but purely for escapism.

Don't substitute hooking up for emotional connection. Sex can be a beautiful form of intimacy, but it is short term, especially with a hookup. Emotional connection is something that many humans crave, whether that's true love and marriage or just a cuddle and a film. Queer people have become great at emotional connection and vulnerability with our friends. Many of us are tactile and are more than happy to have a cuddle, a 'date'-type evening, or even sex with friends. It's okay to seek emotional connection outside of a relationship, sometimes we simply need it. I'd be lying if on occasion I didn't want a guy to stay around a bit longer after a hookup just to have a cuddle. The issue, like with validation, is that it's not sustainable when it starts to be used as a long-term substitute. Much like emotional regulation, more and more hookups become needed in order to sate that need for emotional connection, and that need is going to be hard to keep up with. We've all felt that longing for something *more* from time to time – I know I have. But a big part of living in this world contentedly is learning to be okay in our own company too.

'They don't see you as a person. They see you as an item, a piece of meat, and if you don't meet their requirements, then fuck off. But people don't know how to reject in a sensitive and empathetic way, and genuinely, it's because a lot of these people don't care. They see people as collateral damage.'

Asad Zafar (they/them),
queer charity worker

Treat people with respect. This is one that no one should really have to say. Having respect for people, regardless of the setting, is not something that should be seen as controversial. I'm not talking about kinks, because in some scenarios being 'disrespected' is all part of the role play. I'm talking about respect, human to human. I remember years ago when I wrote some articles about stopping people sending unsolicited nudes to strangers on hookup apps, and the response was alarming. At least half argued that 'it's a hookup app' and 'people are being too sensitive'. I love a nude, I love taking them and receiving them. There's literally explicit material of me on the internet, but it's sent and distributed consensually. Some people want to bypass 'niceties' and avoid small talk, which if two consenting adults agree to, is absolutely fine. The key term there being *consenting*. Being 'disrespectful' in a role play is not the same as just being an asshole.

'I've been at a club and someone has pushed me out of the way so that they could go and hit on my muscular friend. Like, physically put their hands on

me and just moved me out of the way, because that is what they want.'

Romone (they/them),
performance artist

If these points are adhered to, hookup culture *can* be beneficial for all involved. But some forget to consider other people's emotions entirely or that there are actual people on the other side of that screen. Not only can people's rejections be unkind, but so can people's profiles. What you personally desire in a sexual partner should not invalidate the existence of others. Your personal desires should not be used as a means to put others down. When I spoke about this online, the response was mixed. Some people preferred to know in advance if the individual they were about to message was 'masc4masc' as a way to avoid wasting their time. But a lot of other people found this mindset completely disheartening. People have become almost too well acquainted with their 'preferences' that they become careless when declaring them.

Attraction first and foremost is physical most of the time. An initial attraction to someone for most allosexual individuals is based on the way we feel when we look at them and an emotional connection is sought afterwards. But assessing attraction from a few photos and our listed 'body type' is incredibly unrealistic. A lot of modern dating is visually led, meaning that we do indeed prioritise an aesthetic over personality. However, boxing others off entirely based on a few discriminatory metrics is not something that mainstream queer apps should be encouraging, especially when hookup apps are often young people's first experiences of the queer scene.

When younger queer people first witness the use of these filters and such discriminatory behaviour, they will believe it is the norm. I certainly did. I can't remember what my bio used to be on hookup apps when I was younger, but my mindset was certainly influenced by the behaviours of 'more experienced' queer people. One thing I do remember is the acronym ASL. Not American Sign Language – this means 'age, sex, location'. Whenever I would interact with people on an app, this would be the very first response. Their priority was not my name, what I was interested in, or anything else. It was only if my age was in their range, what was between my legs, and if I was close enough to them to be bothered with.

I very quickly adopted that behaviour and believed it to be standard practice on hookup apps. Not to say hey or ask how their day was going, but to respond only with three letters. This was the way I was being treated, so it became how I treated other people. When a young queer person starts experiencing cyberflashing, fatphobia, racism, femphobia, and all the other phobias at an impressionable age, it will give them a tainted first glance into queer life and make it easier to internalise these mindsets. Worse than that, this gives a very poor perception of consent and for some erases the concept entirely. If people start to feel that sending nudes without consent is okay, who's to say how far they'll take it when they're offline? Consent matters, online and offline.

A common response whenever I have spoken about this before is simply 'This is Grindr, what do you expect?' or 'If you don't like it, don't use it', which I guess is valid but is not at all the healthy and progressive mindset to have. Our actions have consequences, no matter the spaces we're in. Our behaviours are passed on to future generations, especially when online platforms have such mixed age groups. If you're at a sex party, you are not automatically consenting to a stranger just walking up to you and cumming on your back or even so much as touching you. That's not how it works. Just because you're in an environment that is mainly for sex doesn't mean you're automatically consenting to every single person in that room touching you whenever and however they'd like.

In my interview with disability activist Andrew Gurza, they discussed the difficulty of navigating casual sex, mainly because of other people's views and treatment of disabled people. Hookup culture is something that became increasingly difficult for Andrew, so they turned to sex workers. This often stirs up controversy (albeit mainly from those who are anti – sex work overall), but for Andrew, sex work gives them the ability to experience pleasure at their own pace without the fear that comes with navigating the hookup scene and other people's discomfort. Sex is something that is fundamental to many of us to support our wellbeing. Yet the stigma regarding the sexuality of disabled people makes it harder to access. What many don't know is that a lot of sex workers themselves are in fact disabled. Having any form of disability, including a mental disability, can make navigating a nine-to-five job difficult. Sex work can be a flexible solution, which is in part why I started it. Whilst my sex work is purely online, it is something that provides me with a lot of stability and helps me manage my schedule. Having ADHD means that managing my time, my headspace, and pretty much everything else in my life isn't exactly easy, especially on the days when my ADHD is worse.

> **'Sex work has really saved my life. I'm so thankful that it's there, because then I don't have to deal with the "Does he like me? Does he not like me like this? What is this?" Sex [workers] can be good for disabled people because they allow you to go your own pace.'**
>
> Andrew Gurza (he/they),
> disability awareness consultant

Are You 'Clean'?

Unless we as queer people go out of our way to educate ourselves, stigma and misinformation spread like wildfire. We have come a long way since the start of the AIDS epidemic, but much of the stigma around STIs and HIV remains, even within the queer community. The slogan 'U=U' (undetectable = untransmittable) is becoming more widely used. If someone who is HIV positive is getting the treatment they need and their viral load for HIV is undetectable in their bloodstream, the virus physically cannot be passed on, including during sex. Essentially you could have unprotected sex with someone who is HIV positive and it would be physically impossible to contract it, even if you weren't on PrEP. Yet, so much fear still remains.

> **'My peer mentor was just this very caring, sweet person who I'd never met before. And he just**

completely opened up his diary and shared what his experience had been. And then there he was sitting, living, breathing, healthy, alive, laughing, all these things that in that moment I thought I would not be. That was extremely, extremely powerful.'

Daisy Puller (she/they),
drag queen and HIV activist

Daisy recalled the time she went home to Australia and had a conversation with her brother about her HIV diagnosis. She remembers seeing the colour drain from his face as she revealed her status and how his facial expression shifted to almost bereavement. Her brother asked, 'Have you come here to tell me that you're going to die?' To which Daisy reassured him that this was not at all the case and explained the incredible treatment and support provided to those living with HIV. The groundbreaking treatments available now mean that those with HIV can live long, happy, and healthy lives just like everyone else. Her brother, relieved, quickly admitted he hadn't thought about HIV since they were kids, with the (fearmongering) ads on TV at the time, and that the very idea of it simply didn't come into his life. The lack of awareness is a double-edged sword. Some queer people are unaware that it cannot be transmitted whilst on effective treatment, and stigmatize those living with it. Whilst many heterosexual people are completely unaware of its existence, even though back in 2020, more heterosexuals tested positive for HIV than gay and bisexual men, and they're also far more likely to be diagnosed at a late stage, perhaps because of the belief that they're simply not at risk of contracting it.[9]

'There was somebody that I'd spoken to for quite a while, and we'd had lots of saucy chats and stuff. When it came down to it, he only wanted oral, and then later told me that was the first time he'd been with anybody who was HIV positive. I realised that he didn't want to do anything more because he didn't understand the risks or lack thereof.'

Daisy Puller (she/they),
drag queen and HIV activist

Something you'll commonly see on hookup apps is the question 'are you clean?', referring to STIs but more specifically HIV. The question itself implies that having HIV is inherently dirty but also neglects the entire premise of U=U. I've had many conversations with people over these apps where they have asked this, and I've corrected them on their language. This is an important and frankly easy thing to do. In the same way that I'd like to think you wouldn't fuck a Tory, I'd like to think you wouldn't fuck someone who's uneducated in this way. Calling out phrases like this is a simple way of calling out the prejudice and addressing the stigma head-on, which is something we should actively want to do to support those living with HIV.

'Within queer and gay circles, being on PrEP is very acceptable and admirable. But being undetectable is still met with a little bit of disdain, a little touch of judgement.'

Daisy Puller (she/they),
drag queen and HIV activist

PrEP is another incredible preventative against the spread of HIV and is one of our most valuable tools for preventing new cases being diagnosed. PrEP stands for 'pre-exposure prophylaxis' and is a blue pill that can be taken daily to prevent the prescribed person from contracting HIV. I have been taking PrEP daily since 2021, and it's probably the easiest part of my day bar turning on my bedroom lights. Even still, stigma and lack of awareness around PrEP is way more common than I was anticipating.

> **'It's unfortunate that it is so demonised. Because a lot of it was in the come-up to getting PrEP commission on the NHS, you saw a lot of these arguments about promiscuity.'**
>
> Asad Zafar (they/them),
> queer charity worker

When I was first prescribed PrEP at a clinic in London, the process was incredibly easy. The medication was accessible and appointments were readily available, often on the same day. Then I moved back to my hometown and realised quickly how different it was in more rural areas. Now, I quite often have to wait over a week or two for an appointment, and on a number of occasions I've had to travel to a hospital a few towns over to get an appointment or risk the wait being even longer. Not only is the medication less accessible, but I found that very few people are even on it. In London almost every gay man I spoke to was on PrEP. It was just a normal conversation. Back home, an overwhelming number of people admitted they're not on PrEP; they hadn't gotten round to booking an appointment or had simply never heard of it.

One person actually called it the 'slag pill', much to my astonishment. They saw it as a means to have unlimited unprotected sex rather than a preventative measure against HIV. I'm not going to sit here and pretend to be a saint – I think throughout my content online I've made it quite clear that I'm not – but PrEP only protects someone against HIV, nothing else. So taking the medication and having unprotected sex means we are still at risk of contracting other STIs.

> **'I think we've got to treat those attitudes with a level of patience, at least [so] we can engage in that conversation. Until that person encounters somebody who has a different point of view, they're going to carry on calling it a "slag pill".'**
>
> Daisy Puller (she/they),
> drag queen and HIV activist

There are multiple factors for why gay and bisexual men in particular are at a higher risk of contracting an STI. Firstly, the type of sex we have. Gay and bisexual men more commonly engage in anal and oral sex. When it comes to rectal and throat gonorrhoea, over 85 per cent of cases are *asymptomatic*, meaning that *no* symptoms will occur. Wheras urethral gonorrhoea (an STI in your dick) is symptomatic over 85 per cent of the time, meaning you'll experience that lovely discharge and burning sensation when you pee (it's not fun). Genital gonorrhoea in cis women is symptomatic around 50% of the time.[10] With the majority of heterosexual sex involving penis-in-vagina intercourse, it means that when gonorrhoea is passed between cishet partners, symptoms are statistically more likely to occur in at least one of the partners, prompting treatment.

Anal sex itself also poses a much higher risk of STI transmission because of the thin lining and lack of natural lubricant. So, we're more likely to contract an STI because of the type of sex, as well as being less likely to display symptoms. Even with regular testing, being asymptomatic means we are more likely to have an infection without knowing it. So a big part of the higher rates of STIs amongst gay and bisexual men is actually due to the biology of the sex we have, rather than the misconception of 'sleeping around.'[11]

Calling out stigmas, misconceptions, and prejudices in any form is the least we can do, including for sexual health. Similar to other discussions of privilege, a person living with HIV won't have a choice but to be forced into difficult conversations, as it's a stigma that affects them directly. It's a discomfort that's thrust upon them. When someone who is not living with HIV encounters these stigmas, we have the option to either avoid or face the discomfort. Do we address the stigma and have an uncomfortable conversation, or do we avoid the conversation and discomfort and let the stigma persist? Sure, you may start the conversation with the other person being completely reluctant to listen. They may even block you. We cannot help how other people will react, but we also shouldn't assume how people will react.

Let's Get High (and Horny)

Our relationships with sex, nightlife, and drugs are all heavily intertwined. With widespread prejudice, our entire existence was forced into the shadows. The night became the only time we could thrive. It was the only time we were free from societal expectations and internal shame. We could dress how we liked, say what we liked, act how we liked, and kiss who we liked. From an outsider's perspective, it looks like we just really like to party, and certainly we know how to do it right. But the reality for a lot of queer people can unfortunately be much darker.

> **'A lot of it can be to do with queer people not having somewhere safe to go home to, so we want to make the night last as long as possible. We feel the most ourselves at night, or we're just having the best time, so why would we want to go home?'**
>
> Felix Mufti (he/they),
> writer, performer, and activist

For some, the escape the night provided often wasn't enough. You could dance the night away, but you would still remember the reality you were getting away from would resume the very next morning. So, to prolong the night, people often turned to alcohol. At first, having a drink on a night out can be fun and can just help you feel freer. With lowered inhibitions comes less shame, and soon all the cares in the world are a distant memory. Your only thoughts are of the sound of the music, the beat vibrating through your bones, the beams of vibrant flashing lights, your friends' laughter, the taste of another person's lips.

> **'There is a huge substance abuse problem in our community. Not only is it normalised but it's**

encouraged. Other people aren't going to call you out on it because they're doing it too.'

Felix Mufti (he/they),
writer, performer, and activist

In time, the slight buzz of alcohol doesn't quite cut it anymore. We long for a more potent and longer-lasting high. Drugs become a way of completely altering the reality around us so in that moment our shame isn't even a distant memory, it simply ceases to exist. Drugs become a way of ensuring the bliss of the night lasts as long as possible. The thought of sleeping doesn't even enter our head, our only thought is of being there and embracing a shame-free existence for as long as we can.

'I definitely used alcohol and drugs as a coping mechanism for how traumatised I was.'

Dani St James (she/her),
chief executive of the trans+ charity Not a Phase

The sense of euphoria this can bring makes the thud back to reality even more apparent. The dopamine hits we receive come to a grinding halt, and both our body and mind don't know what to do with themselves. Soon we can find ourselves longing for the night again, itching to get back on the dance floor feeling nothing but sheer elation and ridding us of the intense shame that comes with being queer in a straight world. Dani's experience is one that is sadly all too familiar for queer people: turning to whatever to cope with incredibly difficult and dark experiences.

'Vulnerable queer folk who have resorted to chem use to give them that high can then become dependent. That's where it gets dangerous, because you need to realise what your red line is. Is this something I'm doing to have fun, or is this something that I'm depending on to help me survive because I can't deal with the harsh realities of this world?'

Asad Zafar (they/them),
queer charity worker

Around 30 per cent of LGBTQIA+ people struggle with an addiction of some kind compared with only 9 per cent of our non-queer counterparts. The way we're treated causes shame; our shame causes mental health struggles and, in turn, means that substances are more commonly used as a form of escape, making us even more vulnerable to addiction. The aim of this section is not to shame or judge behaviours but instead to help us understand why we turn to them in the first place. Too often are queer people just labelled sluts, drug addicts, or reckless. Substance abuse isn't approached with empathy and compassion but with stigma and judgement, the single viewpoint being that it's merely a choice that's made. It's seen as an action in isolation, rather than a reaction.

When we hear the word *addiction*, most of us assume it's to substances. But there is another type of addiction that many of us suffer with silently without even realising it, known as a 'process addiction'. This is exactly what it sounds like: you become addicted to a process, often as a direct response to certain emotions or stimuli, just like exercise addiction. It's not an addiction to a substance such as alcohol, drugs, or nicotine. It's an addiction to particular actions often used as a coping mechanism and as a dopamine boost, and sex is one of them. Sex itself is something that releases a vast array of chemicals that shoot around our body. Given the often all-encompassing nature of sex and the way it stimulates our senses, it can become a way of escaping negative feelings for some people.

My discovery of a process addiction came at a very poignant time when I realised that my relationship with sex had become rather complicated. I mentioned earlier that one of the keys to ensuring healthy casual sex is to not use it for emotional regulation. Unfortunately, I unknowingly began to do so. I was having a tough time and would open a hookup app to look for casual sex instead of sitting with my negative emotions. I began avoiding my feelings entirely and hoped they'd disappear in the arms of someone else. Over time, this developed into a process addiction. It had become almost uncontrollable: I would get the same fidgety feeling to open an app that I would get when trying to quit nicotine. No matter what I'd try to distract myself with, the overwhelming urge to use the ultimate distraction was just unavoidable. And relying on sex as a coping mechanism wasn't just about looking for a hookup when I was horny; it was about regularly looking for a hookup whether I was horny or not as a way of avoiding negative feelings.

The unique risk, for gay and bi men in particular, of using sex for emotional regulation is that it can intersect with our susceptibility to addiction and lead to what is known as 'chemsex'. This is where recreational drugs are used to enhance and prolong sex. It combines the two different highs that we can get from sex and substances to create an experience that truly makes us lose all concept of time and reality. Whilst it isn't unique to gay and bi men, it's incredibly prevalent in these spaces. I interviewed Ignacio Labayen de Inza, the cofounder of the charity Controlling Chemsex and a man who hasn't used drugs since 2015. He started the charity after noticing a serious lack of support for those battling with chemsex. Having worked with hundreds of people to help them overcome their chemsex addiction, Ignacio noted that for many people it starts as a coping mechanism and soon develops into a full-fledged addiction. It's a way of escaping reality and temporarily alleviating low self-esteem, the latter being something a lot of gay and bi men struggle with.

> 'If I do chems, I feel sexy. If I do chems, I can have the kind of sex I like. If I do chems, it's very easy to meet people, because you go to a house and there are five or ten people who come and go, or even just one person. Chemsex is about not being at home, feeling lonely, watching Netflix the whole weekend. Chemsex is about "I want to feel valued, I want to feel sexy, and I don't normally feel like that." Clients tell me they never meet people on apps because people don't like them. Or they go to the sauna, and they say they're always in a corner, scared, not knowing how to approach anyone. But then one day, someone offers "something", and then they feel safe. They don't care about anything. They're on the "fun" side of the cubicle, not on the outside waiting. They go around

the sauna like the sauna is theirs. And then the next time you go to the sauna, you don't want to go without chems, you can't go without them.'

Ignacio Labayen de Inza (he/him), founder of the charity Controlling Chemsex

Many apps have become facilitators for chemsex, allowing users to post HH or HnH (high and horny) in Europe or PnP (party and play) in the United States and Australia, with virtually no safeguarding measures or support in place. This can be actively looking for someone who wants to engage in chemsex or looking for what is known as a 'chillout' (a chemsex party). These can occur after the clubs have closed in the early morning and continue late into the afternoon and sometimes for days at a time. Or they can just be arranged on their own, with some now not going to clubs at all and instead purely trying to find a 'chillout'.

There are three main drugs that are commonly associated with chemsex: mephedrone (MKAT), methamphetamine (crystal meth/Tina/T), and GHB (G). These all have very potent effects and equally potent side effects, as well as being highly addictive. Ignacio openly admitted that his addiction was to GHB as well as being a heavy meth user, and it ultimately ruined his life to the point that the combination of these two substances almost killed him. He found himself keeping it at home and using it day and night until he lost everything. It took him years to recover, but he has since been sober for more than ten years. It may not sound like it, but Ignacio was one of the lucky ones: he survived.

'Chemsex is not that you go buy drugs, you take drugs, you have sex, and that's all. Chemsex is not about that. It can start like that, but chemsex is about self-esteem. It's about loneliness. It's about connection. It's about a need for validation. It's about internalised homophobia.'

Ignacio Labayen de Inza (he/him), founder of the charity Controlling Chemsex

Ignacio explained chemsex perfectly: 'It's not about the substance, it's about the purpose.' The three substances mentioned above are the most notable as they carry the most risk, but there are others that can be classed as chemsex if the purpose is the same.

'Some may think, "Without drugs my sex is boring", or "I don't relax enough to be a bottom, and I want to be a bottom." There are some people who get drunk because they can't really handle sex unless they have some drinks to be comfortable. Technically, that could be chemsex. How long are the effects of poppers? Ten seconds. But we [at Controlling Chemsex] have been supporting people who *have* to go through these ten seconds for masturbation, for everything. If they don't have the bottle of poppers, and the person they want to meet doesn't either, they don't meet them.'

Ignacio Labayen de Inza (he/him), founder of the charity Controlling Chemsex

For those who aren't familiar, poppers are liquid amyl nitrate, often in a very small bottle, and the scent is carefully inhaled (*not* drunk, because that can literally kill you). The aim is to provide a short-term high, and the main reason poppers are so popular amongst gay and bi men is that they relax your muscles, which can make bottoming easier. Even though there are serious health risks, they are so common that for most gay and bi men, they are just a normal part of sex. Chemsex is incredibly complicated; some are able to take part recreationally with the ability to remove themselves whenever they want, but for others it can become all-consuming.

Before I became aware of chemsex, I noticed that I'd too often see other queer people sharing a photo on their social media of an attractive and seemingly well-put-together man with the caption 'gone too soon'. Flurries of condolences would fill the comment section over the loss of a dear friend. I remember thinking, 'What could possibly be causing this?' There were no news articles about a hate crime or an accident involving them, so why were so many gay men leaving us too soon? It was chemsex. Reports found that chemsex claims three lives a month in London alone, with at least one call a day to ambulance services being related to chemsex drugs.[12] This is the heartbreaking reality of chemsex: queer lives are being lost. What's worse, gay and bi men in London are almost *twice* as likely to take part in chemsex if they are HIV positive, the main reasons being the debilitating stigma that still exists in society, and chemsex alleviating some of the stress of revealing their status to partners. This is how serious and real the stigma of HIV remains.[13,14]

Despite the prevalence of substance abuse and addiction within queer spaces, we are starting to hear more and more people talk about their journey of sobriety. Many queer people hit a very dark place before reaching for support. Dani admitted that it wasn't until close friends of hers made her aware or even cut ties before she realised she needed to become sober or she 'would have ended up dead'. In the early stages of her sobriety journey she was attending seven or eight recovery meetings a week, and she 'went very heavy into the program of recovery, the twelve-step meetings, for about two years'. Today, Dani is the founder of a leading trans+ charity in the UK as well as other incredible businesses and a true pillar of our community. Ignacio, whose addiction was more specifically chemsex, went from using GHB day and night at home and his addiction taking over his life to running one of the leading chemsex support charities in the UK, helping those battling with their addiction every single day. Some queer people, however, do not make it.

For anyone battling with chemsex:

> 'The first message is: there is life after chemsex. I haven't done anything since 2015 and I'm very, very happy with that. The majority of the people in our team, they also struggled in the past themselves, and they don't use chems anymore. We can also see this from our clients when we support them, that many of them get over it and they have a completely

normal life. The second message is that there is support available. Because some people think, "Where am I going to go? Shall I go to my GP? But my GP isn't going to understand. They'll treat me like I'm a heroin user. So there is no support for me." But there is a support for you and specialised for you. And the third message is: there is *free* support. For example, all the support that we provide at Controlling Chemsex, all the services that we offer, are free. Some people think, "I will have to go to rehab. I don't have the money. I will need to go to a private therapist, but the private therapist is going to charge me £120." It's important that you know, if you need support, it is available and it's free.'

Ignacio Labayen de Inza (he/him),
founder of the charity Controlling Chemsex

Ignacio also gave me the following points for anyone who wants to support someone battling with chemsex:

Do your research. Get as much information as possible. There are many misconceptions around chemsex, so it's important to keep yourself informed and know what you're likely to be dealing with.

Know that it's not personal. Someone battling with addiction is likely to lie to you. They will confide in you and say they'll never do it again, but do it again two days later. It's not that they don't care about you. This is just the reality of addiction.

Be realistic with your expectations. Overcoming addiction takes time and patience for everyone involved, and giving them a lecture will not make recovery easier. It may instead push them away.

Just be there for them. Family and friends can play the role that a professional cannot. A professional, such as the team at Controlling Chemsex, is only going to be with them for one hour per week in a session. It's important to have a solid support network around them for the rest of the week.

Sexy and Shame-Free

There is a common theme throughout this chapter: stigma and shame. Many stigmas are placed on our community, saying that we're 'sex freaks', we don't care about STIs, or all we do is party. Some queer people do just like a night out, enjoy sex, and are happy single. But for other queer people, we're just desperate to find an escape from the harsh reality of the world around us. The focus needs to be on why we have our vices to begin with, not simply shaming the vice itself. Whether our actions are trauma responses or not, they need to be met with non-judgement.

> **'At the end of the day, everyone is looking for happiness, and we all want to be happy, but we are broken.'**
>
> Ignacio Labayen de Inza (he/him), founder of the charity Controlling Chemsex

With queer people already being more likely to battle with addiction, we do not need any additional shame added. Dani admitted to spending the first two years of her recovery beating herself up over things she had done whilst she was high or drunk. Those who battle with substance abuse often already feel a great deal of shame, especially when it comes to reaching out for support. Adding more shame and stigma does not make that process easier. Addiction is something that needs to be approached with empathy and understanding.

Quite often I'm met with 'we're not all traumatised' and 'I have my struggles but I didn't resort to it' as an attempt at justifying the ostracisation of those who *do* battle with addiction. If you've thought these or anything similar in the past, I want you to think back to what I said in the introduction (yes I'm mentioning it again, and I will keep doing it till it sinks in): just because something doesn't impact you does not mean that it doesn't impact others. It's incredibly unlikely as a queer person that you've reached adulthood completely unscathed. Felix noted that they specifically have an addictive personality and addiction runs in their family. Even if you believe you have managed to come to terms with your own queer identity relatively pain-free, and as a result haven't resorted to substances, that does not negate the experiences of others. Even if our experiences are the same, our ability to cope with them may not be. That is one of the main components of empathy: recognising and understanding struggles we may not have had to endure ourselves.

'I enjoy sex. It's something that I like to do. It's a topic I like to explore and I like to help other people explore.'

Felix Mufti (he/they),
writer, performer, and activist

Navigating my sexual experiences has been incredibly liberating and honestly has been one of the biggest contributors to finally accepting myself as I am. Sure, there have been some bumps in the road, but exploring my body and what I enjoy has, naturally, made me spend more time with my body. I see it from more angles (and in more outfits) than I ever thought I'd feel comfortable with, and you know what? It's been transformative to finally think, 'Yeah, I am desirable, I am fucking sexy', and fundamentally, I feel shame-free.

Unpacking shame around sex is just about giving people the grace to explore things for themselves, without judgement. Some people want to explore being slutty and embrace kinks purely because it's fun, and if no harm is being caused, let them. We all have our vices, and we all do things that can make existing in this difficult world a little bit easier (or a little bit more fun). We just need to learn not to lump everyone together with the same stereotypes and expectations, and instead treat people as individuals – with empathy, and without judgement.

Chapter 7

Love and Rejection

Our shame is the main reason we have such unique internal battles and why we think and act the way we do. Because of our shame, one of the most heartbreaking realities of growing up queer is that so many of us truly believe we're unworthy of love. We are told we are wrong, and we carry that into our adulthood, long after we've come out.

The overarching feeling of being unlovable manifests in many ways but most prominently in the place it's going to feel most at home – relationships. Once we've reached a place of acceptance in our identity and that our relationships may look different from what we may have seen, we begin to yearn for love. For many of us, that unlovable feeling can become a void we must fill in order to feel complete, even more so if our upbringing was devoid of love because of our queer identity. Yet we never saw any representations of healthy queer relationships. We rarely saw queer people at all. We're given no manual on how to navigate queer dating; our only blueprint is a heterosexual relationship. But this can feel like being given instructions to build a wardrobe but with the parts to build a chest of drawers. Sure, some of the screws may be the same and the type of wood could look similar. But ultimately, you're not going to be able to follow the instructions.

> **'We have to find our own ways of feeling enough or feeling good enough, and it has to be from within before anyone else tells us.'**
>
> Daisy Puller (she/they),
> drag queen and HIV activist

Those who don't want to differentiate between queer and non-queer love will say, 'But why is a queer relationship any different?', as fundamentally we're still people looking for love. The difference isn't even about being the same gender or presenting differently. It's about how we're wired. Taking the feeling of being unlovable into a relationship won't suddenly make us feel lovable. It's not just feeling unlovable, it's not even feeling worthy of love to begin with. So much of our unresolved trauma and shame is buried so deep down that it can manifest in subconscious ways.

Nobody Wants to Date Anymore

Having a successful relationship doesn't just happen, it requires work. Not just on the relationship but on ourselves. There tends to be a lot of controversy around the idea of not dating unless we are fully healed. To an extent I understand the premise, but there's a lot of nuance to it. Every single person handles trauma differently, and so everyone's individual journey will be different. That is why being provided with generalised dating advice isn't automatically going to solve things. For some the advice will work, and for others it simply won't; it's down to the individual and first understanding how we are wired.

I'm not about to provide you with some long-kept secret to having a successful queer relationship. Whilst the vast majority of work in a relationship is carried out as a team, the reality is a lot of the work also has to be done by you and you alone. Many of our experiences when we're younger shape our approach to relationships as adults. The most common trope is having 'daddy issues'. This is where our relationship with our father (or lack thereof) growing up can lead us to idealising a form of 'father figure' in a partner. For queer people in particular, our shame and frequent societal rejection make us more likely to experience both anxious and avoidant attachment styles than non-queer people.[1] More importantly, these attachment styles are often caused by our parents, even if unintentionally.

Anxious Attachment: You fear losing or being abandoned by a partner and resort to seeking reassurance and closeness, often perceived as being 'clingy' or codependent. This attachment style can be caused by parents who are inconsistent, do not provide emotional support, or are frequently absent.

Avoidant Attachment: You fear abandonment, much like with anxious attachment, but also fear commitment and losing independence. When you sense a risk of being hurt, you respond by pulling back and distancing from someone to protect yourself. This attachment style is often caused by parents who aren't physically affectionate or are overly critical and emotionally unavailable.

Understanding our attachment style will help us navigate our dating life a lot more confidently. Given the most common causes of these attachment styles, and just the general experience of being queer, it's pretty clear why we're more likely to struggle with them. It's not the case that queer people 'just don't want to date'. Many of us have so much trauma to unpack that we simply aren't ready for a relationship because we don't know how to effectively handle our own feelings.

> **'We're trapped in this idea that it's up to other people to make us feel good about ourselves. It's up to other people to validate us.'**
>
> Daisy Puller (she/they),
> drag queen and HIV activist

Right Time, Wrong Person

Love and relationships are supposed to be a beautiful addition to our lives, not a missing piece, but this is much easier said than done. The show *Heartstopper* has been a beautiful piece of work to give hope to younger queer people, but to many older queer people, the show feels bittersweet. For me personally, I think it's beautiful and the kind of soppy romance queer people deserve to see, but for many of us the experience just doesn't resonate. For young queers, the love story seems attainable, but for queer adults, it feels like a fairy tale. Our experience was googling feelings we didn't quite understand to figure out what was 'wrong' with us. We got butterflies over someone we didn't think we were allowed to feel them for. We couldn't relate to what our friends were saying about dating but pretended to go along with it anyway. We were too young to be speaking to strangers online who were much older than we should've entertained . We had to live with this overbearing secret, which, for a time, we truly thought we'd have to take to the grave.

LGBTQIA+ youth are twice as likely to feel lonely compared with non-queer people.[2] So, for many queer people, love *does* feel like a missing piece, it *does* feel like a void that needs to be filled. We've all known someone at some point who 'just can't stand being single' or is a 'serial dater'. Maybe they're seen as jumping from one relationship to the next. Whilst not always the case, this can be another example of a process addiction, whether it's the need to constantly be in a relationship, serially date, or spend countless hours on dating apps – the constant liking and swiping in the hopes we may just find the person we're going to marry, or at least to occupy our brain with so we don't have to feel things. Soon we can become dependent on the mental boost we get from dating and spend our time on that rather than processing any negative feelings we may be experiencing.

'Do I wish Prince Charming would come down and tell me that he loves me and I'm the greatest thing

ever? Yeah, of course. But if that doesn't happen, you can find joy in other ways too, and you can cultivate joy and queer joy in ways that is not around a dude.'

Andrew Gurza (he/they),
disability awareness consultant

The hardest part is that our yearning is often at war with our shame. We yearn for the love that we feel unworthy of, and this can lead to us settling for less than we deserve. Our internalised belief that we're unlovable means we may begin to settle for even the slightest bit of validation. You may be wildly incompatible with someone, but that occasional kind word can keep us on tenterhooks. We feel comfortable with poor treatment because that's all we've known. We also begin to fall for the idealised version of someone that we create in our heads. We can fall for their *potential* rather than their *actual*. For some, positive treatment may be so rare that we instead settle for the closest to it that we can get. Maxine Heron noted that often trans women 'subsidised a lot of emotional closeness with men for a physical closeness'. Whilst this is a common and harsh reality for many trans women, it is one that other queer people can also succumb to. With the dating scene being so difficult, the appetite for love needs to be fed, even if it's not a full meal. Instead, we may have to settle for something that doesn't completely satisfy us. This can manifest in poorly matched partners or unfulfilling casual sex.

> **'I think it's really important to not date or see anybody in any capacity who would not be proud to be seen with you in a public place.'**
>
> Maxine Heron (she/her),
> writer and trans advocate

Both of these can lead to losing all sense of hope. I know this feeling, and I've gradually come to enjoy my own company. But every now and then that niggling feeling of loneliness can creep in. Queer events and being around other queer people can be great, but sometimes I'll clock a couple, and rather than feeling happy, I'll feel envious. And it's easy to think, 'When is it my turn?' The world is so romanticised that we can be made to feel lesser if we've not yet found love. And for queer people, finding love can be incredibly difficult. Take out the trauma, the prejudice, and every other struggle we face – we are still a minority. How many straight couples meet in the same town, or at least within a thirty-mile radius? Quite a lot. For queer people, we may have to resort to looking farther afield. Finding someone we're truly compatible with isn't easy at the best of times. But when queer people are still such a small proportion of society, finding compatibility is going to be harder. Unfortunately, it's just maths, and yes, it sucks, but that doesn't mean we should give up entirely.

Instead, we need to learn to be comfortable with our own company. There is a difference between being alone and feeling lonely. Being alone is a physical state, loneliness is a feeling, and the two are not mutually exclusive. The feelings of loneliness can creep in, and that's natural. But it's important to learn to feel comfortable being alone and finding the joy that comes with living life as it is, with or without a partner.

Hopeless Twenty-First-Century Dating

Most of society is still learning how to navigate dating with the new wave of technology, but as a community, we are still learning how to love at the same time as the prevalence of dating apps, social media, and increased pressure on appearance. Shame drives perfectionism. Low self-worth drives us to do things that make us feel worthy.

> 'So I'm not fussy when it comes down to the actual deed of it, but relationships are so much more than that. And for me, being able to laugh every day – my partner needs to be my best friend. I need to be able to get up and wake up and laugh and talk about stuff. And I think that's really hard in the gay community.'
>
> Danny Beard (he/they),
> drag queen and performer

We discussed the idea that gay men in particular can project expectations onto others, specifically onto potential partners. A desire for perfection, to compensate for shame, often means being more selective in choosing partners not based on how we're treated but how we're perceived. We strive for the most muscular partner, the most conventionally attractive partner, the famous partner, the successful partner, and so on. Our standards for our partners mean that finding authentic love can prove challenging. We're already a minority, so striving for very specific criteria can make queer dating even more difficult. Whilst we feel unworthy of love, we may simultaneously struggle to deem anyone else worthy of our own. So let's talk about navigating modern dating.

'Let's See a Photo!'

The importance people, gay men in particular, place on physical attractiveness doesn't just contribute to pressures in sexual scenarios but dating in general, including a fear of what other people will think. Our overcompensation for gay shame seeps into what we expect from our partners, and gay men often strive for perfection even if those expectations are of others. People in general often subconsciously want approval from others of those they're dating. That's why we get that little anxious feeling when we're about to show our friends a photo of them – that awkward 'wait, let me find a good photo' pause. We in some way want other people's approval, and gay men feel this even more so.

> 'I think some people are worried what others will think or say if they have a partner who's a little bigger than them or who is plus size. There's a lot of good people in our community, they just have this thing in their head of what their partner should be visually. They don't sit back and think about what they want in a person, not outside.'
>
> Ady Del Valle (he/she),
> plus-size model and advocate

This is something I personally have battled with in the past, and to this day I sometimes have that little voice creep in: 'I find them attractive, but *should* I find them attractive? Do they look like what I've been told is desirable? Are they the hot one out of their friends? Is my ex dating someone more attractive? Will others judge me?' And on it goes. We fear that someone will say we are 'punching' (meaning we are punching above our weight by dating someone 'more attractive'). We also fear that someone will discuss our partner as being a 'downgrade', as so many often do. The same judgements that we make of others we fear will be made of ourselves. We live in a judgemental society with appearances being perceived as one of our most valuable assets.

People will mock other couples based purely on believing one person is better looking than the other, rather than considering the emotional chemistry, love, support, and adoration they may share. When we grow up seeing judgement everywhere we turn, we can begin to internalise it. These don't have to be active thoughts, they can be passive. They can be little thoughts niggling in the back of our minds, adding pressure to our dating pool to be 'perfect'. These thoughts, if left unchecked, may affect our actions and the way we treat others. After the layers upon layers of pressure over body image, expression, and every other stressor we subject ourselves to, the only plausible way that many of us feel we can even alleviate the pain is by conforming to the ideals. If you don't conform, you are othered and experience restricted access to certain spaces and opportunities – not restricted through refused entry, but by the way you're treated based on your appearance. Understanding our desires is not an easy task but is one that gay men need to unpack the most.

'I think it's about not discriminating against anyone and not making anyone feel like they're in a position to not be loved or to feel like they're not enough. I think that's the bare minimum.'

Uzo Emenike (he/she/they), musician

Dating Apps

A small device that fits in our pocket can give us access to thousands of people at our fingertips. We are no longer living in a world where the primary place to meet someone was at a bar, bumping into them in the supermarket, or being introduced by a friend. Apps have become seen as the quickest and easiest option. Queer people are far more likely to use a dating app than non-queer people, primarily due to the difficulty finding partners in person.[3] Being a minority, especially in a rural area, means we are far less likely to just stumble across our future spouse out and about, so many of us resort to online dating.

But online dating can begin to feel monotonous and even hopeless at times. Having thousands of people at our fingertips means that we begin to see people as 'options' rather than people. Twenty years ago, we couldn't have ten conversations with dating prospects taking place simultaneously, all whilst reviewing their profiles like a CV. Having multiple 'options' in front of us means it's harder to take the time to get to know someone on a truly personal level, especially with our personality being more difficult to convey online. For gay men in particular, the focus we put on physical attractiveness means that before even saying hello to someone we've already decided that they're not the one for us.

Dating apps and instant messaging also give us the impression that we have 24/7 access to someone, anxiously checking our phones to see if they've replied. Authentic dating within queer spaces then becomes much harder to come by, but it's not impossible. It's about dating with more intention and taking the time to get to know people on an individual level. A common experience is matching with someone, exchanging a couple of messages, and never speaking again. Or never speaking to begin with. We cannot change other people's trauma, nor can we change their behaviour. The only person's behaviour we can change is our own. I've been more than guilty of letting out a big sigh at the thought of still being single, when all the while there are multiple waiting for me on a dating app. I think this is something we've all been guilty of at one point or another. Dating with intention means we make an active effort to get to know someone and ask them on a date. Going on a date with someone and realising they're not for us is not a waste of time. If we all met the person we want to commit to on our first date, dating apps wouldn't exist to begin with. That's the reality of dating: it takes time, commitment, and resilience. So don't hesitate in asking that match out on a date, it's the best way to find if you're an in-person match too.

Social Media

Despite being where most of my career is based, I don't shy away from acknowledging the negative impacts social media can have.

On nearly every platform, you're met with a highlight reel of people's best moments without ever seeing their worst –

especially with relationships. Opening social media and seeing a happy queer couple should make us feel hopeful; instead, we'll open the comments to jokes about 'blocking' them for it not yet happening to us. (And I'll admit, the jokes can be funny, but they're all just masks for how people really feel.) When we constantly see happy couples, whether in a single photo or a six-second video, whilst remaining single ourselves, it's natural to feel envious. But what we are seeing is merely a snapshot. We're not seeing the reality of the relationship, how they met, or their highs and lows.

> **'We always hear a gay man say, "Oh, I'm so lonely. I don't know why." It's like, well, have you considered that you're the problem?'**
>
> Andrew Gurza (he/they),
> disability awareness consultant

Andrew's statement here might sound harsh, but it carries a lot of truth. Quite often the defeat we may feel over dating is not the sole responsibility of others. I've noticed that queer people have a tendency to bring other queer people down. We will see a couple doing literally nothing wrong, simply looking happy. The comments and reposts will be engulfed in mocking, criticisms, and even discourse picking their relationship apart. Tearing down other people's joy may provide a temporary relief from your own feelings, but it doesn't and will never address them. Your negativity will return, and the perfectly innocent couple may now begin to lose their trust in queer people. Queer love is such a beautiful and sacred thing that needs to be cherished and celebrated, not torn down. Rather than projecting our negative feelings around queer dating onto others, maybe it's time to address why we have those feelings. Because I can guarantee some random couple isn't going to be the sole cause of your unhappiness. Instead, uplift queer people and celebrate them, and in our own time we can unpack why we feel the need to bring others down and address it ourselves.

'Can I Buy You a Drink?'

Many queer people feel a lot of pressure to partake in alcohol- and substance-oriented social scenes because they're almost all we have. Sure, there are plenty of things we can do that aren't alcohol oriented, but queer spaces are our safe space, and dedicated queer spaces are rarely without a focus on drinking. This makes meeting a partner in organic and sober scenarios far less likely.

Going for a drink is also a pretty common date. Alcohol loosens inhibitions and makes us less nervous, which in turns makes conversation easier. But this is not the only option. If we put more thought into a date and make it more fun, alcohol won't even be needed. Alcohol can be a simple way to ease the tension, and there's nothing wrong with that so long as it's not relied upon. Learning to date authentically as ourselves in an environment that we create can make for a more fulfilling dating experience.

We are allowed to mourn the love we don't get to experience. We are allowed to feel sad that our dating experience isn't the same as our non-queer counterparts'. But focusing on it too much won't serve us in the end. We need to process our feelings, rather than letting them linger to the point we feel hopeless. It is within our power to date intentionally. Dating does look different for queer people, but we absolutely can try to put more purpose behind our choices and do so without the focus on alcohol.

Rejection Is Inevitable

> **'I used do everything I could to avoid rejection. But now I know it's important, because every time I have faced rejection, I've had to learn and grow from it.'**
>
> Char Ellesse (she/her),
> founder and content creator

Rejection is probably the most difficult part of dating, and everyone faces it at some point. It is very easily internalised and viewed as a reflection of our worth. When queer self-worth is already disproportionately low, rejection can feel like a complete invalidation. However, rejection is instead a reflection of another person's desires or 'preferences', which, as we know from what we talked about in this book, have nothing to do with *us* and all to do with *them*.

> **'You have to be okay with the fact that their perception of you doesn't have any correlation with your actual worth and your actual attraction.'**
>
> Romone (they/them),
> performance artist

Rejection doesn't feel nice (it's not meant to), but it's natural and okay that it takes place. The conditions of this, however, are the way the rejection is communicated and how it's received. Rejection does not need to be unkind; it's actually very easy to communicate a rejection politely and with compassion. Thank them for their interest and apologise that you aren't interested back. Your response doesn't need to be specific, personal, or lengthy. More importantly, it doesn't need to be unkind. Just because you are not attracted to someone doesn't mean you need to devalue them with a personal rejection. At the same time, the way we handle a rejection matters too. If you are met with a blatantly rude rejection, then feel free to hand their ass to them. But if you're met with a polite rejection, becoming defensive and lashing out is not going to serve you. The only achievement is that you'll become agitated, and they'll likely just block you or walk away, and they'll be well within their rights to do so. Even if it upsets you, it's important to navigate it yourself. Simply acknowledge that the rejection is not about you. I know it may sound like a cop-out, but it genuinely *isn't about you.* Other people's desires and capacity for attraction are not your responsibility. Their attraction is a reflection of their personal desires and views.

'You want everyone to like you, but you don't even like everyone.'

Char Ellesse (she/her),
founder and content creator

Char spoke in depth about the experience of dating as a queer Black woman and how she often has to consider if an individual even dates Black women to begin with – this is something she has even experienced from Black men. At the same time, Char admitted that people of colour who do date outside of their race may be told that they're 'letting the community down' by doing so. The reality of dating as a Black woman, in Char's experience, is that there are a lot of different layers and things to navigate. She then quoted one of the guests on her podcast, Candice Brathwaite, in response to criticism someone may get for dating outside of their race.

> 'Go where the love is, because at this point, we all just need love. So, if you have the capacity to be attracted to someone outside of your race, do it. There's just a lot of layers to dating as a Black woman and also as a dark-skinned Black woman, because colourists are everywhere.'
>
> Char Ellesse (she/her),
> founder and content creator

'Go where the love is' is such poignant quote for dating, in particular queer dating, and can apply to other forms of prejudice in our spaces. You are not going to be attracted to everyone, and that is okay. You're not expected to like everyone. There are people out there who *will* be attracted to you. My favourite quote from Romone during our interview was 'I'm not everybody's cup of tea, but when I am, people want to refill.' I want you to read that as many times as you need to for it to sink in.

> **'If someone rejects you, it's nothing to do with you. I always think it's nothing to do with me, it's to do with their situation and is out of my control.'**
>
> Tyreece (he/she/they), fashion creator and performer

Dating can often feel like being in a whirlpool of question marks, insecurities, and anxiety. We can tie so much of our self-worth to being perceived as desirable and, in turn, feeling worthy of love. My best friend once told me, 'The person you're dating deserves to feel like nothing less than the most beautiful person in the world', and that is something that has always stuck with me. This isn't just about how we're treated but how we treat others. We are all equally worthy of love. Being kind to others costs nothing, unpacking our unconscious bias costs nothing, understanding that no one is perfect costs nothing.

You deserve someone who is going to love you through thick and thin. You deserve friends who see you for *who* you are, not *what* you are. You deserve to be surrounded by people who will uplift you and help you see that you truly are worth the love that queer people so often feel undeserving of.

Those with a strong sense of self will find rejection easier to navigate. It doesn't mean it won't feel disappointing, but it means we'll be less likely to take it personally. We'll be able to recognise that they simply weren't our person, and that is okay.

Self-worth simply means we know our value and that the *right* person will come along and recognise us for that.

You Are Worthy

But how do we develop a strong sense of self? How do we feel enough? How do we, finally, feel worthy of love? The brutal honesty is that, unfortunately, there's no quick fix. I can give you all the Pinterest inspirational quotes I like, but getting to a place of sustaining your self-worth on your own takes a lot of work and time.

> **'Self-worth has to come from you. You are never going to feel fantastic when you're living for other people and constantly trying to curate your identity around how other people want you to be. You're always going to feel like something is missing, and you may not even be aware of it, I was not aware of it. The feeling of embracing your true, authentic self is going to outweigh any rejection and any doubts that you have about your identity.'**
>
> Shell Rowe (she/her),
> content creator

Shell put it better than I ever could. Internal validation is about being able to sustain your self-worth without needing the approval and praise of others. For me personally, it wasn't about seeing the value in accepting myself; it was seeing the consequences of not doing so that drove me to change. I saw first-hand how fragile it was to rely on external validation. Without the approval of others, I felt like I was nothing, and that was *not* how I wanted to live my life. I wanted to live my life for me. This isn't to say you're going to feel on top of the world every single day – that simply does not happen. Even now, despite being confident, I have my bad days, and I think accepting that is part of it. Someone with a strong sense of self-worth isn't permanently happy in who they are; rather, they recognise that bad days will happen and will pass.

I ended the introduction on the concept that to accept yourself, you need to stop judging. Views on image and gender expression are often a result of social conditioning. When we're told that only one body type is desirable, we are likely to feel insecure if we don't meet that standard. This can take us down two paths: either we can accept ourselves for who we are and, in turn, accept others too, or we can succumb to the standards we're conditioned to and demonise anyone who doesn't follow suit.

> **'I took forever to get to the place I'm at now with confidence in myself. I'm okay if they feel that way because I know who I am, I did the work for myself. And if they don't feel comfortable with it, that's okay, it just means they have a lot of work to do with themselves – it has nothing to do with me.'**
>
> Ady Del Valle (he/she),
> plus-size model and advocate

Self-acceptance also doesn't automatically mean nonconformity. You can have muscles, you can be masculine, and still accept others for themselves. Your gender performance isn't the problem; it's the potential insecurity that manifests in many and is then projected onto others. There are many reasons people may work on their body that are not necessarily related to insecurity, shame, or pride. The issue arises with the motivation itself. If the drive to aspire to muscularity and masculinity is born out of insecurity and shame, then the shame around body image or perceived femininity never truly goes away. It is instead shrouded under a facade. We don't learn to truly accept ourselves, we instead yearn for the standard that brings acceptance from others. With the shame still deep within, its manifestation is no longer in insecurity but in projection. We begin to perpetuate the shame that made us feel inadequate, the same internalised thought that only the societal standard matters.

> **'If you feel insecure and if you are projecting that you don't see yourself as worthy or valuable, you're going to draw people in who like that about you and like that you don't have any self-worth, and they're going to take advantage of that.'**
>
> Charlie Craggs (she/her),
> author and trans+ activist

Ultimately, self-worth means not allowing the opinions of others to interfere with how you feel about yourself (as much as you can). Both judgements and validations from others should not determine the way we view ourselves. By not judging others, the fear of others judging us subsides. By not relying on external validation, the need for others to uplift us subsides.

Overall, we set ourselves on a path of truly understanding that our self-worth is exactly that: how we value ourselves.

> 'Rather than trying to focus on how I can be digestible to other people, I just focus on finding peace within myself and understanding that some people aren't going to be able to digest me.'
>
> Romone (they/them),
> performance artist

Chapter 8

The Fight Isn't Over

This book isn't a fix, cure, or 'ultimate guide'. It's a stepping stone. Reading this book might even be the *first* step, and a big one at that. For a lot of people this will have been an uncomfortable read. There are *few* people who will be able to close this book and not feel called out for some form of behaviour or thought pattern, including myself. I am far from perfect. I am working on myself every day and still have my unconscious bias pop its head up and trigger a thought based on false perceptions, prejudice, and stereotypes. I'm still navigating internalised fatphobia despite being a very public body image advocate. I still navigate internalised homophobia despite calling for the acceptance and uplifting of all queer people. I still navigate understanding other people's cultures, religions, and backgrounds. I'd like to think I've been very transparent in this book, as the last thing I want is for anyone to feel this book is just pages of a privileged white boy preaching tolerance from a pedestal. I've been open about my own unconscious bias, in the past and to this day. We are not born intolerant; we are taught to be through negative representation or the complete absence of it. And I hope this book is a way to fight against that.

Unpacking our internal monologue and why it says what it does is a long process. Social conditioning happens during our most formative years, and trying to rewire our brains to think differently is not as simple as flicking a switch. Even after attending therapy and talking about what demons you're battling – therapy gives us tools, and it's on us to actively use them to change our habits and thought processes. Their continued use is important. You can't just buy a houseplant and expect it to grow and thrive without constant care – it needs nurturing. You can't just water it the day you buy it and call it a day – it needs commitment. What you take away from this book is like that plant. Will you nurture it? Will you water it, feed it, give it sun, trim it, and keep it healthy? Or will you forget it's there and watch it gradually wilt away back down to the earth? This book is a starting point, and it's up to you what you do with it. Will you take the discussions, apply them in the real world, and take active steps to unpack your prejudice? Or will you put this book on your shelf to gather dust until the real struggles of our community fade into the back of your mind, until it's as though you never picked it up in the first place?

'We can't underestimate how powerful support and community is in difficult times.'

Daisy Puller (she/they),
drag queen and HIV activist

In this chapter, I want to give you the tools to pursue active change. Pulled from everything we've talked about, I have developed very universal, actionable first steps. It may feel that some of the following points don't apply to you, but if that's so, I want you to think about why. Is it because you already contribute to uplifting and supporting queer people who are different from us, or is it because you feel the prejudices other people face don't have a direct impact on yourself? The reality is when one of us loses, we all lose. Queer rights did not merely happen; they were fought for. As a community we had to stand in solidarity to make our collective voice louder, ensuring that we *all* get the respect and equality that we deserve. Unfortunately, the reverse is the same. When one subsection of our community starts having their rights targeted and stripped back, that's not where it'll end.

> **'The infighting, unfortunately, kind of gives people ammo to say, "Look at what this community is doing. It's fighting itself. It can't stand together." When we're othering one another, it just gives outsiders the right to do so as well.'**
>
> Dee Whitnell (they/them),
> sex educator and trans+ activist

Being the most marginalised in society means that, ultimately, we have a lot of differences: racial, cultural, economic, sexual orientation, and so on. We have a tendency to respond to this in two ways: either we focus on supporting each other and have greater compassion for other minorities, or we can let exclusion breed exclusion. A divided community should never be our goal. Let's learn from each other, understand our privilege, and ultimately use kindness to get what we should all collectively want – equality.

Why Pride Matters

Pride started as a protest. Over the years, it has transitioned into a celebration, an opportunity for us to take to the streets to proudly declare to the world who we are and feel safe doing so. But originally, no one was dancing in the street with a gin and tonic, blasting pop music, and partying till sunrise. Pride started as a fight for equality. The entire day was full of marches, banners and placards, speeches, chants, and event arrests. It had real power and grit to it. I love a party as much as anyone else, but Pride is so much more than that.

Despite the Pride festivals held throughout the summer, prejudice and disdain towards the LGBTQIA+ community remain. Hate crimes against people of a different sexual orientation more than doubled between 2018 and 2023.[1] On top of this, the UK dropped from first place in 2015 to twenty-second in 2025 on the ILGA-Europe ranking, which details legal and policy protection for LGBTQIA+ people on the continent. It is not enough to view Pride as merely a party, especially when we are seeing a global regression in a lot of queer rights. Pride gives us visibility and shows that we're not going anywhere, but that's no longer enough. Visibility alone doesn't bring about change. UK Pride festivals have taken place every year since the country was first on the ILGA-Europe ranking.

Despite the visibility and celebrations, our rights have still regressed.

> 'The ones who are on the fringes of society are usually the people who are pushing forwards the most, because we're the ones that need it the most.'
>
> Charlie Craggs (she/her), author and trans+ activist

In Europe, we have even seen public LGBTQIA+ events made a criminal offence. If reading that sentence gave you a sinking feeling in your stomach or a hot flush of fear, those feelings are a reality for many queer people around the world. In many countries, Pride parades have never been legal. In fact, in some of these countries, just being queer is still illegal and in some cases punishable by death. So no, it's not enough to just revel in the existence of our rights and become complacent. We are fighting for queer rights globally. As Asad said, 'Until we're all free, none of us are free.'

Representation for All

This is probably one of the most commonly discussed topics throughout all the interviews I conducted for this book. Queer people from all races, sexualities, genders, and backgrounds all echoed the same thought: seeing ourselves represented when we were younger would've helped us accept who we really are sooner. For the vast majority of people, poor representation isn't even acknowledged, mainly because it's being viewed through a very specific lens. In chapter four we discussed the representation of ethnic minorities and how white people tend not to notice a lack of diversity since whiteness has already been represented.

> **'True inclusivity isn't just about inviting people in – it's about making them feel like they belong.'**
>
> Ryan Lanji (he/him),
> cultural producer

Seeing things through a different lens took time. Me five years ago likely wouldn't have noticed the lack of diversity in most spaces; now, it is one of the main things I look for. Queer people and allies need to actively encourage representation – not only encourage but call out lack of representation. I saw a music video a few years ago celebrating queer nightlife, and there was not a single plus-size person in sight. The issue I took with it was that it was specifically celebrating the sweatiness and sexual nature of queer nightlife, something that plus-size people are often excluded from. The discourse that followed included people resorting to the overused phrase 'it's not that deep'. A phrase like this diminishes the importance of a conversation and more often than not is used by someone who isn't impacted by it. The video itself featured predominantly slim and conventionally attractive queer people. Unsurprisingly, the majority of people using that phrase or discrediting the conversation fit the very image that was portrayed in the video. So what's meant by this is that the issue isn't 'that deep' to them personally. Those who are not directly impacted by a topic being discussed have a tendency to reduce or completely refute its existence. If you've not experienced a specific marginalisation, then you're not going to have personal experiences of the impact. That is where queer empathy comes in.

> **'Representation is an antidote to shame. And I think that's hit the nail on the head, because I spent so much time feeling shame that this is what I look like.'**
>
> Char Ellesse (she/her),
> founder and content creator

I want to reiterate one of my main points from the introduction: just because something doesn't impact you directly does not mean that it doesn't impact others. Quite often the impact of poor representation isn't immediate, it's collective and over a long period of time. People aren't going to suddenly be rid of body dysmorphia by seeing someone who looks like them in one music video. But if, over time, they gradually see their body represented in more and more places, including being seen as sexually desirable, they can begin to internalise it. Just like how we can internalise negative representation, we can internalise positive representation, but it requires a collective effort. So whilst to some it may be seen as people complaining about the lack of body diversity in one video, to others it's about seeing the bigger picture. It's about holding people accountable for their contribution to poor representation. It's about seeing something through someone else's eyes and realising that whilst I personally may be represented in this, no one else is. When only one type of representation is normalised, that becomes the societal standard to aspire to, and anyone other than that standard is made to feel less than.

> **'Seeing yourself represented in spaces makes you feel valid and makes you feel seen, and kind of gives validity to your experiences. And I feel like when you take that away, you just have a lot of lost people that don't know where to go and don't know where the community are.'**
>
> Romone (they/them), performance artist

Unpack Your Unconscious Bias

Ask yourself: 'Why?'

This is one of the most simple and effective ways of challenging our unconscious bias. When a prejudice or opinion comes into your head, ask yourself why. When you see a type of person and instantly think of something negative, ask why. What about that individual made you think that? Maybe it's a past experience, maybe it's because we've not seen someone like them before, maybe we've been told negative things about them. I want you to consider if those beliefs are based in reality. I can almost guarantee the answers you're thinking of for when asking yourself 'why' for your own bias are the same answers someone would use against any queer identity. 'I just don't agree with it' or 'I don't understand it' is not a valid reason to perpetuate hate against someone. Quite often we find that our unconscious bias is not based on reality, fact, or evidence. It's not based on a real threat or objectively immoral behaviour. It is instead often based on stereotypes, misconceptions, and opinion. On top of this, freedom of speech is *not* freedom from consequence. 'I'm entitled to my opinion' is often a follow-up from someone saying something completely abhorrent. And they're correct, it is their opinion and they're well within their rights to share it. We have just as much right to respond. People aren't mad because of a supposed lack of free speech; they're mad because they now have consequences to face as a result. If after reading this book you still see no issue with plainly stating 'no fats, no fems' at every given opportunity, honestly go for it. Just be prepared for people to call you a dickhead.

Prejudices do not exist in a vacuum, they come from somewhere. Our views on gender, sexual orientation, race, body image, religion, gender expression, and every other characteristic we may have an opinion on are more often than not a manifestation of past experiences. Whether they're personal experiences or stem from representation or any other environmental factor that can contribute to a formulated opinion. Challenging our thoughts and asking ourselves why we think the way we do is one of the most valuable ways of unpacking our unconscious bias and setting us on a path of empathy.

Accept That It's Not Your Fault

Having an unconscious bias isn't your fault. You are not born with prejudices. Children grow up curious and carefree. They often start the process of picking on each other only when they see something they're not used to. It's society's fault. It's poor representation. Prejudices are passed down from generation to generation, and they're then broadcast on a wider scale to reinforce the negative way we think about each other. I'm not saying we don't have to accept responsibility for our prejudices, because we do. They may not be our fault, but we and we alone are responsible for unlearning them and making change. So don't beat yourself up over it. Speaking to ourselves negatively will not serve anyone. Instead, focus on putting the work in to unlearn those prejudices. That's where true allyship starts.

Look Objectively at Others' Behaviour

It's easy to begin to mimic and echo the views of friends, family members, colleagues, public figures, and even partners. But I want you to pause and look at how they act. Creating a 'safe space' between friends not only allows us to confide in them but also to say things we may not ordinarily say to others. Taking the time to unpack our own unconscious bias also requires consideration of the potential prejudices that may surround us. It's important to have people in our lives who check our worst impulses, not feed them; who make us aware if we're in the wrong, not remain idle. We cannot grow as people and work on our own problematic behaviour if people around us echo and enable the same views. Just because our peers agree with us does not mean we are in the right.

We all joke about being bitchy and talking about people, but we know deep down that being judgemental isn't very nice. Speaking negatively about someone else's appearance does not increase our own value, and we know that if someone else was speaking negatively about the way we looked, we wouldn't like it. As I've mentioned already, I used to be an incredibly judgemental individual, partially because of my need for acceptance in the community but also due to who I was around. I grew up around a lot of judgemental people and it encouraged the same behaviours in me.

If we take the time to truly observe the viewpoints of those around us, we may begin to realise that we've internalised them. In chapter five, I spoke of a guy I went on a date with a long time ago and how his friends had internalised the strict gay body standards so intensely that they would judge him if he didn't keep up. When we have an emotional connection with someone, be it platonic or romantic, our objective view on them and their behaviour is warped. We can begin to make excuses and justify problematic behaviour. If we take a step back and remove the connection from the equation, we can start to see people objectively again and for who they truly are. Our peers aren't the sole cause of our actions – that's not a fair conclusion to make. Ultimately we're responsible for our actions. But our peers can influence our perspectives and behaviours. If we are surrounding ourselves with judgemental people, we feel safer being judgemental. If we surround ourselves with shallow people, we feel safer being shallow. If we surround ourselves with people who have unchecked internalised homophobia, racial prejudice, transphobia, and so on, we feel comfortable echoing the same problematic views. Taking a step back to view our peers objectively means we can begin to evaluate who should and should not be in our lives. Who brings out the best and worst in us. Who helps us grow, and who keeps us stagnant. Who encourages empathy, and who encourages prejudice.

Diversify Your Environment

Surrounding ourselves with different kinds of people can help us garner a better understanding for other people's experiences. I grew up with only white, masculine, and muscular gay men as representation. It wasn't until I began using TikTok during lockdown that I started to be exposed to different kinds of queer people online. I moved to London and saw this in person. I then began to understand why the progressive pride flag was important. This transformation doesn't happen overnight; unpacking my bias and learning about the experiences of others wasn't instant, and it never will be. But actively making the decision to diversify our surroundings is a step in the right direction.

> **'On social media, follow people you identify with and make connections. Not everyone has that immediate circle around them, so make connections online.'**
>
> Ady Del Valle (he/she),
> plus-size model and advocate

Specifically when it comes to body image insecurity, follow people and consume media that make you feel good about yourself and feel seen. When our feeds are flooded with idealised bodies and aesthetics, it's easy to internalise this and begin to feel we're not enough.[2] Once we start to realise we're not alone, shame can start to be addressed, and then we are less likely to externalise it and project it onto others. Representation isn't a short-term fix, it's a long-term solution. Over time, we can begin to understand that within the queer community there are so many different types of wonderful, colourful people who may look entirely different from us but are fundamentally just people with unique experiences. Ones that we can begin to understand and empathise with.

It's also important to be mindful of the motives behind the types of media we are consuming. There is a *lot* of misinformation online aimed at stoking further division. Not everything we read online is true. With the growth of AI, now not everything we see or watch online is even real. When consuming any media that contributes to you forming an opinion on any topic, consider how reliable the source is. A lot of prejudices can come from false information or biased reporting that only aims to reinforce stereotypes, division, and prejudices.

See People for Who They Are, Not What They Are

Queer people are people. No matter our identity, heritage, or aesthetic, we are not a mere object of desire. We are people. Queer people are not a fetish or something to fantasise about.

> **'[When] you are reduced to just being someone who people see in explicit content, they're not thinking about the fact that you have interests and you have a favourite colour and a family. These are really menial things, but they're not thinking about you beyond the fact that you have a certain anatomy that they can gain from.'**
>
> Maxine Heron (she/her),
> writer and trans advocate

No one should be fetishised without consent. Just because it feels nice that people like my body doesn't mean I like it when they fetishise my weight gain. Liking muscles also does not justify the mistreatment of those who don't have muscles. Bisexual women do not exist to be an object for men to fantasise threesomes with, nor do trans women exist for men to explore their fascination. If an individual is enthusiastically consenting to being fetishised, then that is their personal prerogative. But we're all human and still deserve to be treated with respect.

> 'If I feel like someone's fetishising me in a space where there's a conversation to be had, then I'll say, "Hey, why do you think that? But why is that hot? Where's that coming from?" or "Why is that that way for you?"'

Beth McCarthy (she/they),
artist and performer

How to Be an Active Ally

I asked Danny Beard, 'Why should we be allies?'

> 'Quite frankly, because we should. Because I think if I was in that position, if that was my journey, I'd want people to be on my team.'

Danny Beard (he/they),
drag queen and performer

Do the Work

Whilst I've done my absolute best to highlight queer experiences from as many parts of our community as possible, this book is a drop in the ocean compared to the stories and history of queerness. To garner a true understanding of our queer family, we must actively put in the work to educate ourselves. It is not the sole responsibility of a queer person of colour to list all the ways in which their race intersecting with their queerness makes navigating queer spaces more difficult. It is not the sole job of a fat queer person to tell you why body shaming them isn't okay. It is not the sole job of trans people and lesbians to explain the multitude of ways in which they have fought for collective queer rights, only to be shunned by transphobic and misogynistic views.

There are so many incredible resources that can help us better understand intersectional experiences, and they're not hard to find. I'm just hoping that this book will be useful for many years to come, and in the future, I'd like to think there will be even more resources to choose from. For now, I am simply going to ask you to do your own research. Finding the information is the easy part. Open a search engine and search for films, articles, books, documentaries – anything about queer people and their experiences. With this in mind, I'd be remiss if I didn't shout out the incredible contributors to this book. I implore you to please go to the acknowledgements at the back of this book. If any of their quotes or stories spoke to you, I'd highly recommend finding them online and supporting their work.

LGBTQIA+ history is not actively taught, and so it can feel

elusive. But as a community, it's important to put in the work to truly understand that history and where we come from. The history of drag queens, the protests and riots for queer liberation, the AIDS crisis, queer racism, misogyny, the shunning of trans+ people, the pivotal role of lesbians, the erasure of bisexuals, and the intersection of queerness and religion – these are just a few things we're not taught about but everyone, queer people and beyond, should feel duty bound to know.

Check Your Privilege

Hopefully this book has helped you have a better understanding of what privilege actually is. These conversations aren't meant to invalidate your experiences, contrary to what some people seem to believe, but instead they're meant to help us understand that some of our inherent characteristics can give us societal advantages.

When analysing the Wheel of Power and Privilege, we can see how some people's identities make them subject to far more societal disadvantage than our own. As a cis white gay man myself, while I do not have the privilege of being heterosexual, I still hold a great deal more privilege than intersectional queers. Too often will intersectional queers feel unseen or seen for only one part of their identity. As Ryan Lanji said, recognising intersectionality is important to ensure 'no one feels like they have to choose between their identities'.

You may wonder why checking your privilege is necessary. Knowing your privilege is about helping us have more empathy for those who have less privilege. It's not about you, it's about all of us.

Have Difficult Conversations

Becoming aware of our privilege in society also means we understand the power our voice has. Using our privilege to uplift others is allyship at its core. People are more likely to listen to their peers than to a stranger. A homophobic straight man is more likely to listen if his friend calls him out than if he's called out by a queer person he doesn't know. Challenging people is where a lot of the work takes place. Being aware of our privilege means we acknowledge that some people don't get to opt out of conversations; they are cornered into them. Whereas those in a privileged position can opt out and not engage.

> **'What's going to change the world is talking about it when we're not around. It's having a conversation with someone who might need to have their mind changed by someone they trust.'**
>
> Dani St James (she/her),
> chief executive of the trans+ charity Not a Phase

When someone is introduced to a concept they aren't familiar with that goes against their belief system and view of the world, it counteracts their unconscious bias. The difficulty with rationalising with someone experiencing this is that, quite often, unconscious bias isn't rational. Rarely will an unconscious bias be something that can be backed up with research, evidence, statistics, case studies, or anything based in reality. Some people may be so heavily influenced by their unconscious bias that they will go out of their way to find justifications for their opinions, even if the reasoning they do find is fragile and lacks substance. As such, the unconscious bias of others can feel like banging your head into a brick wall. But that doesn't mean we shouldn't try. As Maxine Heron was quoted saying in chapter two, 'Never underestimate people's capacity to learn.'

Speaking to a lot of intersectional queers about prejudice opened my eyes to the level of patience many of them have. It's very easy to resort to insults and dismissal when discussing prejudice with someone we don't align with. I've been more than guilty of that. I cannot begin to count the number of times I've had to stop myself from typing 'omg, shut the fuck up' when reading an ignorant comment. Sometimes that's exactly what I did (and occasionally still do). It's understandable for us to want to respond this way. When our entire lives are questioned by people who know nothing about us, over and over again, our patience is going to wear thin. But that's not how progress is made. When a muscular gay man comments on a post of mine critiquing my body or gender expression, I've been trying to avoid clapping back and instead attempting to engage in a conversation. 'Why do you think that?' and 'Do you think that's a nice thing to say to a stranger?' are two common responses I make. Sometimes when someone says something, it hasn't come from a place of malice but from lack of understanding. What can be a microaggression to us may not make sense to someone else. Whilst some simply won't engage in the discourse and are comfortable spreading hateful views online, for others it prompts them to look at themselves. When challenged on their behaviour and the impact it has, some will realise that it wasn't the nice thing to do. Even if their opinion is unchanged, the very least we can do is remind people that spreading hate online serves no one.

> 'You have to have compassion for the both of you in that dynamic, not even so you can come out of the other side of it being right, but so that you can actually just understand why it is that both of you are placed in the way that you are. My bias is that I am a trans woman, and that's why I feel this way. Someone else's bias might be that they're not and that they've never met a trans person, so they're believing what they've seen on TikTok.'
>
> Maxine Heron (she/her),
> writer and trans advocate

Sometimes there are people who simply want an argument or to be controversial for the sake of being controversial, and so are willingly ignorant. These are the people I'll still quite happily tell to fuck off. But many simply lack the education and therefore do not have the understanding, being unintentionally ignorant. It's important to distinguish between the two, as giving attention to the former is going to leave you emotionally drained with zero progress made. But if bigotry comes from lack of awareness, then it's our job to make them aware – not by letting people know we exist, but by explaining why it's okay we exist. It's a job that none of us should have to do, but one that is necessary. Maxine's quote is a perfect example of this. For a lot of us, accepting people for who they are often comes naturally because of who we are today and who we may surround ourselves with. But for those who simply have not had the exposure to different viewpoints or different people before, their bias is that they simply do not get it. Sometimes, even if we don't want to, listening to their side can help us understand how they got to where they are.

Daisy said in our interview that she understands why many of us are stuck in our ways. We as a community and individuals will, for a long time to come, have to justify our right to exist to at least someone. Our very existence is challenged daily, so when we go out to our known safe space, nightlife, we're doing so to escape and feel free. So when we're in that space, maybe we don't want to be challenged. Maybe we don't want our thoughts questioned or our mindsets critiqued, we just want to escape. But whilst we ourselves may want to escape the prejudices we as individuals are subjected to, that doesn't mean we shouldn't challenge other prejudices we may be guilty of upholding. That is the difference between sitting in our privilege and using it to uplift others.

When people do not naturally consider inclusivity and diversity, it's because they haven't seen it themselves nor have they been made aware of its value. A lot of queer 'safe spaces' have a tendency to feel safe for only certain demographics of queer people. These are not true safe spaces. They are instead only as safe as we make them. The only places I have ever felt truly accepted and free of judgement have been *queer* spaces. Not gay, *queer*. Gay spaces absolutely have their place, and for some they can be a haven. But the main distinction between the two is who they're a haven for. Gay spaces are often safe spaces for gay men, and normally a specific type of gay men, depending on their tribe. Queer spaces truly celebrate everyone: different expressions, different genders, races, sexualities, body sizes, and disabilities. This, to me, is what queerness looks like:

standing together as a community and embracing each other's differences. Here, no one looks the same. That's what queerness is, being different. It's imperfect.

Our unconscious bias makes us believe that only certain queer people have true value. The power to create inclusive spaces and to change people's behaviours is in our hands. Tyreece said that 'if everyone's getting involved, that makes it have more weight' in relation to fighting for inclusion and queer rights, because we have power in numbers. We get to encourage this by having difficult conversations and calling things out when we see them. We may think we don't, but we all have a role to play in queer progression.

> 'The power to create spaces that we want to be in is actually in our own hands. I've done it with when I was hosting club nights with young people that were first coming to London, and if they were being catty or bitchy, I'd be like, "Wait. No, babes, this is not what we do here." You can cultivate the kind of environment that you will thrive in and that everybody else will thrive in.'
>
> Daisy Puller (she/they),
> drag queen and HIV activist

Stand Up and Turn Out

These are more tangible forms of allyship that involve actively taking part in the movement. Whilst donations are a great form of support, they are not the only option. Many other forms of support simply require time, and often not a great deal of it:

- Sign petitions
- Email your local political representative
- Turn up to protests
- Donate to fundraisers and charities
- Share important information with peers
- Listen to those affected

> **'If I am ever on public transport and I see another [visibly] queer person – I just keep my eye on them, and I usually keep my music down, just in case I ever have to step in.'**
>
> Charlie Craggs (she/her),
> author and trans activist

Is Your Voice Needed?

The explosive growth of the internet paired with right-wing viewpoints has galvanised people into thinking their opinion is a birthright on every single topic. Even if the opinion isn't well formulated, they still think it is their right to have and share it. Technically they're correct: we are all entitled to share our opinions – but that doesn't mean we *have* to. Too often people will contribute their viewpoint on a topic they have little if any knowledge on. They'll share an opinion about a subject that has absolutely no bearing on their life.

One thing that can create a lot of frustration, especially amongst liberals, is our ability to pick apart and dissect every single piece of discourse. But too often, people will even attempt to pick holes in arguments they fundamentally agree with. This leads to infighting and minuscule disagreements about a shared view with a shared goal. This is not a productive use of our energy. Sometimes it's necessary and people need to be held accountable, and sometimes it's unnecessary. Our ability to hold people accountable is both our strength and our weakness. Some topics are more important than others, some are more urgent than others. We can be so determined to be right and righteous on a micro level, that we forget that sometimes we need to take a step back and prioritise our advocacy.

I also want to bring back the idea of 'no speaking about us without us' mentioned earlier in the book. Shiv recalled a time when they were contacted to take part in panels for Black History Month, despite them being South Asian. They recognised that despite being a person of colour, no matter how many queer Black people they speak to they will never fully understand that experience and therefore cannot speak on their behalf. There is a difference between speaking *up for* someone and just speaking *for* someone. Speaking up for someone means you are having difficult conversations to support them when they're not around and amplifying their experiences. Speaking *for* someone means that you could be taking up space and attempting to discuss their experience instead of them, rather than alongside them. Being an ally means amplifying marginalised voices.

Queer Empathy: The Bottom Line

I hope that, at the very least, this book has achieved the three intentions I laid out in the introduction: Allow you to recognise where prejudices within queer spaces come from, understand the true impact they have, and help you develop empathy to encourage real change in the way we treat each other. We can attempt to listen to and understand someone's different experiences all we like, but without the ability to empathise, then no true change can be made. As I said in the introduction, I cannot make an innately unempathetic person suddenly care about others. But what I can at least attempt is to provide the starter kit for you to be able to take the existing empathy you have and extend it to different kinds of queer people. Take these stories, experiences, and consequences and absorb them, share them, and use them to bring about change.

There have been a couple of common themes throughout this book with the aim of prompting a more empathetic viewpoint towards our fellow queers. I want to end this book by prompting these one last time:

Just because it doesn't impact you does not mean it doesn't impact others.

Too often are we unable to put ourselves in someone else's shoes. We all have different backgrounds, upbringings, families, friends, hometowns, workplaces; all kinds of different wiring in our brains. Not only can our experiences differ, but so can our ability to handle them. One person's threshold for hardship may be entirely different from your own, and their mental health might be much harder to navigate.

If we've diversified the people we surround ourselves with and the media we consume, then we can begin to hear first-hand accounts of the experiences other queer people go through. Even without taking this step, the various experiences discussed within this book should help to provide a greater understanding of the unique stressors that different queer people face.

> **'I'm not someone who cares about what other people think, but I am someone who cares about how the people around me feel.'**
>
> Felix Mufti (he/they),
> writer, performer, and activist

Prejudice doesn't justify prejudice.

Read that again.

It doesn't matter how you identify, experiencing prejudice yourself doesn't absolve you of perpetuating further prejudice. It's our responsibility, every single one of us, to understand the discriminations that take place around us and ensure we are not actively contributing to them. I've discussed many different prejudices within this book, many of which I'm ashamed to have once believed – not through active hatred but because of sheer lack of understanding. Some of us may unknowingly perpetuate harmful ideologies, stereotypes, and stigmas that could be harming another member of the community. Be it intentional or not, it's our duty to recognise it and take active steps to overcome it. The reason behind the existence of our prejudices can help explain why we think the way we do, but does not justify it, especially not acting on it. Queer people, regardless of how we identify, can in some way understand how it feels to experience prejudice over something we have no control over. Empathy is key.

One experience shouldn't determine another.

Our prejudices and mindsets often come from our past experiences. Whether it's with people of different body types, religions, sexual orientations, expressions, or any other notable attribute. Our experiences in the past have a tendency to determine our experiences now.

Some things in our past may leave more of a scar than others, and the impact can be even more psychological than we realise. Sometimes it's trauma, sometimes it's an unconscious bias. Either way, it's something we should unpack – for ourselves, if anything, but more so for others. We cannot get to a point of being truly empathetic and understanding of one another if we are still holding on to past experiences and then holding them against an entire group. When we're constantly pitting person against person, tribe against tribe, community against community, we just continue to hold up the same divides we need to break down. But if we take the time to understand our past and empathise with our differing experiences, we can begin to see people for who they really are and not what our brain is telling us they *will* be.

> 'As a community, I think it's important to not let our trauma inform how we treat other people.'
>
> Romone (they/them),
> performance artist

It's okay to admit you're wrong.

This is the final piece of advice I want to give you, because many people are too afraid to do it. Admitting we're wrong allows us to learn and grow. We can take the feedback and evolve as a human. Putting our pride and ego aside isn't an easy thing to do to begin with, especially as queer people. Having a higher craving for validation gives us a bigger fear of invalidation, and holding our hands up and admitting we were wrong can feel like a big invalidation. But it's important to embrace this feeling. Taking accountability isn't weak, it's brave. Being in the wrong doesn't automatically determine your character, it is instead determined by how you handle it.

What unites us as queer people is our shared nonconformity and frequent ostracisation from wider society, but that does not mean our experiences are synonymous. The ability to place ourselves in someone else's shoes can lead us on a path of empathetically viewing queer people's experiences. When we view people with empathy, we can begin to think of ways we can help rather than merely judge. Judging people does not achieve anything other than bring shame on those being judged. Shame doesn't encourage support, it doesn't encourage people to reach out or seek help, and it doesn't encourage people to change their behaviour. Shame only brings isolation and a poorer mental wellbeing. Some will view shame as throwing a bucket of water onto a fire in the hopes of stamping it out, when in reality they're throwing a bucket of fuel.

It is our divisiveness that becomes our ultimate downfall. We need to learn empathy not only for those who are different, but also for those who are taking the first steps in learning. We need patience and grace. Change and progress takes time. Unlearning unconscious bias, learning the history of queer people, and fundamentally changing our way of thinking is never going to be instant. There is no point in us actively encouraging people to put the work in if we won't give people the time to do so. Whilst we need to accept that our own unconscious bias isn't our fault, we also need to recognise that other people's isn't their fault either. This doesn't mean we can't bring certain behaviours or errors to people's attention, but we can do so in a way that acknowledges that they are still learning and actively putting in the work. It's not giving them a pat on the back; it's instead giving them the time and grace for the change to take place.

Ultimately, we're all just trying to make our way in the world, and some people's paths have more bumps in the road. Whilst I hope this book can help enact even the smallest bit of change, unfortunately it's unlikely to be transformative within our lifetime. Some may have picked this book up and felt seen, some may have felt affronted, and hopefully some reflected on their own thoughts and behaviour. No one can make you understand different experiences. No one can make you develop empathy. No one can make you put the work in. Only *you* can make the decision to take the starter kit within this book and actively do something about it.

The community should feel safe for everyone. For too long have those on the fringes of society put in the most work to give us the freedoms we have today. Now it is our turn to return the favour.

A Note on the Contributors

I'd like to personally thank the following people for adding their identities, experiences, and backgrounds to this book:

Danny Beard (he/they), drag queen and performer

Yasmin Benoit (she/her), model and asexual activist

Charlie Craggs (she/her), trans+ activist and author

Ady Del Valle (he/she), plus-size model and advocate

Char Ellesse (she/her), founder and content creator

Uzo Emenike (he/she/they), musician

Andrew Gurza (he/they), disability awareness consultant

Maxine Heron (she/her), writer and trans advocate

Ignacio Labayen de Inza (he/him), founder of the charity Controlling Chemsex

Ryan Lanji (he/him), cultural producer

Le Fil (he/they), artist and drag performer

Beth McCarthy (she/they), artist and performer

Felix Mufti (he/they), writer, performer and activist

Daisy Puller (she/they), drag queen and HIV activist

Romone (they/them), performance artist

Shell Rowe (she/her), content creator

Shiv (they/them), journalist and broadcaster

Dani St James (she/her), chief executive of the trans+ charity Not a Phase

Tyreece (he/she/they), fashion creator and performer

Dee Whitnell (they/them), sex educator and trans+ activist

Asad Zafar (they/them), queer charity worker

Acknowledgements

For as long as I can remember, writing a book has been a life goal of mine. I've been writing articles for publications, charities, and personal blogs for years. I've always enjoyed being able share things with the world that may help people, even just a little bit. But a book is another story, over 70,000 words compared to the 600 or so I'm used to writing. It's a project that I'm incredibly grateful to have been given the honour to work on to the point that even writing these words at this very moment, it still doesn't feel real. So, to that end, there are a few people I want to thank.

My mum has been my biggest cheerleader since day one. Whether it was playing *momager* by helping me with social media when I was first starting, to being the second person in the world I ever came out to. My mum first and foremost showed me the value in selflessness and helping others, and these are the qualities I am incredibly grateful to have. If it wasn't for my mum putting me first, then I likely wouldn't have the life I have today. One of my biggest motivators to this day has been to make my mum proud, so hopefully being a published author will do it.

My dad always encouraged me to do what I love. Whether I was naturally good at it (or not) I was just made to feel that if I put my mind to something, I could achieve it. That sense of determination and resilience is why I've never given up. Not to mention the amount of university essays he proofread for me (thank god) because it's never been my strong suit. I likely wouldn't have received the grade I did if I hadn't had my many, many, *many* grammatical and spelling errors brought to my attention. It's a good thing my lifelong dream wasn't to work on a project tantamount to a dissertation . . . oh wait!

Speaking of spelling errors, hi Ryan! My incredible editor came into my life exactly how I needed him to: encouraging, honest, and gay as fuck. When I first started pitching this book in 2023, I said to my literary agent that it was incredibly important to me for the editor to be queer. No one on the planet will relate to every single experience in this book on a personal level, but I wanted the person editing it to have real emotional ties to the queer experience. After over thirty rejections, Ryan popped into my inbox. He had been following me on social media for a few years, and I was even on his list of people to reach out to about writing a book. So when he came across the pitch for *No Fats, No Fems,* he later admitted to me that in that moment, he thought "I have to have this". Over 2 years later, here we are. I want to thank Ryan from the bottom of my heart for believing in me, encouraging me, and being patient with my ADHD-riddled little brain for doing absolutely everything last-minute. None of this would be possible without him.

My literary agent, Jason was introduced to me by my friend Yolanda 3 years ago. Little did I know that this introduction would lead me to having my words printed round the world. Jason believed in me from the moment we met and was just as excited as me to bring this project into the world. Both Jason and I were sceptical about the idea of being able to find a queer editor. Even after thirty rejections, and a couple of offers from non-queer editors, I was still determined to wait. Following mine, Jason and Ryan's first ever meeting, me and Jason both stayed on the call to debrief. "I get why you wanted to wait now," he admitted to me. He saw the passion Ryan had for the project and that it was personal. Despite Jason always having my best interests at heart, he trusted me in wanting to wait for the right person. He knew the importance of this project to me and did whatever he could to ensure we would do it justice.

Now, I want to thank some friends. Firstly, my oldest friend Alex. She is the first person in the world I ever came out to and has been my rock ever since. Despite us having very different lives, we somehow just click (mainly because we're both insane). She is incredibly supportive, understanding, and accountable – the kind of friend I describe in this book that you *need* to have. She checks my worst impulses instead of feeding them, as I do with her. Alex is a cishet, white, Christian woman, and I've never met someone so willing to learn in my life. She reminds me every day that we all have the ability to do our own research, explore new topics, and to understand things that we may not instantly get. It is because of people like Alex that I know this book will be worthwhile.

Asad and Romone (who you've heard from throughout this book) are two of my closest friends. When I first moved to London, I barely had any friends let alone queer ones, and I had no experience navigating the queer social scene before, having moved up from Kent. Their lived experiences are incredibly different from my own, but from the moment I met them both, they've felt more like family than friends. They've supported me, encouraged me, educated me, and laughed with me (or, in Romone's case, laughed at me). Having queer people in my life is something I will never take for granted, and these are two people I love with all my heart.

I want to thank you, the reader. I would not be writing these words if you didn't believe in me to begin with. I wouldn't have the career I have as a sex educator and advocate if you didn't trust me to be the person to do it. Your endless support means more to me than I could ever explain, so thank you.

Finally, I want to thank every single contributor in this book. I am incredibly grateful to each and every person who opened up about their queer journey, as without them, this book would not exist. They shouldn't have to share these experiences, but I feel honoured that they chose to share them with me. I truly hope I have done you all proud.

Notes

Chapter 1: I Don't Want to Be Gay

1. Christopher C. H. Cook, 'The Causes of Human Sexual Orientation', *Theology & Sexuality* 27, no. 1 (2021): 1 – 19.

Chapter 2: Gender, Sex, and Everything in Between

1. United Nations. 2019. "OHCHR | Intersex People." OHCHR. 2019. https://www.ohchr.org/en/sexual-orientation-and-gender-identity/intersex-people.
2. World Health Organization. 2024. "Violence against Women." World Health Organization. March 25, 2024. https://www.who.int/news-room/fact-sheets/detail/violence-against-women.
3. Josh Parry, 'NHS England to Stop Prescribing Puberty Blockers', BBC News, 12 March 2024, https://www.bbc.co.uk/news/health-68549091.
4. Valeria P. Bustos et al., 'Regret After Gender-Affirmation Surgery: A Systematic Review and Meta-Analysis of Prevalence', *Plastic and Reconstructive Surgery – Global Open* 9, no. 3 (March 2021): e3477.
5. Sarah M. Thornton, Armin Edalatpour, and Katherine M. Gast, 'A Systematic Review of Patient Regret After Surgery – A Common Phenomenon in Many Specialties but Rare Within Gender-Affirmation Surgery', *American Journal of Surgery* 234 (August 2024): 68–73.
6. Julia M. Serano, 'Transmisogyny', in *The SAGE Encyclopedia of Trans Studies*, ed. Abbie E. Goldberg and Genny Beemyn (Sage Publications, 2021), 868, https://doi.org/10.4135/9781544393858.n296.
7. 'The 2022 Year in Review', Pornhub Insights, accessed 8 November 2024, https://www.pornhub.com/insights/2022-year-in-review.
8. Nina McLaughlin, 'Pornhub Has Revealed What Brits Were Searching for Most in 2024', JOE, 10 December 2024, https://www.joe.co.uk/life

/pornhub-has-revealed-what-brits-were-searching-for-most-in-2024-467654.

9. 'New Data: Rise in Hate Crime Against LGBTQIA+ People Continues, Stonewall Slams UK Gov "Inaction"', Stonewall, 5 October 2023, https://www.stonewall.org.uk/news/new-data-rise-hate-crime-against-lgbtq-people-continues-stonewall-slams-uk-gov-.
10. Kelsey Libert, 'Data Finds Republicans Are Obsessed with Searching for Transgender Porn', Lawsuit.org, accessed 25 June 2022, https://lawsuit.org/general-law/republicans-have-an-obsession-with-transgender-pornography/.
11. 'The Third Gender and Hijras', Harvard Divinity School, accessed 15 September 2025, https://rpl.hds.harvard.edu/religion-context/case-studies/gender/third-gender-and-hijras.
12. Tessa Wong, '377: The British Colonial Law That Left an Anti-LGBTQ Legacy in Asia', BBC News, 28 June 2021, https://www.bbc.co.uk/news/world-asia-57606847.
13. Leonore F. Carpenter and R. Barrett Marshall, 'Walking While Trans: Profiling of Transgender Women by Law Enforcement, and the Problem of Proof', *William & Mary Journal of Women & the Law* 24 (2017): 5–38.
14. 'L020A Seg Sylvia Rivera, "Y'All Better Quiet Down": Original Authorized Video 1973 Gay Pride Rally NYC Cc B1', Christopher Street Liberation Day, Washington Square Park, New York, 24 June 1973, posted 18 September 2017, by Love Tapes Collective, Vimeo, https://vimeo.com/234353103.

Chapter 3: The Alphabet Mafia

1. Nikolai Endres, 'Kertbeny, Károly Mária (1824 – 1882)', GLBTQ Encyclopedia Project, 2004, http://www.glbtqarchive.com/ssh/kertbeny_km_S.pdf.
2. Peter Cava, 'Cisgender and Cissexual', *The Wiley Blackwell Encyclopedia of Gender and Sexuality Studies* (John Wiley & Sons, 2016), 1–4, https://doi.org/10.1002/9781118663219.wbegss131.
3. Prishita Maheshwari-Aplin, '5 Things You Might Have Missed from the 2021 Census', Stonewall, 12 January 2023, https://www.stonewall.org.uk/news/5-things-you-might-have-missed-2021-census.
4. Brian A. Feinstein and Christina Dyar, 'Bisexuality, Minority Stress, and Health', *Current Sexual Health Reports* 9, no. 1 (2017): 42–49.
5. Jes L. Matsick and Jennifer D. Rubin, 'Bisexual Prejudice Among Lesbian and Gay People: Examining the Roles of Gender and Perceived Sexual Orientation', *Psychology of Sexual Orientation and Gender Diversity* 5, no. 2 (2018): 143–55.

6. Yasmin Benoit and Robbie De Santos, *Ace in the UK Report (2023)* (Stonewall, 2023), https://www.stonewall.org.uk/resources/ace-report.

Chapter 4: Preference or Prejudice?

1. Channing Gerard Joseph, 'Swann, William Dorsey', Oxford African American Studies Center, 2021, https://doi.org/10.1093/acref/9780195301731.013.79001.
2. Chong-suk Han and Kyung-Hee Choi, 'Very Few People Say "No Whites": Gay Men of Color and the Racial Politics of Desire', *Sociological Spectrum* 38, no. 3 (2018): 145–61.
3. Gayle Kaufman and Voon Chin Phua, 'Is Ageism Alive in Date Selection Among Men? Age Requests Among Gay and Straight Men in Internet Personal Ads', *Journal of Men's Studies* 11, no. 2 (2003): 225–35.

Chapter 5: The Body Image Crisis

1. 'Fatphobia', *Cambridge Advanced Learner's Dictionary*, accessed 13 August 2025, https://dictionary.cambridge.org/dictionary/english/fatphobia.
2. Matthew B. Feldman and Ilan H. Meyer, 'Eating Disorders in Diverse Lesbian, Gay, and Bisexual Populations', *International Journal of Eating Disorders* 40, no. 3 (2007): 218–26.
3. Michael P. Chaney, 'Muscle Dysmorphia, Self-Esteem, and Loneliness Among Gay and Bisexual Men', *International Journal of Men's Health* 7, no. 2 (2008): 157–70.
4. Ruth Knight et al., 'The Impact of Sexual Orientation on How Men Experience Disordered Eating and Drive for Muscularity', *Journal of Gay & Lesbian Mental Health* 28, no. 2 (2024): 210–32, doi:10.1080/19359705.2022.2118921.
5. Dalit Lev Arey, Yuli Peleg, and Tomer Gutman, 'Male Body Image in Focus: Muscularity-Oriented Eating Behaviours, Muscle Dysmorphia, and Exercise Addiction in Gay and Heterosexual Men', *Journal of Eating Disorders* 13, no. 1 (2025): 151.
6. Martin Cordes, Silja Vocks, and Andrea S. Hartmann, 'Appearance-Related Partner Preferences and Body Image in a German Sample of Homosexual and Heterosexual Women and Men', *Archives of Sexual Behavior* 50, no. 8 (2021): 3575–86.
7. Scott M. Strong, Devendra Singh, and Patrick K. Randall, 'Childhood Gender Nonconformity and Body Dissatisfaction in Gay and Heterosexual Men', *Sex Roles* 43, no. 7 (2000): 427–39.
8. Stuart Haggas, 'Goldicocks: The Penis Issue', LGBT HERO, accessed 16 September 2025, https://www.lgbthero.org.uk/fs160-the-penis-issue.

9. Zachary A. Soulliard, Micah R. Lattanner, and John E. Pachankis, 'Pressure from Within: Gay-Community Stress and Body Dissatisfaction Among Sexual-Minority Men', *Clinical Psychological Science* 12, no. 4 (2023): 607–24.
10. Cordes, Vocks, and Hartmann, 'Appearance-Related Partner Preferences'.
11. Christopher John Hunt, Karen Gonsalkorale, and Brian A. Nosek, 'Links Between Psychosocial Variables and Body Dissatisfaction in Homosexual Men: Differential Relations with the Drive for Muscularity and the Drive for Thinness', *International Journal of Men's Health* 11, no. 2 (2012): 127–36.
12. Graeme Kane, 'Unmasking the Gay Male Body Ideal: A Critical Analysis of the Dominant Research on Gay Men's Body Image Issues', *Gay & Lesbian Issues and Psychology Review* 5, no. 1 (2009): 20–333.
13. Kane, 'Unmasking the Gay Male Body Ideal'.
14. Jan Antfolk, 'Age Limits: Men's and Women's Youngest and Oldest Considered and Actual Sex Partners', *Evolutionary Psychology* 15, no. 1 (2017): https://doi.org/10.1177/1474704917690401.
15. Yash Bhambhani et al., 'Examining Sexual Racism and Body Dissatisfaction Among Men of Color Who Have Sex with Men: The Moderating Role of Body Image Inflexibility', *Body Image* 28 (2019): 142–48.
16. Melanie A. Morrison, Todd G. Morrison, and Cheryl-Lee Sager, 'Does Body Satisfaction Differ Between Gay Men and Lesbian Women and Heterosexual Men and Women? A Meta-Analytic Review', *Body Image* 1, no. 2 (2004): 127–38.
17. Samuel M. Fogarty and D. Catherine Walker, 'Twinks, Jocks, and Bears, Oh My! Differing Subcultural Appearance Identifications Among Gay Men and Their Associated Eating Disorder Psychopathology', *Body Image* 42 (2022): 126–35.
18. Morrison, Morrison, and Sager, 'Does Body Satisfaction Differ'.
19. Letitia Anne Peplau et al., 'Body Image Satisfaction in Heterosexual, Gay, and Lesbian Adults', *Archives of Sexual Behavior* 38, no. 5 (2009): 713–25.
20. John E. Pachankis et al., 'Sex, Status, Competition, and Exclusion: Intraminority Stress from Within the Gay Community and Gay and Bisexual Men's Mental Health', *Journal of Personality and Social Psychology* 119, no. 3 (2020): 713–40.
21. Aaron J. Blashill and Steven A. Safren, 'Sexual Orientation and Anabolic-Androgenic Steroids in US Adolescent Boys', *Pediatrics* 133, no. 3 (March 2014): 469–75.
22. Peplau et al., 'Body Image Satisfaction'.
23. Pachankis et al., 'Sex, Status, Competition, and Exclusion'.
24. Michael Martin, 'What Is the Average Penis Size?', Ro, updated 10 November 2024, https://ro.co/erectile-dysfunction/average-penis-size/.

25. Fogarty and Walker, 'Twinks, Jocks, and Bears, Oh My!'
26. Fogarty and Walker, 'Twinks, Jocks, and Bears, Oh My!'
27. Fogarty, Samuel M., and D. Catherine Walker. "Twinks, Jocks, and Bears, Oh My! Differing Subcultural Appearance identifications among Gay Men and Their Associated Eating Disorder Psychopathology." *Body Image* 42 (2022): 126–135.

Chapter 6: Slutty or Liberated? (Probably Both)

1. Takeshi Furuichi, Richard Connor, and Chie Hashimoto, 'Non-Conceptive Sexual Interactions in Monkeys, Apes, and Dolphins', in *Primates and Cetaceans: Field Research and Conservation of Complex Mammalian Societies*, ed. Juichi Yamagiwa and Leszek Karczmarski (Springer Japan, 2014), 385–408.
2. '80% of Gay Swan Couples Successfully Raise Their Young, Compared to 30% of Straight Swan Couples. (Gender Showcase, 9 – 12)', Gender Inclusive Biology, 3 February 2020, https://www.genderinclusivebiology.com/newsletter/80-of-gay-swan-couples-successfully-raise-their-young-compared-to-30-of-straight-swan-couples-gender-showcase-9-12.
3. Ryan Schacht and Karen L. Kramer, 'Are We Monogamous? A Review of the Evolution of Pair-Bonding in Humans and Its Contemporary Variation Cross-Culturally', *Frontiers in Ecology and Evolution* 7 (2019): https://doi.org/10.3389/fevo.2019.00230.
4. Ryan Scoats and Christine Campbell, 'What Do We Know About Consensual Non-Monogamy?', *Current Opinion in Psychology* 48 (2022): 101468.
5. Zachary Zane and Justin Lehmiller, 'How Common Are Foot Fetishes, and Why Do People Have Them?', *Men's Health*, 7 October 2020, https://www.menshealth.com/sex-women/a19523651/foot-fetish/.
6. Phillip L. Hammack and Liam Wignall, '"Be Dog Have Fun": Narratives of Discovery, Meaning, and Motivation among Members of the Pup Subculture', *Sexuality & Culture* 28 (2024): 2537 – 2556, https://doi.org/10.1007/s12119-024-10242-y.
7. Richard Vytniorgu and Jaime Garcia-Iglesias, 'Bottom Shaming, Shame Anxiety, and Sexual Wellbeing', *Lambda Nordica* (2025): https://doi.org/10.34041/ln.v.990.
8. Soulliard, Lattanner, and Pachankis, 'Pressure from Within'.
9. 'Heterosexual HIV Diagnoses Overtake Those in Gay Men for First Time in a Decade', press release, Terrence Higgins Trust, 7 February 2022, https://www.tht.org.uk/news/heterosexual-hiv-diagnoses-overtake-those-gay-men-first-time-decade.
10. Mario Martín-Sánchez, Christopher K. Fairley, Jason J. Ong, Kate Maddaford,

Marcus Y. Chen, Deborah A. Williamson, Catriona S. Bradshaw, and Eric P. F. Chow. 2020. "Clinical Presentation of Asymptomatic and Symptomatic Women Who Tested Positive for Genital Gonorrhoea at a Sexual Health Service in Melbourne, Australia." *Epidemiology & Infection* 148. https://doi.org/10.1017/S0950268820002265.

11. Gus Cairns, 'Belgian Study Asks: Is It Worth Treating Asymptomatic STIs?', aidsmap, 27 June 2024, https://www.aidsmap.com/news/jun-2024/belgian-study-asks-it-worth-treating-asymptomatic-stis.
12. Sam Leader, 'A "Silent Crisis": "Chemsex" Related Drugs Claiming LGBT+ Lives, Yet Few Are Taking Notice', ITV News, 12 March 2025, https://www.itv.com/news/2025-03-11/a-silent-crisis-chemsex-drugs-claiming-lgbt-lives-yet-few-are-listening.
13. A. R. Howarth et al., 'The Association Between Use of Chemsex Drugs and HIV Clinic Attendance Among Gay and Bisexual Men Living with HIV in London', *HIV Medicine* 22, no. 8 (2021): 641–49.
14. Rusi Jaspal, 'Chemsex, Identity and Sexual Health Among Gay and Bisexual Men', *International Journal of Environmental Research and Public Health* 19, no. 19 (2022): 12124.

Chapter 7: Love and Rejection

1. Geva Shenkman, 'The Mediating Role of Insecure Attachment in the Gap in Parenthood Desire Between Lesbian and Gay Individuals and Their Heterosexual Counterparts', *International Journal of Environmental Research and Public Health* 20, no. 5 (2023): 4084.
2. 'LGBT+ Young People Twice as Likely to Be Lonely and Worry Daily About Mental Health, Research Finds', Just Like Us, November 2021, https://justlikeus.org/news/2021/11/25/lgbt-young-people-twice-likely-lonely-worry-daily-mental-health/.
3. Risa Gelles-Watnick, 'About Half of Lesbian, Gay and Bisexual Adults Have Used Online Dating', Pew Research Center, 26 June 2023, https://www.pewresearch.org/short-reads/2023/06/26/about-half-of-lesbian-gay-and-bisexual-adults-have-used-online-dating/.

Chapter 8: The Fight Isn't Over

1. 'New Data: Rise in Hate Crime Against LGBTQIA+ People Continues'.
2. Giulia Fioravanti et al., 'How the Exposure to Beauty Ideals on Social Networking Sites Influences Body Image: A Systematic Review of Experimental Studies', *Adolescent Research Review* 7 (2022): 419–58.

About the Author

MAX HOVEY is a London-based writer, creator, and queer advocate. He dedicates his platform to sparking discussions about and promoting body acceptance, sex positivity, mental health awareness, and other topics relating to LGBTQIA+ issues. His writing and work have been featured in the *Independent*, *Attitude* magazine, *GQ*, *Bustle*, and more. *No Fats, No Fems* is his first book.